CLINT EASTWOOD
AND ISSUES OF AMERICAN MASCULINITY

CLINT EASTWOOD
AND ISSUES OF AMERICAN MASCULINITY

DRUCILLA CORNELL

FORDHAM UNIVERSITY PRESS ■ *New York 2009*

Fordham University Press has no responsibility for the persistence or accuracy of URLs for external or third-party Internet websites referred to in this publication and does not guarantee that any content on such websites is, or will remain, accurate or appropriate.

The final, definitive version of Chapter 5 has been published as "Parables of Revenge and Masculinity in Clint Eastwood's *Mystic River*" in *Law, Culture and the Humanities* 1 (2005), pp. 316–32, by SAGE Publications Ltd. All rights reserved, © 2005. It appears online at http://lch.sagepub.com/cgi/reprint/1/3/316.

Library of Congress Cataloging-in-Publication Data

Cornell, Drucilla.
    Clint Eastwood and issues of American masculinity / Drucilla Cornell.—1st ed.
        p.   cm.
    Includes bibliographical references and index.
    Includes filmography.
    ISBN 978-0-8232-3012-9 (cloth : alk. paper)
    ISBN 978-0-8232-3013-6 (pbk. : alk. paper)
    1. Eastwood, Clint, 1930– —Criticism and interpretation.   2. Masculinity in motion pictures.   I. Title.
PN1998.3.E325C67   2009
791.4302'33092—dc22

                                                                    2009002461

Printed in the United States of America
11   10   09   5   4   3   2   1
First edition

Contents

Preface

As for so many of my generation, Clint Eastwood was simply a part of the social landscape in which I grew up. My ex-husband met him on the set of *Rawhide*, and my mother campaigned for him when he ran for mayor of Carmel, California. My father, like so many of his Republican cohorts, simply idolized Eastwood—he was "their man." Still, I never really paid much attention to him, because he was part of a landscape that I thought I had long outgrown as a feminist. Indeed, my first opportunity for serious engagement with Eastwood's work as a director came only a few years ago during a visit with my father in Laguna Beach, where the small movie theatre was playing only two films, one of which was Eastwood's *Mystic River*. My father surprised me by warning me to avoid the film, commenting that something bad must have happened to Eastwood—he claimed *Mystic River* was the worst film he had seen since *Closely Watched Trains*, a film that I had dragged him to see when I was nineteen. He said that Eastwood seemed to be making some point about men, but dismissively he confessed that he had no idea what it was supposed to mean. Naturally, I immediately went off to see the film—and I agreed wholeheartedly that Eastwood was, indeed, addressing some of the most profound questions of American masculinity. But unlike my father, I thought I got the point.

The very man who seemed to be such a disappointment to my father had become to my mind one of those rare men who actually struggle with what it means to be a good man at a time when all the props that held up ideals of masculine goodness had fallen into disarray. Eastwood seemed to have changed and grown in his work both as an actor and as a director. Let me emphasize, however, that this is a book that engages almost entirely with Eastwood as a director. Indeed, the film scholar Dennis Bingham has commented that Eastwood provides us with something like a twelve-step program away from the mistakes of traditional masculinity.[1] This book, I want to stress, is not focused on Eastwood's personal journey as a man, nor as he was produced as a cultural icon nor on the specificity of his acting style. I have a different project, which is to study Eastwood as a director as he is relevant to certain major philosophical and ethical themes that I have personally articulated throughout my life's work. The particular tenure of this project compels me to take up all of what I consider to be the pressing issues of masculinity as it is caught up in the very definition of ideas of revenge, violence, moral repair, and justice. Eastwood grapples with this involvement of masculinity in and through many of the great symbols of American life, including cowboys, boxing, police dramas, and ultimately war—perhaps the single greatest symbol of what it means (or is supposed to mean) to be a man.

Thus, I still have hope that my father may actually read this book and that it may take him to a deeper appreciation of Eastwood's work as a director as well as the dilemmas facing any aspiration to ethical manhood. Indeed, I am hoping that this book will be widely read by men, perhaps more widely read than some of my other feminist work. Masculinity has recently become a very popular and important topic for social critics, and I have long wanted to address some of these issues myself. But when I tried to think about writing on masculinity in general, I felt lost in a project too large for myself—and so, having written with Roger Berkowitz on *Mystic River*, I decided to undertake a smaller project that nevertheless provides me with the space for at least preliminary reflection on almost all of the great symbols of American masculinity. If I could not write about all men, maybe I could handle just one.

This book, then, is not a traditional book of film criticism or a cinematographic biography; neither is it Eastwood's unauthorized biography. As a work of social commentary and ethical philosophy, it is inspired in large part by the work of my late colleague Wilson Carey McWilliams, who turned his brilliant analysis of American political thought primarily toward the world of literature, arguing that it has always been in our cultural products that Americans express our greatest political ideals and concepts. In the late twentieth and early twenty-first centuries, of course, the new medium of film has clearly dominated the scene of artistic cultural production.

Eastwood takes us through some of the great images and symbols of American life through his engagement with classically American film genres from cowboy movies to police thrillers to boxing heroics. In a world in which we seem to be losing our grasp on shared symbols along with community itself, Eastwood's films work with those fragmented symbols that remain in order to engage masculinity with the most profound moral and ethical issues facing us today. Over and over again he returns us to that simple question: what does it mean to live a life as a good man in a complex and violent world? I concede that much is to be said for the broad literature that has criticized the idea of the director as auteur, the originator and sole author of the images and narrative line of his films. However, although Hollywood imposes real limits on what will be allowed to reach the screen, through all my work I have argued against a theory of the subject that pretends to tell us exactly how we are limited and constituted so that, underneath it all, we cannot find even a remnant of the subject who creates. Indeed, if one wished to put this idea of the subject that is irreducible to any theory of it as constituted as a social object or, in Eastwood's case, a cultural object, we could be reminded here of Jacques Derrida's endless emphasis on the iterability of all linguistic and symbolic forms, including those which both limit and allow a range of subjective agency. This insight into the inevitable iterability of linguistic and symbolic forms even as they are repeated to give us a meaningful world could be used in two ways to understand my own insistence that it is possible to study Eastwood as a director. First, there could be no theory of the subject that so encompasses Eastwood as a cultural production that all of his agency as a director is simply eclipsed. Second, genres are indeed symbolic as well as cinematic forms, and it is precisely Eastwood's subtlety in reworking these forms (while seemingly repeating them) that shows the power of iteration to break up as well as to ground the bounds of meaning.[2] Whatever other factors may have contributed to his films, there is no doubt that Eastwood's interests and choices have stamped his work with a distinctive trajectory that builds upon, disrupts, and reenvisions the very masculine stereotype for which he is known so well. Indeed, what makes Eastwood's work so interesting is how he engages with accepted genres and pushes them to their limits.

I am taking Eastwood's engagement with these fundamental moral and ethical questions as a point of departure working toward the possibility that men and women can reenvision our greatest ideals in a configuration that does not doom us to a world of loveless relationships or the stultifying reality of male violence, whether in the chaos of war or in the halls of our universities and high schools, as well as the violence that erupts in our own homes. Thus, this book is not simply organized in any strict sense around film genres (though it does include chapters on the Western, the Romance, and the war movie) but also around the ethical issues raised by certain related constellations in Eastwood's films, focusing on their meaning for all of us as we attempt to see our way through what I have elsewhere termed the glaring phantasmagoria of advanced capitalism that no doubt provides Hollywood with its very condition of possibility.[3]

Having said this, I am not reading Eastwood as primarily a political filmmaker, or one of course who has explicit deconstructive motivations, but rather as a filmmaker caught within the integral connections between ideals of masculinity and the fundamental moral and ethical issues of our time. The importance of Eastwood's cinematic journey is that he reconstructs the images of manhood in such a way that it is almost impossible to avoid the question—what does it mean to be, not just an ethical person, but specifically an ethical man?

Throughout his directed films Eastwood challenges and explores the deep thematic networks of white masculinity as they have come to be encoded in genre films. By so doing the dilemmas of white masculinity, particularly the dilemma of what it means to be a good man, are brought to the fore rather than being erased in uncomfortable stereotypes. In a century ridden by the traumas of an almost unimaginable violence against any ethical ideal of humanity, which have undercut the stereotypes of the white male hero who makes it against all odds, we cannot expect to rest assured in easy fantasies that we can recapture the good old days when what it meant to be on the right side of the law could be shown in a simple light. Eastwood's engagement with conventional genres does not shy away from the trauma of the conventions of manhood that have been undermined. It is the struggle to engage with all the complexities of what it means to be a good man that makes Eastwood's movies so powerful when we are oftentimes thrown between images of meaningless violence, including sexual violence, that portray nothing more than an empty shell of the masculinity they are supposedly propping up. Perhaps that is Eastwood's ultimate strength as a director in that he reworks genres so that the stereotypes of masculinity fall away—and, by so doing, remain faithful to a glimmer of how men might be different, and this difference is always shown from within an ethical conflict. It is this fidelity to ethical conflict as meaningful if never easily resolved and to the connection between masculinity and the struggle to be ethical that makes Eastwood movies so relevant now. It is this fidelity to moral conflict and its connection to a crisis in masculinity that in a deep sense motivated an "ethical feminist"[4] to write this book.

Acknowledgments

First I would like to thank Elrich Kline for his tireless editing and reediting of this book. It is no exaggeration to say that he went through every page with me. He also carefully watched all the movies that are analyzed in the pages that follow.

Mieke Krynauw worked with enthusiasm to respond to readers' reports. Her careful attention both to those reports and to our response to them has made this book more accessible.

My daughter Serena Cornell watched all the movies with me and carefully wrote down the quotations from the movies because I did not know that you could get the scripts from the Internet. When I asked my daughter what her favourite Clint Eastwood movie was, she said, "the one that you did not ask me a hundred times to listen to so I could write it down." Her actual favourite is *Million Dollar Baby*.

When I realized that I could get the scripts from the Internet, my goddaughter Laura Shaffer used them to recheck the quotations that my daughter had had to transcribe. This book was truly a family affair because my daughter had to then go back and check the Internet transcriptions against the transcriptions she had made.

My students Sam Fuller and Nyoko Muvangua played a crucial role in preparing the final manuscript. Their careful work has undoubtedly played a major role in ensuring a well-ordered manuscript. I am in their debt for their hard work.

Dr. Jaco Barnard-Naude and Dr. Ken Panfilio read many of the chapters and gave me comments. The book has undoubtedly been improved because of their careful insights.

Jessica Benjamin offered insightful comments from her own original work on psychoanalysis and feminism, and her recent work on psychoanalysis, retribution, and acknowledgment.

Dorothy Pietersson has been an indispensable help to me in running my daily life and always being there for my daughter. I thank her from the bottom of my heart.

Roger Berkowitz not only collaborated with me on one of the chapters but has also given me critical commentary on the entire book. I thank him not only for his comments but also for his intellectual companionship for the past fifteen years.

CLINT EASTWOOD
AND ISSUES OF AMERICAN MASCULINITY

Introduction: Shooting Eastwood

Clint Eastwood has been acknowledged as one of this country's most original and provocative directors, but this classification fails to recognize the real depth of Eastwood's complex trajectory as a director. He grapples with all of the most significant ethical issues of our time: war, vengeance, the role of law, relations between the sexes, the meaning of friendship, and indeed with what it means to lead an ethical life as a good man in late modernity. Most of Eastwood's movies do focus on men—on a certain brand of manliness—but from the beginning of his directorial journey he has been more complicated than he has appeared, working with some of the most sophisticated literature that addresses the meaning of straight white maleness throughout the history of the United States.

Eastwood became famous for the Dirty Harry movies. Indeed, his famous phrase in the first film of the series—"Make my day," which is spoken as he stares down a suspect over the barrel of a .44 Magnum—has saturated the everyday vernacular of the English language, even appearing in American politics. Ronald Reagan famously used that phrase as a slogan in his election campaign. The projection of the image of magnum force is explicitly phallic in its identification of man with gun. We see the gun from the side, initially, in what seems like a frozen image; this goes on for a seemingly unbearable span of time, as we wait for the gun to be cocked and aimed. It is cocked, it's pointed, and we hear Clint Eastwood's voice before we even see his face: "But being this is a forty-four Magnum, the most powerful handgun in the world, and would blow your head clean off, you've got to ask yourself one question: 'Do I feel lucky?'"[1] It's not surprising, given these powerful images from the Dirty Harry movies, that Eastwood as an actor is identified by some of his critics as representing the perfect image of remorseless masculinity and the phallic power of the outlaw-hero who must never be drawn into the domestic world of women.

> Eastwood may spend large portions of a film pursuing a woman, and he may ride off with a woman at a film's conclusion, but if an Eastwood character is ever married in a film's "back story," he is inevitably estranged, divorced, or widowed. Because Eastwood's masculine presentation is incompatible with the daily frustrations and accommodations of conventional family life, a stable loving relationship becomes for his characters an unrepresentable element in an impossible past.[2]

The very power of these images, however, has taken even the most sophisticated authors down a wrong path when it comes to viewing Eastwood's complex engagement with violence and masculinity in his directorial trajectory. Indeed, in his first film as director, Eastwood begins to examine what it means for men to experience remorse—often through their own investment in the saving power of phallic fantasy—and even when that fantasy is most mundanely played out in an actual sexual relationship.

Consider Eastwood's directorial debut, *Play Misty for Me* (1971),[3] a movie that has been identified as an originator of a particular genre of thriller in which obsessive femininity is shown as being the ultimate danger to masculine survival. But unlike some of the films to follow, such as *Fatal Attraction*, Eastwood breaks open the psychical fantasy of the women on whom these films are based. We do not have the traditional elements of the paradigm, in which a basically innocent man is lured by carnal temptations to a woman who is often portrayed as having phallic power—the "evil woman" in *Fatal Attraction* is a lawyer—and out-of-control female sexuality. In these movies, of course, the "good man" is restored to home and family while the "evil woman" is brutally killed. This brutality is seemingly necessary given her fantasized sexual potency, which incredibly withstands bullets and multiple knifings as in *Fatal Attraction*. In Eastwood's *Play Misty for Me*, however, the stereotype of masculine innocence is reworked and questioned, and there is no glorying in the death of the female antagonist. Although it is his first directed

film, *Play Misty for Me* already highlights Eastwood's penchant for spinning the themes of a genre into a sort of commentary on the genre itself.
Dave (Eastwood) explicitly plays out the perspective of a man's blindness
to a woman's view of what goes on in a sexual relationship. The main
character is, of course, a deeply troubled—in fact, psychotic—woman.
However, unlike other later films in this genre, Eastwood plays this narrative not only for the thrill of suspense, but rather for the tragedy of
Dave's failure to read the signs of her anguish, of her growing desperation—a failure premised on his inability to understand what it might
mean for a woman to take on a sexual relationship with a man.

Indeed, remorse runs throughout the film. Eastwood devotes considerable time to Dave's attempt to make good on a relationship that he
had, in his own mind, already failed. Here we see Eastwood grappling
(as he will later in *The Bridges of Madison County*) with how to portray on
film a scene of *lovemaking* rather than sex. In *Play Misty for Me* Dave
seeks to win back the heart of his lost love, believing that she has rightly
condemned him for his failures of attentiveness, sensitivity, and fidelity.
Whatever one makes of the sentimentality of filming the two lovers in
the forest with Roberta Flack's "First Time Ever I Saw Your Face" in
the background, the opening of that scene is Dave's explicit sorrow at
his betrayal of their relationship. Ironically, it is this remorseful focus that
distracts him from what is going on in the other woman—for whom a
one-night stand has turned into obsessive attachment. Even as the movie
ends in his stalker's inevitable death, after her psychosis has run completely out of control, the last scene projects more than just her plummet
into the ocean. It is not simply that he can finally be done with her.
Instead, the film closes by acknowledging the horror of what has happened not only to Dave as the one who was stalked but also to Evelyn,
as the tragic consequence of Dave's misreading her understanding of the
meaning of sex.

By *Million Dollar Baby*, Eastwood's concern with remorse and repentance has become an obsession, which is expressed through a father's
daily letters to a daughter who refuses even to open them and sends them
back. But then as we have seen remorse, repentance, and moral repair
are present in Eastwood's representations of masculinity from the very
beginning of his career as a director. For now I would like to draw
attention to another early film, *Tightrope* (1984), which was produced
but not directed by Eastwood. In this film the Eastwood character is a
man deserted by his wife and abandoned as to be a single parent to his
children. We will return to this film in more depth in Chapter 2, and

will also explore my reasons for examining it in this book even though Eastwood did not direct the film, but for now I want to emphasize that *Tightrope* contradicts the critical implication that Eastwood characters are never portrayed in stereotypical domestic situations or in sustained romantic involvements with women. *Tightrope* opens with Wes Block (Eastwood) playing ball with his two girls, who convince him to adopt yet another stray dog to add to their nearly uncontainable menagerie. The chaos of Block's life as a single parent would seem to underscore the need for a mother or caretaker to care for the children while their father is away at work—but the woman who actually enters Block's life is far from the milk-toast good woman you would expect to save him. Beryl Thibodeaux is a fearless woman, even when facing Block's own terror at the perverted "dark side" of his own sexuality. She provides one of the most positive and affirmative images in film of a strong-willed feminist activist viewed as a potential lover. Rarely does Hollywood portray a sexy, witty feminist, who runs women's self-defense classes, as a desirable sex object expressly *because of* her strength and *because of* her feminism. Block does not need to "save" her; indeed, he ultimately catches the murderer only because *she* has effectively stalemated the murderer's attack.[4]

Eastwood maintains a focus on the vulnerability of men's phallic pretentions throughout his films. This focus runs through the various themes that he engages, including the so-called "masculine" responsibility to save others or to prevent them from being ensnared by a boyhood or manhood gone wrong. In *A Perfect World* (1993), Red Garnett (Eastwood) attempts to intervene in the fate of a young boy, but the ultimate failure of his effort underscores the hubris of control that lies at the heart of phallic fantasy.[5] Once again in this film we see a strong feminist character; this time it is Sally Gerber, who earns Garnett's respect during the manhunt that provides the film's dramatic tension, despite his initial sexist dismissal of her. As we come to fully understand the implications of Garnett's relationship with the escaped prisoner Butch, we see why he is so haunted by this case. At the end of the film, with Butch slowly dying in a field, the criminologist Sally Gerber attempts to comfort Garnett, telling him, "You know you did everything you could. Don't you?" Garnett responds, "I don't know nothin'. Not a damn thing." The echoes of these lines find us a long way from pretentions of a cocky, assertive masculinity.

What I am suggesting is that by reading Eastwood's involvement in these films against the grain of even his best critics, we can grapple with some of the most searing issues of masculinity that confront us in late twentieth and early twenty-first century America. Yes, Eastwood rides off into the sunset at the end of some of his films, a solitary figure with no need or promise for the complexity of a lasting connection, but he also struggles visibly with the contradictions of masculinity in relationships with both men and women.

This concern with the right relations between men and women (and, in the later Eastwood, between the generations) is a touchstone leading us to many of the dramatic high points in Eastwood's directed films. Eastwood comes into his own artistic position in the America after the closing of the frontiers, where the drama of the cowboy has an even more powerful hold on the imagination as American life transforms historical reality into pure fantasy. As Lee Clark Mitchell has pointed out in his classic study, the Western genre itself was an elegy to what was never actually there except as a set of ideals for masculinity—and, indeed, for a kind of cultural and moral horizon that reminds the audience of what it means to be a man. As Mitchell writes,

> More generally, the central terms "West" and "Western," which have forged American cultural identity, are less self-evident than initial impressions might lead one to believe. Actual landscapes are everywhere recast in the Western, which conceives of setting not as authentic locale but as escapist fantasy. The West in the Western matters less as verifiable topography than as space removed from cultural coercion, lying beyond ideology (and therefore, of course, the most ideological of terrains).
>
> The one aspect of the landscape celebrated consistently in the Western is the opportunity for renewal, for self-transformation, for release from constraints associated with an urbanized East. Whatever else the West may be, in whatever form it is represented, it always signals freedom to achieve some truer state of humanity.[6]

But Eastwood appears not only in the waning shadow of the cowboy mythos. He also comes to a generation traumatized in the aftermath of two world wars who has lost faith in the idea of progressive historical movement toward a better, more peaceful world—indeed, who has lost faith in the possibility of a world where shared meanings are essential to the aspiration for an ideal democracy founded on the rule of law.

In *Bronco Billy* (1980), Eastwood plays a cowboy who is past his time, one who is left only with the dreams of what it might have been to be a man in the "true West." He must actually live on as a performer of great deeds only in vaudeville acts.[7] Here, Eastwood clearly presents the cowboy (or at least one who still has the dream of living as a cowboy) anachronistically. Indeed, Bronco Billy poignantly struggles to live up to ideals of masculinity that are available to him only in his own parody of his fantasy of the West, his fantasy of himself as a cowboy. It is a story of a man out of sorts with his time.

Of course, Eastwood also has a more playful (and, indeed, ironic) relationship to the ideal of the cowboy, and as we shall see he understands it as both a fantasy and an allegory. In his later film *Space Cowboys* (2000), we see Eastwood explicitly and enjoyably featuring a friendship that has run a difficult life.[8] Four young men form lasting friendships as participants in an early military forerunner to NASA's space program. As Hawk Hawkins (Tommy Lee Jones) tells Frank Corvin (Eastwood) in an opening flashback (a device that Eastwood will develop and use more creatively in his later work as the black and white of memory and dream), someday—someday—the two of them will fly to the Moon. Unfortunately, Hawkins eventually plays too dangerously with his plane, destroying the expensive machine and leaving the men blacklisted by a government bureaucracy that wants men who conform and obey orders rather than those who cherish a desire to "shoot the moon."

Yet as fate has it, many years later the NASA program that did them in needs Corvin to unravel the outdated computer program of a Soviet satellite that has lost its orbit and is falling steadily to Earth. Corvin agrees to help, but only if he and his three comrades get to go into space, fulfilling the dreams of their youth. The film toys playfully with the various ideals of masculinity: Jerry O'Neill (Donald Sutherland) is the proudly strutting (if aging) stud, while Tank Sullivan (James Garner) finds it more than a little difficult to keep the stiff upper lip of a man who has made his way, as a preacher, to God. While at times this movie seems to feature men in a "boys-will-be-boys" fashion, always fighting and keeping their eyes out for young women, its spoofing and self-irony also underscores some of the deeper virtues, such as loyalty, trust, and courage, that make the film much more than simply a light, enjoyable comedy with four great actors making fun of themselves.

The four discover that the Soviet "communications satellite" actually houses an arsenal of nuclear weapons—and, tragically, no simple feat of engineering can avert the pull of gravity that is bringing the spacecraft down. Instead, Hawkins must sacrifice himself to pilot the rockets into space, out of range of the Earth's gravitational pull. As it happens, Hawkins has been diagnosed with pancreatic cancer—and he has made it clear that he does not want to go down slowly, in the same painful manner that his wife did. Hawkins's current love interest, Sara Holland (Marcia Gay Harden), is one of Eastwood's feminist heroines—feminist, that is, in the sense that she is an engineer working in a predominantly male world. She is also a heroine for these men in that she actively supports their dream to shoot themselves to the Moon by travelling, at last, into space.

Hawkins is successful in his final mission, safely directing the missiles out of Earth's pull, and the badly damaged space shuttle returns to Earth without him. Facing a seemingly doomed final descent, the younger astronauts—and there has been much play between older and younger generations—throw open the hatch and parachute to safety. But in his final memorial to Hawkins, Corvin rejects all procedure and pilots the plane to what the "experts" and their manuals would call an impossible landing, because he knows that this would have been the move of his cocky, death-defying friend. Likewise, O'Neill and Sullivan refuse to bail out on the landing, confirming a profound fraternal loyalty that transcends considerations of safety or procedure. There is no question for them that Hawkins was the greatest pilot they had ever known; Hawkins would have landed the shuttle, and for this reason they know what they must do. They pay tribute to Hawkins's memory by living up to his unorthodox thinking about the relationship between a man and his machine.

For all of what may seem like a surface romantic sentimentality in this film, Eastwood is playing with all of the ironies inherent in masculinity, and the dramatic tension is not reducible to the outward play between four talented male actors. Indeed, Eastwood highlights in his own directorial fashion the fact that we can never just step out of that play because ideals of masculinity are embedded in it. When a writer or critic reviews such a rich body of work, she inevitably takes a perspective on it; and indeed, I am well aware that what I am offering my readers is very much my own take on Clint Eastwood as a director. I am, indeed, "shooting" Eastwood in that I intentionally capture and frame his work through four main themes.

The first is the horrifying impact of trauma on our shared ethical life. The second, related to the first, is Eastwood's struggle with evil as a possibility for each of us. The third is the powers of moral repair and repentance as well as the dangers implicit in them—dangers both to one's self and to others one may seek to save, whether from the abusive world that surrounds them or even from themselves. My fourth theme is the relationship between a masculine narcissism enforced through the terrifying threat of castration and the violence that inevitably inheres in the hubris of an exaggerated sense of control over one's self—and in the case of a nation-state, control over other nations and ethnicities.

All of these themes relate to the struggle for ethical meaning, which is oftentimes cast in the complex relation between ethics and law in that moral repair as a possible redemption from the hell of trauma and abuse, and this struggle will inevitably take us to the possibility or impossibility of a shared world of meanings and symbols. These symbols may be created by the victim as he or she seeks a more perfect world, a world that holds out hope for a "beyond" that is not inscribed with the endless repetition of anguish that is written upon a human being who has survived horrific trauma. A commonly expressed fear is that these shared ideals and allegories may so completely collapse that the ideals associated with masculinity, and indeed with ethical personhood, become so utterly vacated that they live on only as parody, as stylized performances without any cause for action. Such parodies were the Spaghetti Westerns of Sergio Leone—no doubt a great influence on Eastwood's own Westerns, but an influence, as we shall see, that he has clearly surpassed. Leone presents us with the living dead, fighters left with style but no standards, faces without souls. Yet Eastwood in his Westerns restores humanity to the face of the cowboy, implicitly stressing that even this face is not immune to the force and impact of trauma. His heroes, often enough, still have no name—but Eastwood reinterprets their namelessness as an identity *lost* in trauma rather than an absence of identity at all. Even if it were the case that wrong life could not be lived rightly (as Theodor Adorno once wrote) we are inevitably fated to make judgments of right and wrong. In Eastwood's directorial trajectory, the struggle to make judgments to hold onto ideals of right and justice—which in turn imply a complex relationship to law and the good man who supposedly upholds it—brings into vivid relief the drama of what we lose if we give up the struggle for ethical life and meaningful relationships, thinking it has already been lost.

It is these themes—as the schemata through which to analyze Eastwood's directorial trajectory—that connect the seemingly diverse genres we will address in this book. Having a certain coherence, these themes underscore how the great ideals of justice, love, and friendship are integrally defined in and through masculinity, the definition of which can and must pass through the ordeal of a foundational questioning of not only their phallic underpinnings but also of masculinity's seeming ability to pull us down the tracks into the horrors of violence, war, and vengeance that undermine ethical life. We turn now to examine Eastwood's cowboy movies in more detail as these movies in turn force us to address all of these themes.

1

Writing the Showdown: What's Left Behind When the Sun Goes Down

High Plains Drifter (1973)

High Plains Drifter,[1] Eastwood's first Western, clearly reflects the influence of Sergio Leone. The Stranger (Eastwood) rides into town as the residents gather nervously around, transfixed by the beating hooves of his horse. As Lee Clark Mitchell reminds us, the Western's beautiful landscape is laden with moral meaning:[2] here the Stranger rides out to a picturesque town built on the shores of a mountain lake, its tranquility suggesting the quiet beauty of the civilized life the town hopes to establish. Yet from the moment when the town gathers around the hypnotic beat of the horse's hoof, it is clear that all is not right about the town of Lago. The beautiful landscape belies the social reality.

On the surface *Drifter* is one of Eastwood's most violent films, certainly in the beginning. First, the Stranger kills three men who harass him while he is getting a shave, and he hardly even aims when he shoots his gun from under the barber's cape. Soon after, a woman accosts him on the street, insulting his manhood. He decides to teach her "a lesson in manners," abruptly dragging her into the nearest barn and raping her until her struggles give way to enjoyment. Here of course there is a risk of the crudest kind of gender stereotype—"rape the woman, kill the man." The opening scenes of violence and rape certainly highlight this gender distinction. *Drifter* would hardly be a film to inspire a positive feminist analysis, but once we understand these events in the context of trauma—and how trauma unleashes the evil of what Sue Grand has called "malignant dissociative contagion"—we begin to understand the power of Eastwood's profound exploration of what happens when a community falls into horrific violence and murder, attempting at the same time both to hide and justify its criminal past.[3]

We only discover the Stranger's past through a series of flashbacks, the first of which comes closely after the rape scene, as he lies down for his first night at the hotel. In the flashback, a group of men (whom we meet later as the outlaws Stacey Bridges and the Carlin brothers) surround the Stranger, whipping him violently as a faceless crowd stands by. Beaten to the point of death, the Stranger reaches out his hand and begs for someone, anyone, to help him. No one moves.

In his work on the Western, Mitchell has written that brutality perpetrated against the male body, and whipping in particular, occurs in part so that we can witness the body's restoration as once again intact.[4] Indeed, standing up to such beatings becomes the hallmark of the hero's masculine self-restraint, the paradoxical power of not acting. But here we see a man prostrate, begging for help. We face at this moment the absolute presence of the perpetrators and the bystanders who allowed the event to unfold—and the bystanders' absolute lack of compassion multiplies the victim's trauma, which involves not only the beating itself but also the deep and profound experience of being denied the status of a human being in the onlookers' eyes. He is being stripped of humanity with each crack of the whip.

Because the story does not cohere—we get only glimpses of meaning through flashbacks—the film can be classified as a broken narrative, but this is not the broken narrative of Sergio Leone's Westerns.[5] For Leone, violent acts seem to have their own meaning with very little narratability associated with them—because there really is no meaning to that kind of violence, and it remains only as a disruptive force. But in Eastwood's *Drifter*, the lack of narratability is itself meaningful because it reveals the effects of trauma on shared meaning. Since what actually happened to Marshal Jim Duncan has been silenced, denied significance in order to allow civilization to flourish on the lake, the town has doomed itself to collapse under the weight of its own guilt. Gradually, the film begins to identify the Stranger with the murdered marshal, who discovered that the mining company that supports the town was operating illegally on government property. To keep him quiet, the company owners arranged for Stacey Bridges and the Carlin brothers to execute the marshal, with the cooperation of the town leaders. Marshal Duncan was publicly whipped, left for dead, and thrown into an unmarked grave.

But Bridges and the Carlin boys turned out to be more trouble than Lago bargained for. After completing the gruesome task for which they had been hired, they terrorized the town until, in another act of desperation, the townspeople arranged to have the gang imprisoned—on charges unrelated, of course, to the murder of Marshal Duncan. Now, having served their time, the gang has returned to Lago for revenge.

Unable to defend themselves, the town leaders hire the Stranger as their gunfighter, offering him anything he wants and declining to press charges against him for killing their hired guns at the barbershop. As the so-called sheriff tells the Stranger, "Forgive and forget. That's our motto." The Stranger agrees to defend the town, but he sets surprising conditions for his service. First, he makes Mordecai "the runt" the new sheriff and mayor of the town. Moreover, rather than taking up the job to shoot the outlaws himself, he trains the townspeople in shooting and has them paint the town red, literally, with red paint. He also has them make a sign that announces, "Welcome Home, Boys." He instructs them to prepare a picnic and a welcome home party. After a few unsuccessful attempts at resisting his instructions, the town goes along with whatever he says (though they never stop complaining about it).

Only Mrs. Belding, the hotel owner's wife, begins to take the Stranger's instructions as more than merely the excessive and arbitrary demands of a violent man who is accustomed to getting what he wants. Reflecting on the murdered Marshal Duncan, she worries that "the dead don't rest without a marker." She even seems to suspect that the Stranger may be connected to Duncan somehow, that he might be the dead marshal's ghost. Alone with the Stranger, only Mrs. Belding can speak frankly with him. "You are a man that makes people afraid, and that makes you dangerous." The Stranger's response is telling: "It's what people know about themselves inside that makes them afraid."

Confronting her husband about the town's part in the murder, she accuses them of hiding behind words like peace, justice, and faith. "Good words. Damn good words," her husband responds, but she will not let him escape the hypocrisy. She reminds him, "We hid a murder behind them." Mr. Belding's only justification for the crime is that sometimes people have to do such things for the greater good: "It's the price of progress." His wife, announcing that she is packing to leave for good, leaves him with the question, "What is the price of a human life?" She does not accept her husband's utilitarian defense of the murder—and indeed, in a flashback we see that she never really accepted it, that she was the only person who attempted to intervene in the murder of Marshal Duncan. Besides Mrs. Belding, only Mordecai had expressed sorrow or remorse at the brutal beating, crying impotently as he bore witness to the event.

Eventually, Stacey Bridges and the Carlin boys ride into a town that is hardly recognizable, on the surface, as the place that had sent them to jail. The Stranger has gone so far as to rename the town, taking a brush to its welcoming sign and replacing the name "Lago" with "Hell." Indeed, being in no mood for a picnic, the outlaws quickly put the town's incompetent defenders to flight and set about completing the image of red-painted buildings by setting fire to the town. As Eastwood shoots it, it does indeed look like Hell.

Abruptly the Stranger appears, outlined in flames that make him the very Devil raised from the pit of Hell. He kills the first Carlin brother, whipping him just as he had whipped Duncan. Indeed, Stacey Bridges stares at the length of rope in recognition, suddenly fearful that the whip buried with Jim Duncan in an unmarked grave had returned to put him in his. The Stranger easily kills the remaining outlaws, but he does not see Mr. Belding, who is angry about the destruction of his hotel and the loss of his wife, taking aim at him from behind a building. It is Mordecai "the runt" who shoots Belding, proving himself more of a man than the people would have believed—indeed, more of a man than any of them—and fully deserving the titles of sheriff and mayor.

The next day as the Stranger rides off, his only smile is for Sarah Belding who prepares to leave behind the horror of a town that has dared to put a price on human life in the name of progress. At the edge of town, the Stranger rides past Mordecai, who has finally marked the grave of Marshal Jim Duncan. Mordecai remarks, "I never did know your name." The Stranger replies, "Yes, you do. Take care." In an end typical of this kind of Western, the gunfighter rides back into the landscape from which he emerged. We know this town will never see him again.

How are we to understand the violent acts that open the film? As I have suggested, Eastwood's Stranger is not simply a replication of the role of No Name in Leone's famous *Dollar* trilogy; he is instead the no-self of the trauma survivor, irreparably marked by the traumatic event. In her excellent work on the reproduction of evil, Sue Grand has written that often the dead self of the trauma survivor can only impose himself on the other unilaterally, at least if there is not meaningful moral repair on the other side. He accomplishes this through acts of cruelty and violence that make him known in his very deadness.

Through the victim's mind and body, the survivor-perpetrator registers his longing for the absent other, "who could have and should have been there" (Benjamin 1995, p. 193) in the moment of execution. Through the disappearance of the victim's interior, the perpetrator recreates the missing other who is *never* there and can *never* be there. The survivor works out his trauma on the human race by "trying to bring others to an equivalent Fall" (Bollas 1995, p. 1184): he lives, masters, transforms, and reobliterates the forgotten forms of his own traumatic past. And the no-self of survival is sustained by the imminence of contact, while evading the dangerous properties of contact by extinguishing the other before too much contact is made.[6]

As the Stranger rides into town, the people are clearly frightened by a presence that reminds them of what they refuse to know; and he imposes on them the eruption of their own fear, simply by living up to the violence that they dread—the violence they know they deserve in retribution for their own dreadful acts. Again, to quote Grand,

> Through revictimization, through a renewed link to a perpetrator, some survivors attempt to be seen in the area of the no-self. Through perpetration, the survivor who becomes a perpetrator attempts to share his no-self by evacuating it into his victim. In both revictimization and perpetration, *there is a meeting which is no meeting in the execution itself.*[7]

Only through the violence that he perpetrates does the Stranger present himself as the *living* dead, but the history of his trauma makes him a very different kind of living dead than the almost automatic, stylized cruelty of No Name in the *Dollar* trilogy. The solitariness that seems to enshroud the Stranger in an impenetrable barrier is for Grand one of the deepest signs of trauma. Indeed, she finds that the reproduction of evil itself occurs in the victim's attempt to answer, as she puts it, "the riddle of catastrophic loneliness" confronted in the wake of a terrible trauma.[8] As she explains,

> The reproduction of evil is the survivor's continual reentry into the moment of execution, where "death is the irreducible common denominator of men" (King, 1963, p. 117). The survivor has been waiting to be known, not merely in the *memory* of the execution,

but in the execution *itself*. It is here that her solitude was defined; it is here that she attempts to be known in her solitude.[9]

The town's anxiety is precisely that of the perpetrators' denial of what they had done, and it signals their fear that something must happen to pay them back for the murder of Marshal Duncan, who died for no other reason than that he tried to do the right thing. Indeed, the Stranger must confront the perpetrators as well as the people who stood by silently during the crime, but he can no longer bear the name of his pre-traumatic self. Thus, his confrontation can take place only through the medium of violence. No one greets him, no one knows him, yet everyone is immediately afraid of him because, as the Stranger remarks, they are really afraid of what they know about themselves, about their own horrific capacity for murder.

How does one share a "no-self" that is living dead, the psychic dead for whom shared meaning has been lost in the experience of absolute cruelty? As Grand explains, both perpetrator and bystander refuse to understand, and it is this refusal that traps the no-self of the survivor into the cold, cruel recreation of violence—in a sense, to make them understand.

> Only in the context of evil is it possible to achieve radical contact with another *at the pinnacle of loneliness and the precipice of death*. Only perpetrator and bystander recreate and encounter the no-self of torture's vacuity, and only they can be *in the presence of that no-self without any pretense of knowing it. In perpetrator and bystander, there is neither the desire for, nor the illusion of "understanding" the no-self. In the perpetrator-bystander-victim relation, the no-self is in the presence of others who confirm the truth of catastrophic loneliness, even as these others do not know this loneliness*.[10]

As *Drifter* opens, the evacuation of the no-self into his victim takes the form of a rape perpetrated to remind the woman of how she played into his own torture—even if she does not know it was his—by participating as a bystander to the act, betraying any moral relationship to him as a human being. Of course, rape as such a gross and tragic violation of a woman's body and therefore as a castrating act to the men who can't protect her seems, even in the context of the analysis I am making of trauma, to be unquestioned in its promotion of violence against women as an inevitable act of vengeance. Like the woman who is raped, Mrs.

Belding ultimately resists the Stranger only to give way to her passion for him. In each case, of course, there is the ambiguity that both women are portrayed in stereotypic narrowness and the only sign of life in the Stranger is his sexual potency. Thus the Stranger can, in a sense, preserve his masculinity, even though that goes against the traumatic undoing of the man he once was. And the men in the town, who can neither protect their women nor keep them from being seduced, are cast in a stereotyped castrated masculinity of their own. The use of sexual violence in this film to the degree that it allows the Stranger to maintain phallic power despite trauma seems to run against the underlying theme of traumatic undoing that the film so graphically portrays.

This town is an allegory, but not in the sense that it represents any overt political reality. As Mitchell reminds us, the complex narrative and dramatic elements of a Western cannot be reduced to allegory in the sense that they have a meaningful connection to some concrete historical reality. Westerns are, however, allegorical in Walter Benjamin's sense of the word, in that the ideals associated with the post-traumatic self of Marshal Duncan remain only as what he is not.[11] Once an upholder of justice and law, it is his return as the fearsome no-self, a physical but not a psychic survivor of trauma, that lends the film its allegorical character. When evil actions overtake ordinary people, when a person suffers the cruelty invoked against Duncan, the sense of it always escapes the simple grasp of narrative knowledge. As Grand explains,

> In this obfuscation of the truth, evil eludes accountability and justice. Secrecy, concealment, denial, ambiguity, confusion: these are Satan's fellow travelers, requiring elaborate interpersonal and intrapsychic collusion between perpetrators and bystanders. The operations of silence potentiate evil and remove all impediments from its path.[12]

Walter Benjamin has written that allegory is the retinue of destruction. But I am thinking of allegory here in the sense that evil, defined by Grand as the annihilation of history and subjectivity for the victim, can never be known directly; and therefore we can approach it only through a series of signs that break up the very sources of meaning upon which we ordinarily rely to understand our world. The film does not, as we have seen, proceed by way of a traditional narrative. Through the Stranger's acts of violence, through the disorientation he imposes on the town as they begin to know what they cannot admit to knowing, we come to grapple with the total evacuation of the ideals represented by the young marshal. The film proceeds allegorically through an elusive and elliptical set of flashbacks that takes the audience back to an event that really happened, but which cannot achieve any kind of reparative closure because the act itself will not be recognized and given voice—let alone given voice by anyone who is expressing true sorrow and is capable of begging forgiveness. Instead, the no-self that remains of Marshal Duncan turns into the opposite of what he was as a man psychically alive, a man of the law. Here we see two well-known versions of law at play. The first in a sense is psychoanalytic. Duncan, at least from what we know of his stance against the mining company, was bearing out the virtues of masculinity, which by the standard of many different schools of psycho-analysis means behaving as a mature man—someone who imposes the law upon himself and lives by it in uprightness. Of course much of psy-choanalytic theory has been criticized for the phallic underpinnings of this masculine uprightness. That Duncan is also the marshal, the one who stands by the law, not in its letter but with its ideals that in turn reflect the deep underlying structures of masculinity, underscores a theme that we will see again and again in Eastwood's films—when the law fails to be true to these masculine ideals, it exiles the one who seeks to uphold his own masculine understanding of the law, even before the exile is made actual. In a deep and profound sense Marshal Duncan becomes a stranger to himself, because the injustice inscribed upon his body completely breaks his ability to identify himself as a potent agent of the law—leaving him the way we see him in the flashbacks, as a victim begging for help.

In a sense, the town's "forgive and forget" motto is willing to take the no-self of the Stranger literally, which further unravels his ability to identify with the so-called order that has been imposed on the town as "law" and indeed with the inevitable "law" of progress. They give him a position as a gunfighter, burying him further in a cloak of invisibility: even his acts of vengeance make no sense, since no one will admit to who he is. His ideality seemingly lingers in its very absence.

The Stranger's ruthless and effective disorientation of the town repli-cates his own traumatic experience, in which his uprightness as an officer of the law was not only dishonored; it was turned into the excuse for his own murder. To achieve vengeance he would have to be recognized, but the townspeople deny him again. Thus, there is in the Stranger both the trauma revealed through flashbacks, the actual bodily violation, and the further violation entailed in the town's refusal to remember him, to remember what they did. In the town meetings that ineffectively seek to take action against the Stranger's seemingly arbitrary demands, their own disorientation recalls the disorientation of a sense of trauma, in which no one can come to terms with what is actually happening because the moral truth has been so thoroughly covered up by hypocrisy and lies.

Thus, the allegory here is an allegory of how evil comes to be reproduced by the very failure of the perpetrators and bystanders to admit what they have done and to seek reparation or forgiveness. There is no way out for the town, which has condemned itself to total disillusionment, disorientation, and an almost literal descent into Hell—which is, in a sense, where they sent the pre-traumatic self of Marshal Duncan, allowing him to return only as the no-self of the Stranger, the living dead. Sarah Belding deserves the Stranger's only smile because her leaving Lago implicitly acknowledges the terrible wrong that was done there—a wrong that she can no longer bear to keep buried with the others, so she commits herself to exile. Perhaps a small smile is all that this exile deserves, for she never does fully acknowledge who the Stranger must be. Although Mordecai puts a marker on Duncan's grave, the no-self of the Stranger rides off without gaining any moral repair. He rides off with only the whisper of a hope that Mordecai does, indeed, know who he is. Perhaps this put-upon outsider, who has been socially rejected and never fully a part of the community, is the only one who might really understand what happened. Still, Lago is in a state of total destruction and disorientation, and the Stranger rides off as alone as when he rode in. There is no repair.

Pale Rider (1985)

In *Pale Rider*[13] Eastwood again reworks some of the cinematic lessons of Sergio Leone's Spaghetti Westerns, and this reworking takes him away from the parodic atmosphere of Leone's work. No Name has now become the stranger qua preacher. The film begins, as cowboy movies often do, with a beautiful setting of majestic mountains, but the serenity of the landscape is immediately broken up by the thundering of hooves. A group of riders charges into the scene at a full gallop. Eastwood contrasts this band of men with the peaceful mining community that they are about to disturb. We see idyllic shots of a woman hanging clothes, men quietly panning for gold, and a young girl, who is walking with her dog outside the town when she sees that something is amiss. The tension rises, and it is as if the community can sense an approaching storm based on a sudden shift in the weather that they have experienced time and time again.

Riding into the settlement, the men overturn everything around them. In one of Eastwood's early cinematic engagements with the disorienting experience of violence, which he suggests through rapid, seemingly random changes in the camera's angle and position that completely scramble the audience's perspective, there is no separation between the perceiver and the object to be perceived, no audience that can merely observe the disruption. Instead, we are there, thrown to the ground and surrounded by the chaos of an ordered world that has been completely confused and turned upside-down. Violence makes the very act of perception impossible, as bodies are twisted and turned and violated in their very capacity to hold the world steady before them.

Riding out as abruptly as they arrived, the men leave havoc behind them. The girl, Megan (Sydney Penny), who appeared earlier strolling with her dog, now stands before a dead animal, brutally and needlessly shot—another sign of the wastefulness of violence. Megan and her mother, Sarah Wheeler (Carrie Snodgress), take the dog home, but it is Megan alone who buries the body in the forest outside the community. There she prays for a miracle, and we begin to understand the reasons behind the seemingly senseless violence. The Tin Pans are squatters with legal rights to their land, but they are being challenged by the owner of a large mining company, Coy LaHood (Richard Dysart)—himself initially a Tin Pan—who wants to displace their simple panning operation to make way for the destructive, large-scale operations of his company. As Michael Kimmel points out, the name Coy LaHood, a mock French name, indicates that the capitalists are identified both by others and by themselves as genteel patriarchs who are out of touch with the American working class, even though they rose from a similar background.[14] Megan prays that a miracle will bring someone to rid the community of LaHood and his murderous men. As she prays, Eastwood plays that oft-repeated, sentimental scene of the classic Western—and yes, a scene that Leone endlessly pokes fun at—namely, the pale rider (Eastwood) quietly moving through a sublime forested mountain landscape.

Meanwhile, one of the Tin Pans, a man named Hull Barret (Michael Moriarty) who hopes to marry Sarah, prepares to ride into the nearby town to settle some bills and pick up goods for his home. There we see how poor the Tin Pans have become, as Barret barely convinces the shopkeeper to extend his credit on the promise of more gold. Leaving the store, he encounters another gang of company men who surround him and begin to beat him. Suddenly, indeed almost miraculously, the pale rider appears to kill or incapacitate the members of the gang, saving Hull from a beating and sending him home.

Hull Barret's appreciation for the stranger's help is matched by Megan's enthusiasm, for she believes the rider is the answer to her prayers; but their interest is not matched by Sarah, who suspects that the man is a gunfighter. Barret agrees, but he actually sees hope in the possibility: with a gunfighter around, it may be possible to face the company thugs and fight like a man. Indeed, as the stranger undresses in the other room, we see six bullet holes in his back, suggesting that he does, in fact, have a very violent past. Yet when he comes out for dinner, he is dressed as a preacher—and "Preacher" he will be called. Even Sarah backs down from her apprehension, inviting him to stay for dinner and to stay for some time as their guest in the community.

This Preacher is no soft man of the cloth, and he insists on joining the men in their mining. Hull Barret is convinced that under a particularly large rock there must be a great treasure of gold, so the two men hammer away at the rock and the Preacher remarks, "There are very few problems that cannot be solved with a little sweat and hard work." But just as they set to the task, the company thugs arrive with a new ploy to do in the intruder, sending an enormous man known only as Club (Richard Kiel) to beat up the Preacher. The Preacher defeats the giant, however, kicking him in the groin and sending him on his way. Seeing that the Preacher will not easily be defeated, the gangs call on LaHood himself to resolve the situation.

LaHood, dismayed to find not only a gunman but a preacher involved with the Tin Pans, exclaims, "A man without spirit is easily broken, but a preacher . . . he could give them faith. One man of faith, and they can dig in deeper than ticks on a hound." Indeed, LaHood is desperate to be rid of the Preacher, but none of his efforts are successful. First, he tries bribery, offering the stranger a nice new church, to which the Preacher replies simply, "Can't serve God and Mammon both." LaHood resorts to threats, referring to a special marshal who upholds the "law"—law in this case being the will of the largest bank account. Here again we see Eastwood returning to the theme of how law, when reduced to the authority of the biggest gun, is completely evacuated of its moral underpinnings and therefore, at least in Eastwood's film, becomes something to be despised by the man who holds onto righteousness against this "might makes right" marshal. The irony of course is that the Preacher is himself an outlaw, at least from law understood as the principles that establish what constitutes crime. He is obviously not someone who has been exiled, at least not completely, from his identification with both the ideals and virtues of masculinity as well as with the ethics of the community that should underscore a conception of law based on some notion of rightfulness not just of power. Finally, LaHood decides to negotiate, thrusting the Preacher into the role of a union organizer considering offers on the miners' behalf. Indeed, the Preacher presses LaHood from an initial offer of $100 up to $1,000 a head for the Tin Pan land—not nearly the value of the land, but a respectable offer at least. Still, the Preacher disclaims authority to close the deal, insisting that he must extend the offer to the men of the community directly.

The men are ambivalent, with several of them arguing that LaHood's money could mean a new start, an escape from the endless violence that they have encountered on the mountain. But as the discussion heads toward a vote, Hull Barret intervenes with a passionate reminder:

> Gold ain't what we're about. It ain't what I'm about. I came out here to raise a family. This is my home. This is my dream. I sunk roots here. And we all have buried members of our families in this ground. And this is their dream, too, and they died for it. Now we're going to take a thousand dollars? And leave their graves untended? We owe them more than that. We owe ourselves more. If we sell out now, what price do we put on our dignity next time? Two thousand dollars? Less? Or just the best offer?

Barret's impassioned plea against the salability of dignity wins them over, and they vote to remain on the land for which they have already paid so dearly. Later, the Preacher congratulates them:

> The vote you took the other night showed courage. A man alone is always easy prey. Only by standing together are you going to be able to beat the LaHoods of this world. No matter what happens tomorrow, don't you forget that.

His encouraging words notwithstanding, the Preacher does not want these peaceful men to face the trauma of violence, and he determines to go into town to meet the marshal alone. Indeed, he must face the marshal on his own terms, for it is becoming clear that this man is the very same who once left the Preacher for dead with six bullet holes in his back. Sarah and Megan, aware that the Preacher is preparing to leave, both declare their love for him. He rejects Megan, but tenderly, because she is only a young girl. Meanwhile, Sarah has explained to him that she will marry Hull Barret because he offers the care and stability that she knows a stranger with no name could never provide. It is clear that her heart would disagree, and the Preacher takes her to his bed for a final night of passion. As we saw in the Introduction, Eastwood critics have often identified the portrayal of masculinity in many of his movies as a sense of being unable to connect to women because of a male estrangement from the domesticity that shapes the stereotypic women's world. We certainly see an example of this model of masculinity in this movie, as both the Preacher and Sarah accept that there is no way of overcoming this estrangement. As I suggested in the Introduction, this particular form of estrangement is slowly replaced in Eastwood films by a more explicit battle within the male characters themselves as to how they can relate to their strong feelings for women. But again I want to underscore here that the Preacher is not the typical cowboy lone ranger who is just above it all. Rather, he is a man deeply inscribed in a trauma that prevents him from meaningful connections with others, aside from the brief encounters made possible by his role in protecting a just world that his own violent past seemingly denied to him.

When the Preacher sets out in the morning to meet the company gang, Hull Barret insists on joining him. Before riding into town, the two take the opportunity to dynamite LaHood's brutal hydraulic mining system, which hammers away at the land, destroying all its natural beauty in the name of maximum efficiency and profit. Here Eastwood draws a striking contrast between the capitalistic self-made man and what Kimmel has called the heroic artisan, the Tin Pan who makes his way in the world with knowledge of the land and tools of his own making.[15]

As they destroy LaHood's grotesque machinery, the Preacher apparently fumbles a stick of dynamite only so that Hull can leap to the rescue, throwing himself from off his horse and hurling the lit dynamite to a safe distance. Indeed, the Preacher's mistake was intentional, giving himself a chance to put Barret's horse to run and allowing Barret to think himself a hero. The Preacher leaves him stranded, however, so that he does not have to face the dangers of the marshal and his thugs.

The Preacher's gun battle with the company gang ends with a classic act of revenge. He shoots the marshal in the same six places where the marshal once shot him, but he adds a seventh bullet—that magical seventh bullet that appears so often in the films of Sergio Leone—shooting the marshal in the head, a form of symbolic castration. One gang member remains, however, and he nearly manages to shoot the Preacher. Hull Barret, who, determined to stand by the Preacher, has walked all the way from the mine into town, finishes off the last man. The film ends in the traditionally sentimental way, with the Preacher riding out of town as Megan shouts a farewell behind him. The man she knew as the Preacher never looks back.

Pale Rider frequently echoes *Shane* (1953), a much earlier Western.[16] *Shane* tells the story of a mysterious gunman (Alan Ladd) who arrives from nowhere to visit the Starretts' farm, ultimately staying with the family and, like the Preacher, offering to help with the farming. While the Preacher helps the Tin Pans demolish a rock, Shane helps Joe Starrett (Van Heflin) remove a troublesome stump, both men hacking away at it together in the a traditional manly way. In *Shane* it is Joey Starrett (Brandon De Wilde), the farmer's young son, who must come to terms with different ways of being a man, while the farmer's wife, Marian Starrett (Jean Arthur), falls passionately in love with Shane. Here, too, there is a battle between the heroic artisans and the new rich, ranchers who want their land.

But here the similarities end. While Eastwood borrows heavily from *Shane*, in that film Shane never takes a position either for or against the ranchers. Eastwood's Preacher, of course, not only takes a position but actually becomes the representative of the miners in their negotiations with LaHood. The Preacher, a no-man who is everyman, comes to stand for what is best in them all, if only they can stand together. The Preacher's faith is not so much in God, but rather in the miners' shared dignity as human beings and as men. He brings this to them as a reminder of who they are, and who they can be. LaHood insists to the Preacher that the "squatters"—as LaHood calls them—"stand in the way of progress," in an echo of the same law-progress theme that we saw in *High Plains Drifter*, but the Preacher is clear that he will have nothing to do with any "progress" that becomes nothing more than the brutal unfolding of industrial capitalism. He takes the side of men against the Man, the side of human dignity against "progress."

In *Pale Rider* there is no training session, as there is in *Shane*, for a young boy who must learn what it means to be a man, who must choose between competing ideals of masculinity. Instead, in this early film, Eastwood begins to experiment with the idea of doubling; he plays the Preacher as a split-off part of Hull Barret and positions Barret to be the father to Megan who the Preacher can never be. The Preacher stands in for Hull Barret's faith in his own masculinity, and in the process reclaims his own connection, for a while, with the people around him. Barret, insisting against all odds that he fight side-by-side with the Preacher, redeems his masculinity and regains his manhood. In *Shane*, by contrast, Starrett is defeated in a fistfight, leaving Shane to go it alone.

Shane is the traditional, sentimental Western hero, but the Preacher is something more. The Preacher does not simply save the day; he also brings heroism into the lives of the men around him. By restoring Hull Barret's faith in his own dignity, he leaves the town with a new leader, someone who will fight on in his stead, live up to his example.

What, if anything, does the act of vengeance, of almost artistically perfect vengeance, restore to the Preacher? At this early point in his career, Eastwood does not show us much. He relies on the traditional sentimental ending: the score has been settled, and the gunfighter rides on. But already we see how Eastwood's twisting of the traditional cowboy template dramatically changes the significance of this scene. Like the archetypal cowboy, the Preacher also leaves town, but he leaves much more than bodies and heartache behind. Indeed, by teaching Hull Barret to have faith in his own dignity as a man, he has taught the Tin Pans moral and political lessons that will stay with them long after he is gone. His departure is, in a certain sense, inconsequential; and his personal vendetta becomes much less important than the values he imparted to the townspeople. If we interpret the film as an initial experiment in the significance of two men representing different ends of the masculinity spectrum, then in important ways Hull Barret has become the best of both of them. It matters a great deal that Barret refuses to be defeated.

In *Pale Rider* faith stands in for exactly those ideals of honor, dignity, loyalty, hard work, and fidelity to the honored dead that are associated with Kimmel's heroic artisan. The violence of LaHood completely disrupts the symbolic world in which the Tin Pans believe: where the ideals that tie them to the land are also worth dying for. But by the end of the film Hull Barret has taken his stand side-by-side with the Preacher, and in so doing he proudly upholds the ideals echoed in the Tin Pans' courageous vote to turn down the company's buyout offer in favor of their own continued history on the land.

Unforgiven (1992)

Unforgiven[17] is Eastwood's most acclaimed Western, and rightly so. As it opens, William "Bill" Munny (Eastwood) bears his dead wife, Claudia, to her grave, while subtitles inform us that young Claudia had married

Munny, a murderous man, despite other decent marriage prospects. The scene quickly cuts to a bordello in the town of Big Whisky, where an inexperienced prostitute giggles at her client's small penis—a dangerous slip, as it proves when her offended client slashes a knife brutally across the face. Called to confront the young man and his associates, Sheriff "Little Bill" Daggett (Gene Hackman) concludes that they are just "boys being boys," and orders them to bring horses to the prostitutes in the spring but calls for no further punishment. A more senior prostitute, however, argues that the women should raise funds to hire a hit man. In her eyes, the cowboys have stolen her colleague's livelihood by marring her attractive features, and they should die for it. "They like to ride us like horses . . . but by God we ain't horses," she proudly reminds her colleagues. The Schofield Kid (Jaimz Woolvet), a young man who responds to the women's ad for a hit man, is not eager to face his enemies alone, and he has heard that the famous outlaw William Munny lives close by. He seeks Munny out as a possible partner.

The Kid finds Munny rolling about in the mud chasing his pigs, con-sistently unsuccessful in his efforts to catch them. The young man remarks, "You don't look no meaner-than-hell cold-blooded damn killer," and Munny replies, "My wife—she cured me of it. Cured me of drink and wickedness." Though he sends the young gunman off in search of another partner, it quickly becomes clear that Munny is in dire straits financially: his pigs are ill, the farm is failing, and he is barely earning enough to feed his children. Clearly in crisis, he decides that it may be necessary to play the hit man one last time in order to save his family.

In an amusing scene, Munny fetches his gun to practice target-shoot-ing, missing the mark again and again while his children stand by, bemused by their father's incompetence as both pig herder and marks-man. Indeed, to even hit the target Munny needs to head back inside for a shotgun. He has even more trouble mounting his horse. Reminding his laughing children that even animals have memories, he suggests that the horse must be paying him back for his previous offenses, though his children do not know what he could mean. They know him only as an incompetent pig farmer.

Leaving the farm, Munny first heads over to fetch his old partner, Ned Logan (Morgan Freeman), who like Munny had settled down with a woman after ending his life of crime. Logan resists his friend's efforts to recruit him for the assassination, telling Munny straight out that if Clau-dia were still alive Munny couldn't bring himself to do it either. Still, out of loyalty to his friend, who repeatedly reminds Logan that this is a one-time deal, he agrees to join in the venture. When they catch up with the Schofield Kid, Munny explains to the young man that it can only be a three-way deal, because he doesn't take a job like this without his partner, Ned: "He don't go, I don't." It is Logan, however, who quickly becomes concerned with the abilities of their new partner: the young man, it turns out, is hopelessly shortsighted, and they doubt his ability to shoot effectively.

Meanwhile, another respondent to the prostitutes' advertisement arrives in town. A British gentleman known as "English Bob" (Richard Harris), he is rumored to be such a remarkable gunslinger that he even has his own biographer, who follows him around doing research for the provocatively titled book, *The Duke of Death*. Sheriff Daggett apparently knows English Bob, and he immediately confronts him as he enters town, beating him brutally and throwing him into a jail cell. As Bob withers painfully in his cell, Daggett tells his biographer what really happened when Bob—Daggett calls him the "Duck of Death"—supposedly shot down a dangerous gunman. As Daggett tells it, the murdered gunman was at the time both incredibly drunk and completely unarmed. The biographer becomes enamored with Sheriff Daggett, who happily takes up the manly role of teacher. He shows the writer what it *really* means to be a great shot, stressing that it is more important to be cool than fast. As Michael Kimmel tells us, English Bob represents a discredited ideal of American masculinity, the genteel European patriarch who has no real place in America even when he tries to take up the role of gunslinger.[18]

Meanwhile, Munny, Logan, and the Schofield Kid have arrived on the edge of town. There they decide to send Munny alone into town to speak to the prostitutes, perhaps even to get a down payment on their assassination job. Munny, who at this point is sick with a cold and shaking—he refuses a little whiskey, even just to relieve his symptoms—is not long in town before Daggett confronts him, suspecting already that he must be another hired gun. Too ill to defend himself, he can barely crawl out of the bar after the beating he receives from Daggett (in a scene that strongly echoes Sergio Leone's *A Fistful of Dollars*). Taking refuge in an empty barn outside of town, Munny is nursed back to health by Logan and the scarred prostitute—who is, in a sense, Munny's double, her physical scars mirroring the many scars on his soul.

Munny clearly struggles with the life he has led, the life he thought he had left forever. Hallucinating during the course of his illness, he calls out one desperate plea to Logan: "Don't tell the kids . . . none of the things I've done." Waking to the prostitute's scarred face, he tells her, "I thought I was gone." Having tenderly cared for him, the prostitute offers him "a free one," but Munny turns her down—a rejection she interprets as a response to her ugliness. Munny corrects her: "You're not ugly, like me. We both have scars. You are a beautiful woman, and if I wanted a free one it would be with you rather than the others. But I just can't . . . because of my wife."

Fully healed, Munny rides out with his partners to hunt down the cowboys, but their first encounter with their prey is almost comical in its depiction of how hard it is, in fact, to kill a man. Indeed, the effort becomes almost as ridiculous as it is horrific. First Munny misses, then Logan becomes so horrified with what he is doing that he freezes, unable to go through with it. He hands his gun to Munny, and with it Munny finally succeeds in shooting one of the young cowboys, though the wound is not immediately fatal. The young man cries out in horror, clearly in agonizing pain as he begs his terrified comrades to give him some water. Munny cannot stand his shouts of pain, calling out, "Will you take him a fucking drink for Christ sake! We ain't gonna shoot." He honors his promise, allowing the men to succor their dying friend, even as the other cowboy marked for death has managed to slip away.

At this point, Logan declares that he has had enough and he is going home, though Munny pleads with him to reconsider. He rides off, and Munny promises that one way or another Logan will get his share of the bounty. Munny and the Schofield Kid, meanwhile, set off in search of the remaining mark, finding him in hiding with some of his friends. As he leaves his friends to relieve himself, Munny tells the Schofield Kid to shoot him. Whether he does it because he would rather not kill another man or because he wants to give the Kid a chance to live up to his boasting, we do not know. The scene, again, involves a sort of horrific comedy: the man is caught, quite literally, with his pants down, and that is exactly how the Schofield Kid shoots him, unarmed and pissing.

After the two escape the man's friends who pursue them for vengeance, Munny stares off into the distance as the Schofield Kid begins to break down emotionally. He attempts to boast, but his words ring hollow and eventually he starts to cry. Munny sympathizes: "It's a hell of a thing, ain't it, killing a man. You take everything he's got, and everything he's ever gonna have." The Schofield Kid comforts himself with the thought that "he had it coming," but Munny can only remind him: "We all got it coming."

As they collect their money from one of the prostitutes, Munny remarks to her that Logan will get his share and she must relate to him some unfortunate news. It seems that while Munny and the Schofield Kid settled up with the cowboys, Logan was captured and beaten by Sheriff Daggett, who left him to die in a casket marking his death as the penalty due to an assassin. Munny decides, of course, that he must ride back into town to avenge his friend. Munny returns to the saloon, telling the customers that if they do not want to die, they should leave while they have the chance. The fickle writer, however, thinking that he has found in Munny an even more thrilling subject than Bill Daggett, wants to know more about the mysterious gunfighter. Daggett takes it upon himself to introduce the dreaded Bill Munny from Missouri. At this point, most of the men in the saloon flee, and those who remain are, in fact, killed—including Daggett, of course, who stays alive long enough for a brief final dialogue with Munny. "I don't . . . deserve this . . . to die this way," Daggett says. "I was . . . building a house." Munny replies, "Deserve don't mean shit." Daggett sneers, "I'll see you in Hell," and Munny doesn't disagree.

This cowboy movie, however, does not conclude with its hero riding off into the sunset. Instead, Munny returns to Claudia's grave, unforgiven. He has returned, if only briefly, to the hell he sought desperately to escape in marriage. We do not learn much about what happens to him now: a text crawl tells us only that Claudia's mother finally comes to the farmhouse, seeking clues as to why her daughter would marry such a horrible man. She finds none, and we are informed only that William Munny disappeared with his children to make a life in dry goods, far away in San Francisco. We are far from the sentimental ending in which the cowboy magically rides out into the landscape, disappearing into the horizon with no family or friends.

Analysis

Unforgiven begins with a still shot of Eastwood burying his dead wife. The dead woman has often played a central role in figurative art, in drama, and in the novel: the story begins here because the woman's death allows the masculine protagonist to pull himself together against all that would undo him. It is a fantasy of wholeness that has the man standing tall only because his woman has "gone under" metaphorically to support him. As Elizabeth Bronfen has written in a brilliant study of the role of the dead feminine other in Western art, "Countless examples could be given to illustrate how the death of a woman helps to regenerate the order of society, eliminates destructive forces or serves to reaggregate the protagonist into her or his community."[19] Yet Claudia's death, by contrast, not only fails to provide William Munny with a firm sense of resolve but actually leaves a hole in his heart that he simply cannot fill without her presence. His desperate attempt to keep her with him, at least in spirit, is expressed in his absolute fidelity to her even in death. He allows himself no sexual play at all, not even (as Logan jokes) with his own two hands, because he is afraid that it may disrupt his frantic attempt to hold on to the fragile post-traumatic self that had somehow came into being through his marriage to Claudia. Thus, fidelity to her is a way to hold on to her memory, and through that memory to hold on to himself as well.

As Munny tells Logan, Claudia knew of his wickedness, and it was precisely her ability to know as the drunken, violent man he had been that allowed him to overcome his former self and become a man worthy of her love. Indeed, the title of the film may give us some clue about what it is in Claudia that her own mother cannot understand. As Sue Grand tells us,

> To find redemption, a perpetrator must despair of absolution. Relinquishing all claims to forgiveness, faithful to guilt and to memory, he must turn away from himself toward the other, committing himself to a life of restitution and reparation. In his remorse, through long acts of reparation, he may find redemption and even absolution.[20]

Thus, it is precisely his refusal to forgive himself—the fact that he remains, to his own mind, unforgiven—that gives such profound moral force to Claudia's accepting him as a husband. Munny realizes that forgiveness is not something he can demand, or even something he can ask for. It must be a gift, and that gift must come from the other. It is his very acceptance of the fact that no one can forgive *himself* for such horrible acts as he has committed that gave him the fortitude and strength of will, mediated through his commitment to Claudia, to become the sort of man that a good woman could love. The film's title, then, should be read as signaling the close connection between fidelity to guilt and the possibility of redemptive love.

The hole in Munny's heart grows ever deeper as he fails to hold on to his fragile post-traumatic self in the absence of Claudia's loving embrace. He fails miserably as a pig farmer, unable to make an honest living and raise children on his own. Indeed, we never really see Munny fully mourn for Claudia—certainly not before he stands at her grave in the final scene, and perhaps not even then. Rather, he seems stuck in a traumatic position in which he has neither Claudia nor the sense of her as someone whom he has lost but can fully remember. For in mourning, as Sigmund Freud tells us, our painful process of grief ties us paradoxically to the lost love object by interjecting her symbolically as a part of ourselves, taking what was good in her and making it a part of who we must remain in her memory.[21] But Munny's fragile psychic rebirth as husband, lover, and father leaves him no way to interject Claudia's love for him, because he simply cannot see himself as the man she loved, as a man who can contain what she believed to be good and, therefore, can contain what was good in her as well. He still needs her to hold him, to remind him that he is more than the perpetrator of violence, more than a slave to liquor. Despite all of his attempts to live differently, he can only know the good in himself through the good in Claudia, and in her absence he has no way to remember that goodness except through undying fidelity to her, as if she had never really gone at all.

Thus, far from propping him up, Munny's dead woman remains as an object that cannot be internalized, who cannot support him in his own goodness as a symbol alone because he relies on her too immediately as the source for what he cannot find in himself. Indeed, without her he slips, as if inevitably, back into his old life—though Logan reminds him that he would never do so if she still lived. (We should recall, here, that Logan himself backs out of the deal despite his loyalty to Munny, since Logan still has a living, breathing wife waiting for him at home.) Munny slowly unravels into a melancholic despair as he gets closer and closer to murdering the young cowboys, which will be an affirmation that, left to support himself (both materially and morally), he can find only one set of answers. Without Claudia in his life, he cannot conjure her goodness in himself. Munny becomes increasingly desperate to finish the job as quickly as possible, perhaps because on some level he wishes to discover if it is really a one-time deal. He does not know himself well enough to know that the money to save his family will be enough. Without Claudia, he simply cannot know what kind of man he is until he puts down his gun and moves to California; even then, we have only the barest glimmer of hope that he has settled down quietly, without incident, trauma, or crime. As it happens, there is no sense of victory or empowerment when the job is done. All we have is the melancholic emptiness of

Munny's own self-beratement and his acknowledgment of the horrific nature of murder. The Schofield Kid, meanwhile, is completely undone by his actions. He can still mourn for himself by crying his eyes out, mourning that Munny cannot share his grief because the killing only returns him to the emptiness of a psychic death he has known for far too long. Munny cannot mourn for himself any more than he can mourn for Claudia, because he cannot represent himself internally as a good man who has lost his way. He is doomed to tearless despair because he cannot mourn a life lost to violence, because he cannot accept that such violence can be forgiven. Thus, he cannot retain in memory an image of himself as whole, as good and decent. To do so would be an act of forgiveness.

Finally, after Logan's brutal murder, Munny's desperate efforts to hold on to his post-traumatic self collapse into complete despair, leaving him to grasp at the only remaining ideal that makes sense to him: fierce loyalty to his friend.[22] It is true, as Lee Clark Mitchell remarks, that a "decent burial" is something of an obsession in cowboy movies, but it is also deeply invested with the ideals of male friendship. Male friends stitch each other together into a psychic and bodily unity even at a moment of complete fragmentation, insisting on a kind of dignity in death that belies the violence and the anguish that brings them to it. Mitchell is critical of *Unforgiven*, disagreeing with the notion that it breaks significantly from the traditional Western template. He argues that although Eastwood portrays Munny's complete incompetence as he begins his journey and cannot keep himself together throughout the quest—he degenerates into illness and then barely fumbles through the motions of the gunslinger's lifestyle—the final showdown works too strongly against this tendency, producing in the end another cowboy fantasy of phallic masculinity as delivered through William Munny's mythically infallible "gun."

Let us review that final scene to determine whether Mitchell is correct. As I have always explained to my students, the difference between the phallus and the penis is as follows: a penis is what a man has in his pants, the phallus is what he *thinks* he has, and the difference between the two is as enormous as the New Jersey Turnpike. My contention is that Eastwood understands this difference; he openly plays Munny as a melancholic character with a hole in his heart, who comes to understand that only by forsaking the worst fantasies of the man with a gun can he ever hope to become a real man worthy of his gender. In the last scene, Munny gives innocent bystanders an opportunity to flee before being caught in the crossfire, in itself a radical break from the stylized violence of the traditional Western in which no one ever has the chance to leave the scene—bodies piling on bodies, whether innocent or guilty, only serve to accentuate the obliterating power of the almighty gunslinger. Of course, those who remain on the scene are inevitably killed, but Munny himself nearly falls to Daggett as he struggles with a jamming gun— another very realistic mishap that would never mar the performance of the infallible and invincible hero of the classic Western template.

Of course, the young biographer remains in the background through it all. Proving himself perhaps the most tragicomic figure in the film, he is dazzled by the myth of William Munny and hopes to gain some insight into his extraordinary success in taking out so many men. Ironically and with great sadness, Munny responds, "I was lucky in the order. I always been lucky when it came to killing folks." Here the biographer stands in for the society that glamorizes violence, the society that creates myths out of the perpetrators of crimes and atrocities. Munny, unlike Bill Daggett or English Bob, claims no honor and boasts no special skill; for him, it only comes down to luck. He takes his vengeance for the death of his friend without a sense of glory; rather it is with a kind of resigned tragic necessity. From there, he rides home to pay his respects to a deeply loved, now buried wife, and later purportedly makes a life in dry goods in San Francisco. His life story certainly does not show up on any bookstands, glorified by the pen of a biographer.

Mitchell's criticism is that the magic of that last scene in which Munny takes out so many men inevitably glamorizes the violence of the traditional Western, in spite of Eastwood's attempt to portray it otherwise. I disagree, because the melancholic Munny remains profoundly imbedded in his melancholia throughout this last scene. The vengeance does not firm him up, so to speak, in a remembrance of his former glory. Mitchell argues that in the end it takes a superhuman effort, an extraordinarily phallic effort, for one man to take on so many others. It defies credibility to call it "luck." Yet Munny has always attributed his success to luck, especially because he was always drunk when he killed and looted in the past. Drunkenness and a sober eye and steady hand hardly go together and, though such phenomenal luck may indeed defy credibility, the "fantasy" it conjures is hardly one of cohesive, dominating phallic masculinity. But what Mitchell really misses is the melancholia in the last scene. Yes, Munny kills Bill Daggett to revenge Logan's murder, but he also does it as an act of fidelity to his friend, since he was guilty of dragging his friend into the assassination plan in the first place. At the heart of his melancholy, the only things holding him together are his guilt before Logan and his shame before the ghost of his wife; this is hardly Sergio

Leone's stylized "No Name" gunslinger. Munny really means it when he agrees with Bill Daggett that he will see him in Hell.

Kimmel has written, "When Eastwood reclaims his manhood, we realize that it is a manhood that no one in his right mind would want. The West is gone, we understand, and so too its supposed western heroes."[23] But although I agree that no one would want this brand of manhood, there is a sense in which Eastwood portrays Munny as a man undone throughout the film. In this sense, he does not regain his manhood by completing what he considers a necessary act of vengeance for Logan, because that kind of violence can never restore the perpetrator to any kind of genuine wholeness—and Munny is well aware of that fact. Thus, it is not at all an aside that the film ends with him returning to Claudia's grave, because only by holding on to his guilt and, yes, to his melancholia—thereby remaining the unforgiven—does he have any chance at another life for himself and his family. And now there is only Claudia's spirit to give it to him.

We now turn to *High Plains Drifter*; my reading of this film will undoubtedly go against the grain of Eastwood's most significant critics. Dennis Bingham, for instance, strongly argues that in *High Plains Drifter* Eastwood's character simply *is* the phallus; indeed, he reads this back into the very idea of the "man with no name," since the phallus can never be directly represented. As a result he interprets the opening scene of *High Plains Drifter* as producing a male spectator who enjoys the fantasy of himself as a man possessed of irresistible and impenetrable narcissism. Thus, for Bingham the spectator is tempted throughout the film to receive pleasure from the Stranger's almost magical acts—acts constructed in a sense by the spectator, since the Stranger never seems to look at the men behind him even as he manages to shoot them precisely in the head. On my reading, however, the spectator is set up in a much more ambivalent position—a position to which Bingham occasionally alludes himself—in that we view the town after the Stranger has ridden past, seeing what he cannot. As Bingham puts it,

> this opening sequence establishes the spectator position for the rest of the film. He or she is placed as a kind of middle term, aligned with the hero who knows the town he has come to and why he is there. The narrative will reveal his motives and unfold the action. At the same time, although the citizens are shown at a distance that establishes them as Other, the film apparatus—and especially the soundtrack—displays the things that cause their apprehension.[24]

But here is where I sharpen my divergence from Bingham: as he begins to read the apprehensions of the citizens very literally into the sounds produced by the Stranger's entry into town, he also assigns the spectator the subjective position as originator of these sounds. Bingham writes,

> As the horse goes by, its hooves and breathing combine to sound like some inexorable machine. When the man gets off his horse, the jingling of his spurs amplified sounds like knives slashing at each other. Also exaggerated is the sound of his footsteps as he walks up the wooden stairs to the saloon. In the position to which the spectator has been placed, it is he or she who causes the apprehension, so effectively has the spectator been aligned with the stranger. The male spectator is . . . a socially constructed image of himself as a male.[25]

Why does Bingham fall back on the spectator's supposed identification with the Stranger? As we have already seen, these are not merely innocent citizens but bystanders to a terrible crime, and it is because of this history that they have become so afraid of this so-called Stranger. As the audience, we are indeed in a middle position: aware that no ordinary stranger would cause such a reaction in an ordinary town, we know that something is off about either the rider or the town, or both. Since our suspicions have not been immediately confirmed, we are not in a position to identify with anyone in a straightforward manner. This middle position, in which we see both the Stranger looking forward and the bystanders terrified by his passing, creates a tension between our stances of identification. We sense a preexisting unease between the townspeople and the lone rider, which seems senseless; and it is the senselessness of that unease that undoes any easy identification with either the townspeople or with the strange rider.

As I have already written, the fact that the Stranger kills three men and rapes a woman within minutes of the film's opening scene makes the movie an easy target for feminists. Indeed, as Bingham writes, the sense in which rape and murder are disconnected in these scenes from any kind of moral rationale reveals those images as pure pornographic projections of the imagination. Sensitive critic that he is, Bingham understands that the masculine spectator threatens to dominate the film's construction, spinning it about the Stranger's entry into town so that, no matter what Eastwood's intention, the scenes reaffirm a tacit toleration of rape. Still, Eastwood's construction actively resists the production of this narcissistic masculine spectator. The pervasive uneasiness of the opening scenes undoes any simple identification or standpoint. Thus, we are indeed distanced from the violence early in the film, but our distance more closely resembles that of the investigator or explorer who must get her bearings in unknown territory than the pleasurable distance of the pornographic spectator. Indeed, we will discover that the woman whom the Stranger rapes was not only among the bystanders who condoned his murder, she had also been personally involved with the marshal prior to the incident, making her complicity all the more painful. By this point, we understand that the Stranger took no pleasure in the rape; the act was permeated with considerable hurt and anguish on *his* part, and our feelings cannot resolve toward the event with anything resembling the pleasure taken in sexual violence by the viewer of pornography. To identify with the rapist is as painful, in a sense, as it is to identify with his victim. We are left, again, in a middle position. I would not argue here that Eastwood is entirely successful with this tactic—and we should recall that this is, after all, one of his first films—but that he portrays a series of overreactions that triggers, ideally, an ambivalence in the spectator that defies the male viewer's tendency to casually identify with the perpetrator of a rape.

Throughout the film, the townspeople are aware of the Stranger's identity on some level. Their nervous questions bespeak more than curiosity; rather, they belie the secret expectation, even eagerness, of the guilty to be punished for what they have done. Only Mordecai benefits from the Stranger's visit, becoming both sheriff and mayor of the town that had ridiculed him. Eastwood twists the viewer's identifications again, putting the law in the hands of the object the town itself (like the viewer) least identifies with the imaginary phallus. Regrettably, dwarfism has all too often stood in for the figure of castration—a representation little people's movements have powerfully contested—but the Stranger is equating the law with something other than power and authority. Instead, he gives the force of law to compassion, to the one man who cried helplessly for Marshal Duncan as he was beaten, the one man who, like Duncan, stood for the *moral* force of the law even when that law had become politically and socially inert.

I agree with Bingham that *High Plains Drifter* should not be read as merely a satire on capitalism. Indeed, it is not satire but allegory, because trauma can only be approached indirectly through the allegorical references of flashbacks. Thus, on my reading we need not view the Stranger as, literally, a ghost, but we see him rather as the psychically dead Marshal Duncan, who has remained in this world bodily but whose soul is gone, along with the ideals for which he stood. Of course, he stood for the ideal that law and justice should be applied to the owners of the rich gold mine as well as to everyone else, and it was this insistence that led to his brutal death as an example of what happens to a person who stands up against the relentless march of industrial capitalism. But the film also provides a lesson about the real cost of moral resignation in the name of progress, because we find among people who have lost their common ideals a sense of catastrophic loneliness and a lack of compassion. It is in light of their shame and guilt over what they have lost (but won't admit having lost) that we can understand the Stranger's infamous statement that they do not fear him, but rather what they have hidden from themselves.

Some of the moves in the film are overdrawn, and we can certainly argue that the rape was a dangerous way to try to show a man's vengeance on a woman who should have known his face. Yet the film is better read in the whole body of Eastwood's work as one of his first attempts to demonstrate the powerful undoing of trauma and the violence of the dissociative personality that remains in its wake. The violent reactions of the traumatized self are exacerbated by the attempts of those around him to go on as if nothing had happened, living by the "forgive and forget" motto of the town, because these attempts read as a denial of wrongdoing and therefore a denial of the possibility for repair. There is nothing to be done but to throw the town forcefully into the very Hell experienced by the trauma victim, to force their reality to represent his inner experience of the world. Read allegorically, the film is terrifying indeed, because it raises some of the most difficult questions of our time; among them the question of what it means to stand by silently in a world rife with violence that is openly condoned by the force of "law" and political authorities. Read this way, the destructiveness of the film is indeed an allegory of what can happen when guilt is simply driven underground with the dead and never faced. "The experience of allegory, which holds fast to ruins, is properly the experience of eternal transience."[26]

By *Pale Rider* the Stranger has become the Preacher, and as we have seen the spectator is invited to identify with Hull Barret and the preacher qua union organizer in a both-and relationship that emphasizes the aspect of doubling in which the two men represent alternative but also complementary ideals of masculinity. Again we return to the issues of technological progress and human dignity, a theme that Sarah Belding in *High*

Plains Drifter puts at the heart of her denunciation of her husband and her decision to leave the town.

In *Pale Rider* Eastwood no longer plays the impassive stranger, because he delivers a double performance—first as an actor, but within his role he is also a gunslinger playing the role of a preacher. He shows genuine compassion for Megan's love for him (because that is what a preacher should do), but in his social role as preacher and organizer he very profoundly returns the men to their faith in a concept of law and ideals that are worth fighting for. Eastwood moves well beyond the impassive acting style into which he was directed by Sergio Leone, beginning a long journey as a character actor. Of course, we don't really know anything about the Preacher, and in that sense he still represents the sentimental icon of the traditional Western: he rides mysteriously out of the landscape and ultimately returns to it. But unlike *Shane*, in which the farmer is never really worthy of his own manhood, Hull Barret comes to represent more permanently what the Preacher could only symbolize briefly before his return into the hills. However, even as Eastwood borrows Leone's themes and plot devices, the key difference between the two films is that Eastwood renders Leone's characters in a non-parodic form that actually produces allegorical renderings of the destructiveness of trauma.

Let us return once more to *Unforgiven* to understand how Eastwood concludes the trajectory of his grappling with masculinity within the cowboy template. Bingham has written that in *Unforgiven* Eastwood not only rejects the unrepresentable, shape-shifting phallus as the principle identification of the film's hero, he also deliberately directs against the identification of the penis with the phallus.

> As part of the project of separating myth from actuality, and symbolic from actual fathers, the film takes care to divide explicitly the mere flesh of the penis from the power and force signified by the phallus. The film wastes no time getting to this issue: the cowboy cuts Delilah the prostitute because as Strawberry Alice Fisher explains, all she did when she saw he had a teensy little pecker, all she did is giggle. She didn't know better. The young woman didn't know she was being paid not only to have sex with a man but also to maintain his fragile self-importance. The cycle of violence is triggered, so to speak, by a woman's failure to respect a man's phallic pride.[27]

Bingham also emphasizes that Munny openly identifies with his own femininity by relating openly with Delilah's pain as the victimized woman. Still, as I have written earlier, his melancholia can be traced to a trauma of perpetration that will allow him no easy outs, even through an honest identification with the victim. Thus, he can tell the girl Delilah that she is still beautiful, but at the same time he has to reaffirm his own ugliness.

I also want to register my disagreement with critics who have written that Eastwood's casting of Morgan Freeman as Munny's sidekick, Ned Logan, represents nothing more than a right-wing commitment to what conservatives call "color blindness." Of course, the black sidekick had been a part of the Western template anyway, and what we really see in Eastwood's usage is a subtle twisting of this character's role in the plot and in his relationship with the white protagonist. Indeed, Bingham admits that certain aspects of the film work against his color-blind reading, including the Schofield Kid's racism-tinged reaction to Logan's discovery of his myopia as well as Logan's eventual whipping, seemingly an echo of slavery. Perhaps more importantly, Munny obviously respects Logan; he is, in fact, completely terrified to work without him.

Chris Packard has described the folk hero of the cowboy:

A folk hero, the cowboy embodies the most precious values in the nation: unrestricted freedom, crafty self-reliance, familiarity with wilderness and horses, good with guns. A savior often of what he deems good, a tireless vanquisher of what he decides is bad, the cowboy's quest teaches boys and men to emulate a cluster of behaviors, values, actions, and frames of reference that connote idealized manhood. Ruggedness, ingenuity, and fearlessness are all qualities the cowboy embodies, while feminine qualities such as domesticity, weakness, and purity are anathema to his unwritten masculine code.[28]

By *Unforgiven*, Eastwood has profoundly undermined the cowboy myth in the only way it could be done, namely by revising some of the traditional figures of the Western—the sidekick, the corrupt sheriff, the young man who needs to be trained. Munny's melancholia remains unresolved by the death of Sheriff Daggett, because the hole in his heart arises from his failure to hold on to a pre-traumatic self that can consistently remain faithful to the ego-ideal of the peaceful farmer. Instead, Munny is eaten up by the more accustomed but more contradictory ego-ideal of the paid assassin, a role he cannot accept but, at the same time, cannot seem to resist. This inner conflict precludes the possibility of a reclaimed masculinity, if one means by that any kind of return to an imaginary wholeness identified with the projection of the phallus. Instead, Munny is left with a hole in his heart, standing once again before the grave of his dead wife, Claudia.

In these films, Eastwood brings us through the major themes of the traditional Western, including the parodies presented by Leone, but ultimately it is the theme of trauma that allows these films to demonstrate a trajectory in which Eastwood attempts again and again to come to terms with trauma and violence. Through allegorical renderings of the disruption caused by trauma, Eastwood bridges a gap between his earlier roles as the amoral, postmodern phallic man—the ultimate trickster who can be anything and everything—and the melancholic, conflicted William Munny of *Unforgiven*.

2
Dancing with the Double: Reaching Out from the Darkness Within

In this chapter we will discuss the nature of evil and its relationship to eroticism, the issue of doubling, and the questions Eastwood poses about the relationship between retribution and mercy. Only two of the films in this chapter, *Blood Work* and *Sudden Impact*, were directed by Eastwood. He produced *Tightrope*, while *In the Line of Fire* merely features Eastwood as the male protagonist; even so, his performances in both films clearly reflect his ongoing engagement with the issues of masculinity and its relationship to violence and eroticism, which we will explore in this chapter.

The doppelgänger is a familiar device in many literary and aesthetic works; and indeed, there are many formulaic representations of the double that often end in a narrative line in which the double must die in order for the dark side of the protagonist to be put to death. Therefore, the good man arises out of the ashes of the bad man, who must be pushed under. But in Eastwood, the engagement between the good man and the bad man becomes infinitely more complex, because the so-called evildoer is not simply reduced to a part of ourselves that can be undone by literally killing it off but instead keeps us on a tightrope where the struggle to be a good man cannot be achieved once and for all. The heart of darkness is in ourselves, and remains something with which we must constantly struggle. Meanwhile, the so-called "bad man" is also more complex because, in the example of Mitch Leary from *In the Line of Fire*, he deeply aspired at one time to be a good man. Therefore, this is no simple portrait of the evildoer, but rather it is a man who is traumatized by his own loss of goodness. He reaches out to Frank, a Secret Service agent who has been in disgrace over his failure to react effectively during the assassination of John F. Kennedy. From Mitch Leary's point of view, both he and Frank have been betrayed by the U.S. government, and their bond is that they have both been set up to be disgraced in a manner that is unfair and emasculating in their own eyes. Leary reaches out to Frank to get the recognition that even though he has done terrible things, he is—as he says in his last message—a good man.

Tightrope (1984)

Tightrope[1] opens to a friendly, warm scene: a group of women, obviously friends but of no clear background or profession, throwing a birthday party. The party ends at an early hour, yet one young woman becomes increasingly anxious on her way home, walking down a lonely New Orleans street. The camera focuses on a pair of tennis shoes that persistently pace her steps, pulling the viewer into her fear and suspense, confirming implicitly that she is right to be afraid. Trembling, she drops one of her packages, but she is instantly relieved to see that the man who picks it up is an officer, in uniform. However, as the camera turns to his shoes, we see that they are not an officer's formal shoes at all but the very shoes that stalked her. She was, after all, right to be afraid.

Cut to another pair of tennis shoes, in the first symbolic foreshadowing of the doubling relationship that sustains the tension of the film. These are the shoes of Captain Wes Block (Eastwood), a police detective, who, off-duty, is playing with his children in the street outside their home.

Shortly thereafter Block is called to a crime scene where the young woman—a prostitute, as it turns out—lies dead, the second murder in what will quickly become a serial chain. Meanwhile, we discover that Captain Block has been associating with prostitutes for some time, long before the beginning of the current investigation. Frustrated and alone after his wife left him, Block has resorted to paying for sex as his only erotic release. Block is desperate to maintain a wall of separation between his two lives: as a cop who pursues the prostitutes' murderer and as a civilian who is caught up in the same erotics of violence that lead his antagonist to actually murder the prostitutes with whom he has sex. These lives are now destined to collide, undermining the stereotypic division between the good man as protector and the dangerous man from whom women and the weak must be protected. Indeed, increasingly eaten up by alcoholic anxiety, Block briefly entertains the terrible fear that he might be the killer himself, perhaps losing control in the midst of a drinking binge.

These dual roles bleed directly into each other as Block goes directly from questioning a prostitute as part of his investigation to paying for her services. All the while his guilt deepens as he begins to suspect that, though he may not have killed anyone himself, the murders may be linked to him; the killer seems to target the very prostitutes that Block himself employs. Indeed, the killer proves eager to engage Block directly: following clues to a gay bar, Block is approached by a male prostitute who indicates that a mysterious third party has offered to pay for his services as a gift for Block. He refuses the offer, but interestingly he also admits to some ambiguity in his own sexuality, challenging the prostitute's assumption that he's never been with a man: "Maybe I have." In fact, Block is more interested in questioning the man, already suspecting that he was hired by the killer. Telling the man to proceed to the rendez-vous where he expects to be paid, Block follows him into a warehouse full of giant Mardi Gras sculptures: pretend knights, cupids, clowns, and generals—an ominous charade of "let's pretend." But when one of the figures drops its pretend ax, the prostitute is hanging from it, dead. Block chases the murderer through the warehouse, but his target eludes him.

Block and the killer are locked in a dance, each pursuing the other in turn. As a criminal psychologist[2] explains to Block, "Once you started going after him, you became closer to him than anyone else." Significantly, she concludes, "There's a darkness in all of us. You, me, and the man down the street. Some of us have it under control, some act it out. The rest of us try to walk a tightrope between the two." Increasingly, Block can sense just how narrow that tightrope is, how near he comes to being consumed by his own darkness. Sex dreams turn to nightmares; fantasy bleeds into murder.

Meanwhile, the activist and rape counselor Beryl Thibodeaux (Gene-viève Bujold) has surprisingly become Block's love interest. Initially rebuffed in her attempts to involve herself in the case, Thibodeaux ulti-mately leads Block to make a public warning suggesting that women should be on their guard. As Block becomes increasingly worried about the safety of other women, he visits Thibodeaux at work, where she teaches self-defense to women, and seeks her advice. Eastwood's por-trayal of a rape self-defense class is realistic and respectful. And soon after when Block meets Thibodeaux working out at the gym, he unabashedly admires her physical strength and discipline. Later, at dinner, he tells her frankly, "When I saw you working out in the gym, I wondered what you were like. I was wondering what it would be like to lick the sweat off your body." While she is not at all shocked by this, she is unimpressed, challenging him to say it "like you don't say it to some woman every night." Still, he clearly interests her, despite his warning, "Maybe you wouldn't like what you find out." Her cool response is a challenge: "Maybe I would."

I find it curious that Dennis Bingham concludes Thibodeaux understands Eastwood immediately through the stereotype of "women's intuition." He reads her almost as an earth mother in her acceptance of and placidity about his cavorting with prostitutes—ignoring, in the first place, the fact that she finds out about it only on their second date. By that time, there is no magic to her understanding of Block's front: she has had three meetings with him, and she has played the earth mother in none of them. Indeed, she has met his erotic interest with a straightforward erotic interest of her own. This is not, as Bingham sees it, the receptive sexuality of traditional femininity. It is an erotic challenge, and it is precisely her strength and her ability to speak her mind that deepens his attraction toward her. Finally, it hardly takes "feminine intuition" to see through the bravado bluff underlying his discussion of licking sweat off her body on a first date.

It is one of the boldest statements of the film that Block's sincere attraction to Thibodeaux is premised on her strength, her feminism, and her willingness to be true to herself. As she explains her own difficulties in finding a romantic partner, she speculates that either she hasn't met the right man or she has a tendency to scare the right men away. Block responds, immediately, "definitely not the right man." She says her mother blames her job for intimidating men, but for her, "It doesn't matter. I like what I do. Helping women, and men, too." Block's only question is, "What makes you so sure they need it?" She responds, significantly, "We all need it." She is echoing, in a sense, the sentiment that there is darkness in the world; there is darkness in all of us.

But there is a specificity to how she confronts violence, particularly from men, that is related to one of the film's profound inversions. For Block, his biggest failure, indeed one that he recognizes and that leads him to alcoholic despair, is that he cannot represent himself as the male protector of stereotype because he is caught up in the nightmare world of violent sexuality himself. Thibodeaux, on the other hand, directly faces male violence and, in a profound sense, brings it into the light of day as someone who teaches women to defend themselves. She undoes the pretense that women can rely on men as protectors in this thoroughly unsafe world. Indeed, the cynicism about the police that leads her to pursue Block in the first place derives from the way the rape and murder of women are trivialized precisely because of their ubiquity. That from the beginning Thibodeaux sees there could be a serial killer murdering the prostitutes indicates her clarity in understanding that this kind of violence is part of day-to-day life and therefore one should always expect the worst even if no specific evidence has emerged to prove it. Thus, as Block struggles desperately to hide his erotic violence, Thibodeaux faces it directly on a regular basis; she teaches other women that they must defend themselves, because they cannot expect men, who are themselves implicated in the eroticized violation of women, to defend them.

Here again I disagree with Bingham, who argues that Thibodeaux is not central to the narrative, because her character first allows us to see the pervasiveness of masculine violence, which none of us can ever truly hide from. Within the action of the film, the doubling of Eastwood and the murderer is brought about by Thibodeaux's confrontation with eroticized violence, suggesting that there are no men that are completely free from the struggle against this darker aspect of sexuality. When she finds handcuffs in Block's bedroom and guesses that he uses them for more than police work, she does not withdraw from him. Her ability to squarely face the darkness of violence gives Block a glimmer of hope that she will not run from the truth about his sexual struggle. Questioning him frankly about his motives in using the handcuffs, she links him directly with the killer, who also uses handcuffs to bind his victims.

When Thibodeaux offers herself to be handcuffed, Eastwood is using her actions to create suspense. At best she seems to be naïve, at worst submissive. But the fear traditionally associated with a woman's surrender in a conventional horror movie is interrupted by Thibodeaux's analysis and her retaining her own voice when she offers up her wrists herself. Again, she chooses not to flee from male violence, because she believes there is simply no way to evade it. Her risk, then, is not a naïve submission but is instead rooted in her conviction that the only way Block can climb out of despair is by admitting his own violent tendencies. Block agrees that the murderer's use of handcuffs indicates his craving to be in control, and Thibodeaux presses him to admit he feels the same way: she suggests he uses handcuffs when he feels threatened, because "nobody can get to you in these." "Stops just about anyone," he concedes.

Thibodeaux picks up the handcuffs and closes them around one wrist suggestively, providing an opportunity that Block, in turn, declines. Her gesture is considered controversial by many critics, precisely because it seems to mimic a classic portrayal of female submission. Bingham concludes that Eastwood the director is out of touch with his character, because it is inconsistent for this sort of character to turn down sex with a handcuffed woman:

> Is her offer a test to see if he will shut out intimacy with her? Does Block refuse because, as his partner in a socially sanctioned dating relationship (one with whom you could have a hard-on any time you want, as the younger daughter innocently puts it) Thibodeaux is in the wrong category for handcuffs? The film posits . . . a feminist as Eastwood's character's redemption, while also saying uncertainly that redemption must come by way of Block's recognition of his condition and his elimination—in the death of the double—of the darkness inside of him. Thus, as a Clint Eastwood film *Tightrope* switches uncertainly from a subject's monolithic independence to his use of a woman for validation. Something a woman really tries to live out her feminism would probably not consent to.[3]

But perhaps it is Bingham's imagination that is faltering here; it might well require a feminist to understand the pervasiveness of male violence and know that Block's only way out is to engage the violence. He can neither run from it nor pretend that it is a problem only for the bad guys. After all, the significance of pornography and sadomasochistic heterosexuality has been hotly debated; indeed, both issues have been sources of great contention within the feminist movement in the United States and elsewhere. But I want to reread this scene through Jessica Benjamin's brilliant article on the complexity of pornography and what it means to engage someone who is consumed by deep dread of his sadistic desires. Thibodeaux's offer turns Block's deeply internalized nightmare, which leads him to act out in a sadistic way that he feels he cannot share, into an intersubjective space of shared fantasy where they can play together with his need to cuff women in order to feel safe. There they can begin to distinguish what is actually fantasy, from the profound fear associated with a yearning to destroy the other in an omnipotent fantasy of control that thwarts the desire for the other, a desire which demands that the other remain.

As Benjamin suggests, we must not slam the door on the question that *Tightrope* raises regarding the relationship between sexuality and violence.

This assessment of sexuality actually slams the door on the provocative question as to how sex can be violence and violence can be
sex. What exactly allows sexuality to carry or transmit relations of
power, violence, and destruction? What is this "thing" called sex?
The collaboration between sexuality and power might somehow
be related to the fact that a violation that would be abominable in
reality can be pleasurable in fantasy. The disjunction between fantasy and reality must be taken seriously if we are to begin to understand the complexity of sexuality and its inveterate association with
violence and revulsion.[4]

This is the significance of the handcuffing scene: Thibodeaux refuses to
slam the door on Block's violent sexuality. It is worthwhile to quote
Benjamin at length:

For the idea of an object that can survive destruction also provides
that destruction must have its say, that fantasy must endeavor to
devour reality in order for the subject to taste the difference
between them. And reality must survive the devouring of the
unconscious in order to be more than mere repression, and thus to
truly include the discovery of an other.[5]

The inner tension of aggression may be modified through a shift in
the outer relationship back to mutual understanding, which
includes communication of fantasy contents. Rather than bouncing
back in retaliation (as in the child's rejoinder to name-calling, "I'm
rubber, you're glue; everything you say bounces off me and sticks
to you"), the other's persistence in receiving communication gives
meaning to the expressive act and so transforms the self's inner
state. The transformation is in the direction that permits the self,
once again, to tolerate the outside, the different. The shift back to
mutual understanding, or out of the fantasy of destruction into the
reality of survival, re-establishes the tension between two individuals even as it dissipates the tension of aggression within the individual. But when the shift back to intersubjective reality fails,
internalization remains the only way to deal with aggression; the
turning inward of aggression forms the basis of the fantasy of doer
and done to, and inner world of persecutors and victims.[6]

Benjamin's argument, then, is not that sexuality must always be tied to aggression—far from it. Rather, fantasy can help to metabolize aggression, but only once the basis for the fantasy—the desire for destruction—is recognized by someone who can contain it without running, who can withstand the onslaught of psychic destructiveness and remain whole, ultimately surviving the aggressive aspect of the fantasy. This is the role that Thibodeaux plays for Block. Block is clearly caught in that deadly repetition of doer and done-to, persecutor and victim, and so is his double, whose murders taunt Block by reminding him of his sexual history with prostitutes, as if to say, "I know who you are. You are a bad man, too." At one point, the murderer even hangs Block's forgotten tie on a statue near the body of the fourth victim, implicating him in the crime. This "you are like me" identification is what Block most profoundly dreads. It pulls him into a psychic abyss in which he becomes one with the murderer, in which he is unworthy of love precisely because he cannot live up to the masculine ideals represented by his career as a police officer, one who protects victims. His despair at his own unworthiness is indicated in a powerful scene after Block's eldest daughter informs him, tearfully, that his ex-wife is getting married. Later that night he drinks himself to unconsciousness, and his daughter finds him sprawled awkwardly on the sofa still clutching his wedding picture. Unable to move him, she lovingly embraces him, but her small frame against his larger body emphasizes the fact that, for all her caring, she cannot offer him the equal position that is necessary to break open his deadly fantasies into the shared space of mutuality.

Block needs something more, and what makes the cuffing scene so powerful is that Thibodeaux's courage before male violence is what allows her to stand up to him. In Benjamin's sense, she accepts the challenge of moving into his fantasy, of embracing his darkness within—not to give in to it masochistically, but rather, to embrace the darkness in order to make it something they can share, and therefore something different that can be played with and explored together. Does it take a strong woman to make that kind of gesture? Does it take a feminist? As a director, Eastwood certainly seems to indicate that it does—and that, frankly, gladdens my heart.

Bingham also worries that *Tightrope* portrays sex and violence as so tightly bound up together. Indeed, it is true that they are intrinsically linked in the film since Block and his double are consumed by the same sadistic fantasy, though neither of them can keep it as a fantasy. Each man feels compelled to act it out in his own way. There is a connection, however, as Benjamin has brilliantly written in *The Bonds of Love*, between aggression, violence, and sexuality, one that psychoanalysis must certainly confront.[7] But it also has to be addressed in actual lived relationships as we struggle to loosen the bonds that deeply connect us to traditional gender roles, roles that lead men and women to have difficulty developing fluid relationships with adults of the opposite sex. Indeed, part of *Tightrope*'s provocation comes precisely from its tying sex to violence and its unraveling the stereotypic way of separating the father protector from the erotic villain. Here again we return to the Thibodeaux character; it is precisely her suggesting that the answer for women is not in male protectors but in self-defense and an honest confrontation with a violent world that leads to only one way out for Block, a mutual confrontation of violence within a heterosexual relationship.

Otto Rank has written more than anyone else about the double in psychological literature. Often the image appears as one's own guardian spirit conjured in the form of a torturing conscience. The double, in Rank's analysis, must be killed off in order for what is good in the pursuer to redeem itself.[8] Often, there is no recognition that the double is indeed a side of one's self, but for Block the figure of the double inspires a sense of self-disgust, truly the guardian spirit of the tortured conscience. As Bingham rightly points out, the film is true to the Hegelian insight that the need for change often begins with self-disgust. Thus, as the double in *Tightrope* is granted his full identificatory status, Block does not disavow the killer's deliberate taunting, but his recognition does plunge him into the deepest chasm of self-disgust.

Yet, self-disgust alone cannot save a man from the violent fantasy of doer and done-to, persecutor and victim, without the help of someone who is willing to dance or play with the very act of doubling. Indeed, Wes Block is far from the stereotypical masculine character who is unassailable and self-sufficient. Struggling to raise two daughters on his own, Block cannot even fulfill his role as fatherly protector: the murderer, sharpening his identification with Block, invades his home and murders the girls' nanny as well as most of the dogs, but ultimately leaves one of the daughters tied to a bed, relatively unharmed. Block struggles with the intruder, but he lives only because the one surviving dog grabs the murderer's leg at a critical moment, allowing Block to escape from a deadly stranglehold. Alone, Block would have been killed.

And now Block is truly terrified (another uncommon feeling in macho Hollywood), and we see him as a loving father whose failure to protect his daughters eats him up inside. He cannot fathom how to make it up to them. His ex-wife, at the hospital, never speaks: she merely glares at him with disapproving eyes. Aware now that the murderer wants to dance in his footsteps, to share the same fantasy, Block becomes concerned for Thibodeaux. When he cannot reach the police assigned to protect her, he drives desperately to her home, where he finds Thibodeaux engaged in deadly combat with the murderer, using the skills she has taught to other women so many times before. Again, Bingham worries that she was not ultimately strong enough to defeat her attacker, but very few people, women *or men*, could successfully fend off a frenzied attack and Thibodeaux certainly holds her own. Indeed, she fares better than her police guards! Ultimately, it is her ability to stave off the attack long enough for Block to arrive that both saves her life and offers Block the opportunity to pursue the perpetrator one last time. As he bursts onto the scene, the attacker runs away. Thibodeaux quickly signals that she will be fine alone. She can take care of herself, and he should do what needs to be done. Again she is not the stereotypic attacked woman, who throws her arms around her rescuer. Instead she makes it very clear that she is all right and he should continue pursuing the murderer, which is after all his job.

The tense final scenes follow the two men, the murderer and his pursuer, through a darkened graveyard, a police helicopter providing scattered light from above. Significantly, the film does not end here; the graveyard is a turning point, signaling the life-and-death battle that is reaching its climax, signaling that someone will die here tonight. That the men pass through the graveyard suggests, however, an escape from death as well: Block has the chance, here, to escape both from bodily death and from the psychic death that he had all too nearly embraced. The men end up, at last, in an active train yard—another clear symbol of life paths intersecting and diverging. They fight to the very end, doubles entwined in each other's arms, and it is unclear until the final second who will actually roll out from under the weight of the approaching train. At last, Eastwood tears off the murderer's mask and sees his face, confirming what he has suspected: the killer is a man he had arrested for rape years ago. Block was responsible for sending him to prison. The face-to-face moment is an important resolution for Block, facilitating his victory over his own fearful identification with the man. Here is a man with a face, a man with an identity, a man truly other and different from himself.

For a critic like Bingham nothing has been recuperated here; he claims that the film is too rife with contradictions. These contradictions, supposedly, play against the necessary resolution found in the double's death, the customary end of the doppelgänger film. Indeed, Block does not walk away with any kind of strong assertion that the story is finished, that his work is complete. Instead he remains in total disarray and disorientation. Left clutching the murderer's severed arm, Block stands up shakily after the battle's bloody end, walking away as if he were drunk or concussed, barely able to stand. By this time, Thibodeaux has arrived at the scene. Despite her own struggle and confrontation with death, she is not hysterical. She seeks no immediate treatment in the hospital, but she remains strong enough to find Block, not her hero, but her partner in an equal relationship, which is clearly presented when they walk off supporting one another.

As already indicated, Bingham argues that Thibodeaux is actually peripheral to the plot and the audience finds out very little about her. In one sense, that is true; we never do learn much about Thibodeaux's past, but dramas show rather than tell. In truth, we know a great deal about Thibodeaux as a person through her ethical commitments to other human beings and her erotically charged relationship with Block, which she pursues fearlessly, maintaining an equal footing with him. As Bingham writes, Thibodeaux's function "is to provide Block with his salvation. . . . [H]is case is too serious to be solved by true love, the constitution of which this film doesn't pretend to know. It takes a feminist."[9]

I am not sure whether Bingham means it takes a feminist to save Block, or that it takes a feminist to know about the constitution of true love. At any rate, we cannot be too hard on Eastwood for failing to capture the essence of true heterosexual love; I think few of us can claim to have a clear idea about it. If Eastwood puts his confusion or uncertainty about true love on view for the audience, then we are in his debt for such a honest portrayal. Indeed, what is interesting about his acting in this film is that he captures, in a profound sense, the persona of the hard-edged macho hero; Eastwood shows that it is only a front, a defense against a deeply fearful rejection of women caused by a fear of being rejected by them.

On a deeper level, the film's endless engagement with performance and masking points both to Block's confusion about his own fantasies and to the fact that real men and women are, like Block, perpetually trapped in such performances. These gender roles are based on ideals that are nothing but empty stereotypes when we actually try to put them on. Indeed, Benjamin has argued in *The Bonds of Love* that it may well take a feminist to understand how such gender roles are performed and why they arise in profound relationships with our first caretakers and love interests. Such gender performances are deeply connected to the process by which a human being comes to define her or himself in relationships with others, separate yet inevitably connected. As the prostitutes play, in an overdrawn manner marking the difference between the good girl and the bad girl, they emphasize just how difficult it may be to find oneself as a whole person, underscoring the broader difficulty that Block experiences in relating to women as whole individuals who can meet him face-to-face.

Benjamin's entire argument in *The Bonds of Love* is that we cannot get out of the violent fantasy of persecutor and victim unless we are truly willing to confront our own destructive impulses—what Eastwood's criminal psychologist calls "the darkness within." The struggle for what Benjamin calls recognition begins as an internal within the psyche, which is not created by a particular action but rather conditioning the interpersonal. The question for her is can we ultimately recognize the other person as more than just the sum of our projections or an object of our own need for recognition? Indeed, to feel recognized *by an Other* is crucial to bolstering intersubjectivity. It is precisely because we are bonded to others from birth that we must struggle to achieve any individuation, and this struggle to find what Benjamin, following Hegel, calls recognition cannot help but go through destructiveness. Benjamin defines mutual recognition as, "a relation in which each person experiences the other as 'like subject,' as another mind that can be 'felt with' yet has a distinct, separate center of feeling and perception."[10] By finding her way to Block in the train yard, by surviving his own destructive fantasies—literally by remaining alive and psychically by exposing his fantasy as fantasy in her courage to enter that space with him—Thibodeaux has shown that she is, in Benjamin's sense, the other whom Block can truly desire.

Far from peripheral, Thibodeaux's story is, in my interpretation, a second track for Block—and that is the significance that I give to the final scene in the train yard. Block can, indeed, go either way; he is walking on a tightrope. Perhaps, at one time, the murderer could have gone a different way as well. In a sense, Thibodeaux draws out the contrast between two different kinds of identification. There is the double, which is always an active identification that can only result in individuation through mutual destruction. On the other hand, there is the act of recognition that struggles through our destructiveness to identify another self, an identity that can share our dreams and our nightmares in such a way that maybe, just maybe, we can reach through it all to touch each other. There is no simple salvation at the end of this film. There is, however, a glimmer of hope, and we can only understand that glimmer if we understand the difference between the identification at the heart of doubling—which tries to assert a oneness that denies difference—and a countervailing act of recognition, in which the other remains on her own track, offering an intersubjective space in which nightmares can be shared and, to that extent, relieved. It takes a strong person to offer this lifeline, a person secure in her own self, in her sameness and her difference. It takes someone who can withstand the nightmare.

It takes a feminist.

In the Line of Fire (1993)

Even though *In the Line of Fire*[11] was neither directed nor produced by Eastwood, I am including it in this book because of its powerful portrayal of the doubling relationship, which Eastwood will return to again and again when directing his own movies. Frank Horrigan (Eastwood) is a Secret Service agent, who was disgraced after he failed to save the life of President John F. Kennedy in 1963. When the film opens, Al D'Andrea (Dylan McDermott), one of Horrigan's new agents, arrives late to work because he had to drop off one of his children at school. But Horrigan will hear no excuses and chides the agent, setting the tone of the mentor relationship between the two, a common Eastwood theme. As they immediately set out on an undercover mission to break up a drug deal, it quickly becomes clear that D'Andrea may not be cut out for the constant trauma that this kind of work entails. Indeed, the torturous adaptations of the soul required to serve our national security agencies are one of the critical themes in this film.

The tension mounts as Horrigan investigates a landowner's tip about one of her tenants, who has pinned an ominous scrapbook of presidential assassinations to his wall. Horrigan discovers a second room in the apartment that contains only one picture: Horrigan standing next to Kennedy's car on that fateful day in Dallas. Uncannily, a doubling relationship is suggested already: Horrigan investigates a suspect who has clearly done his homework on him. Indeed, as Horrigan leaves the scene perplexed and concerned by this development, we catch our first glimpse of the suspect, Mitch Leary (John Malkovich), watching Horrigan as he walks home. As we will see, there is an irony in Leary's obsession: he both protects and menaces at the same time. He tracks Horrigan as a tactical piece in the game he is playing, but he also sees himself as a friend who watches Horrigan's back.

Horrigan returns to his apartment and Leary calls him, saying, "I'm dying to talk to you. I feel like I know you." Why? Horrigan asks. "You being intimately involved in the assassinations of two presidents," says Leary, giving Horrigan the kind of threat he needs to call a meeting of his Secret Service staff. At the meeting we meet Horrigan's strong female alter ego, Agent Lilly Raines (Rene Russo), who has just joined the team. Horrigan does not initially greet her with the most respectful attitude, remarking, "Secretaries get prettier and prettier around here." She fires right back, "And the field agents get older and older." In a theme that will recur in Eastwood films, it is Raines who will press her superiors to keep the aging, disgraced agent on as an integral part of the investigation and to assign him to the team responsible for protecting the president.

Running alongside the motorcade, Horrigan is barely able to keep up, his age obvious. Leary is in the crowd, of course, watching Horrigan gasp and double over in his efforts to keep up with the president's car. Later, he calls to say, "I was worried about you today. I thought you were going to pass out. What did happen to you?" Here he refers not to Horrigan's struggle on the road that day but to his challenge that fatal day in Dallas. Leary continues:

> What did happen to you that day? Only one agent reacted to the gunfire, and you were closer to Kennedy than he was. You must have looked up at the window of the Texas Book Depository, but you didn't react. Late at night, when the demons come, do you see the riffle coming out of that window, or do you see Kennedy's head being blown apart? If you'd reacted to that first shot, could you have gotten there in time to stop the big bullet? And if you had—that could've been your head being blown apart. Do you wish you'd succeeded, Frank? Or is life too precious?

Leary draws Horrigan deeper into a relationship that Horrigan cannot resist because he connects to Leary through his taunts, comments like "The world can be a cruel place to an honest man. It's nice to have a friend." Humiliated by Leary, who calls himself "Booth," and his references to Frank's tragic failure, Horrigan nevertheless needs to keep him on the line. "What about you, Booth? What's your story?" Horrigan asks. Leary tells him, "It's an epic saga," before terminating the call to prevent the agents from tracing him.

Meanwhile, Horrigan's increasing respect for Raines keeps pace with his growing affection for her. As in the other Eastwood movies we have examined, the Eastwood character does not ally with his female counterpart because she is a weak woman who needs his protection. Equally significant, Horrigan's friendship with D'Andrea also deepens as the young agent proves his ability by offering creative new ideas about how to track Leary, who continually eludes their attempts to pin him down.

Horrigan's developing friendships with Raines and D'Andrea highlight the need for connection that allows Leary to draw parallels with Horrigan during their conversations. While the new relationships do help to pull Horrigan out of his isolation, they do not stop Leary's identification with him, which draws Horrigan into an emotional abyss. "We've got so much in common," Leary says. "We are both honest and capable men who were betrayed by people we trusted." Horrigan doesn't thinks he was betrayed; he believes there is truth in the report that claimed he should have reacted to save Kennedy. It is Leary who insists that, like him, Horrigan got a raw deal. But Horrigan has a question of his own for Leary: "Who betrayed you?" "Some of the same people," Leary replies cryptically. "But I'm going to get even. I'll have my day in the sun. The question is, will you have yours? I think you're in for a lot more pain."

Indeed, Horrigan has suffered his fair share of pain. We have learned that his wife left him, taking their daughters with her, because she could not handle his moody behavior, which was a direct result of his dealing with a dangerous, stressful job. In some ways, his job has lost meaning for him. Indeed, he suggests that he may be willing to give up his position, which has now become work, to find happiness with a woman. When Raines tells him that she ended a very serious relationship because her lover did not approve of what she did for a living, Frank asks her, "What would happen if I gave up my job for you? Maybe I've vowed never to let my career come between me and a woman." But Raines does not accept his romantic gesture. Some of Eastwood's critics have suggested that the line would have more impact if Rene Russo were not thirty some years younger than Eastwood and if his character were not already on the brink of retirement. But indeed Russo is not quite as young as some of these critics suggest; she made this film during her career renaissance, which came in her mid-to-late forties after a long absence from Hollywood. And although Horrigan at times seems exhausted by his job, he also shows unflagging commitment to tracking down Leary. Thus, Horrigan's willingness to put a relationship before his career stands as a challenge to a certain kind of masculinity, which presupposes that women are the ones who give up their jobs for men, not vice-versa.

By now it is well known that the film spectator is supposed to identify with the camera's gaze. In *In the Line of Fire*, the camera creates an uneasy identification with Leary, the man planning an assassination, as we are frequently left gazing at Horrigan through Leary's eyes. We are pulled into Leary's own ambivalence toward Horrigan, as we simultaneously identify with Leary and worry for Horrigan, thereby participating in Leary's conflicted concern. He watches Horrigan, seemingly as his tormentor, yet at the same time he protects him as a military man guards a fellow soldier. While some would argue that Leary puts Horrigan in the masochistic position—objectified and weakened, even feminized in his vulnerability and uneasiness—these critics overlook the deep ambivalence within Leary: his look is both threatening and caring at the same time. He wants Horrigan to remain his equal, if only because he simply wants to continue with the game, but perhaps also because if he can save Horrigan then he can redeem himself as well.

Horrigan is increasingly on edge, because he too recognizes that Leary's game is a chance for salvation, a chance to replay his protection of a president, hopefully with a different outcome this time. But he is so tense with anticipation that he jumps, literally, at the sound of balloons popping, raising a false alarm that publicly embarrasses the president. Raines, gently informing him that he is being removed from the case because his superiors consider him paranoid, reminds him that it is part of his job to protect the president's dignity. She recalls the time when, as part of Kennedy's entourage, he pretended to be the lover of one of the president's girlfriends to save Kennedy from being discovered by his wife. But Horrigan explains that he has hardened since then: "I was different. The whole damn country was different. Everything would be different if I was half as paranoid then as I am today. Fuck!" Leary may be taunting Horrigan as he threatens to reenact his biggest failure, but Horrigan cannot help but see those taunts as a promise, a possibility. Despite Horrigan's resistance, it is that possibility that draws him ever closer to Leary.

Motivated by watching Horrigan play his piano alone, Leary calls Horrigan again because he cannot bear the thought of his utter loneliness—which mirrors, of course, his own. He says that Horrigan does not have enough in his life, and Horrigan can only lamely point out that he has the piano. So just what is Leary offering him? "There's no cause worth fighting for," he tells Horrigan. "All we have is the game. It doesn't work, Frank. God doesn't punish the wicked and reward the righteous. Everyone dies. Some die because they deserve to, others die simply because they come from Minneapolis. It's random. And it's meaningless." Despite himself, Horrigan is drawn into this conversation. He retorts, "If none of this means anything, then why kill the president?" Leary has already remarked that this president is not worth either man's time; he is almost beside the point. Now he replies, "To punctuate away the dreariness," and concludes the conversation, affirming his profound identification with Frank: "You are the same as me."

Horrigan soon realizes just how similar their lives have been, learning that Leary too has been a government agent. During a search of Leary's former home, Horrigan and D'Andrea nearly have a shootout with other intruders, who turn out to be CIA agents looking for one of their own—Leary, a former wetboy assassin, gone rogue. But even as Horrigan believes they are closing in on Leary, D'Andrea announces he has had enough: he's quitting the Secret Service because he is not up to the job. We do not pity D'Andrea; we identify with his fear. Still, D'Andrea has come to count on him as a friend and an ally. He almost pleads with him to stay at his side: "Come on, pal. I need you."

In their next conversation Horrigan is eager to press Leary with his new information. "I know who you are, Leary." At first, Leary is relieved. "I'm glad, Frank" he replies. "Friends should be able to call each other by name." But Horrigan presses further, "I've seen what you do to friends," referring to what he learned from the CIA about the fate of the man sent to help Leary readjust to civilian life. "You slit your friend's throat." Leary is straining now, becoming defensive. "You talked to Coppinger, Frank? Did you delouse? The man is a professional liar." By now Horrigan clearly has the edge: "I saw a picture of your friend lying on the floor with his throat cut." Leary becomes furious, breaking down under what he takes to be Horrigan's contempt. "What you didn't see, Frank," he screams, "what you couldn't possibly know, is that they sent my best friend—my comrade-at-arms—to my home to kill me!"

Horrigan responds coolly, "Your voice is shaking." Leary is desperate now for him to understand. "Frank, you of all people, I want you to understand because we both used to think that this country was a very special place." Horrigan protests, trying to distance himself, but Leary does not relent: "Do you have any idea what I've done for God and country? Some pretty FUCKING HORRIBLE things! I don't even remember who I was before they sunk their claws into me. I don't even remember who I was before they sunk their claws into me." On some level, Horrigan does understand—or perhaps he's merely trying to provoke Leary further when he remarks, "They made you a real monster, right?" Leary agrees, concluding, "That's right and now they want to destroy me because we can't have monsters roaming the quiet countryside now, can we."

Leary almost pleads with Horrigan: "Do you know how easily I could killed you, Frank? Do you know how many times I've watched you go in and out of that apartment? You're alive because I have allowed you to live. So show me some goddamn respect!" Angry, Leary answers the question he posed earlier about what Horrigan sees when the demons come: "I see you, Frank, standing over the grave of another dead president."

If Horrigan's provocations are a tactic, then the tactic finally works. Investigators trace the call, leading to a death-defying chase across rooftops in which Horrigan, aging and out of shape, finally misses a jump and barely catches a ledge, where he hangs, helpless, as Leary stands over him. Indeed, it is only because Leary offers Horrigan his hand that Horrigan lives to continue the game, standing face-to-face with his quarry at last, with every opportunity to shoot him and put an end to it all. Leary taunts him, placing Horrigan's gun in his own mouth and reminding Horrigan that if he shoots now the president will be saved. Hesitating to kill a man who has just saved his life, Horrigan affirms that this president is only incidental to the game between them. Yet when D'Andrea arrives on the scene Leary does not hesitate: he pushes Horrigan away and shoots D'Andrea twice, killing him immediately. Leary then gets away as Horrigan runs to his murdered friend.

Of course, now Frank is eaten up by a double guilt over his failure to kill Leary, because he risked the president's life and ended his partner's life at the same time. But he has also been drawn into a more complete identification with Leary: his betrayal at the hands of the Secret Service is complete, as his superiors think he is too close to the case. Against his protests, his superiors have him transferred to San Diego. He could never admit what Leary so persistently reminds him, that the report blaming his failure to protect Kennedy from assassination had been a betrayal, that he had been a scapegoat for broader failures of security. Now, like Leary, he has been completely rejected by the authorities to whom he dedicated his life in service. Perhaps for this reason alone, he cannot let go.

In San Diego he continues his investigation, breaking a code revealing bank deposits that Leary had used to get powerful Republicans to invite him to a fundraiser where he planned to assassinate the president. Defying his orders, Horrigan arrives just in time to take the bullet meant for the president—his only cheat, as Leary puts it, is wearing a bulletproof vest. After a brief pursuit, Leary gains the advantage and takes Horrigan hostage in an elevator with him. Implying that, one way or another, his death is imminent, he says that he is glad to have Horrigan there: "I don't want to leave the miserable world alone." Horrigan disavows any friendship, but Leary insists that Horrigan owes him a debt of gratitude. "Without me," he argues, "you'd still just be another sad-eyed, piano-playing drunk. I brought you into this game. I let you keep up with me. I made you a goddamn hero today. I redeemed your pathetic shitty life today." Leary wants Horrigan to acknowledge that he has been honest with him, unlike the government that manipulated and betrayed them both. He wants Horrigan to recognize him as a man of honor, even if he has twisted his sense of honor into a bizarre parody of itself.

In the final scuffle, Horrigan ultimately gains the upper hand. Leary hangs out of the elevator, and in an echo of the earlier rooftop scene Horrigan offers Leary his hand. "Do you want to save me, Frank?" "To be honest and fair with you," Horrigan replies, "no. But it's just my job."

Horrigan is a hero, and indeed his career is redeemed. Unfortunately, he is too old to run with the president's entourage and after all of the publicity surrounding the assassination attempt, he can no longer do undercover work, so he is effectively forced to retire. Yet when he returns home, he finds a chilling message from Leary on his answering machine, revealing that he never intended to win the game. Leary had hoped Horrigan would outlive him all along. Leary's last words to Horrigan, spoken into the machine:

> By the time you hear this, it will be over. The President is most likely dead, and so am I. I wonder, Frank, did you kill me? Who won our game? Not that it matters. For among friends like you and me, it's not whether you win or lose, but how you play the game. Now the game is done and it's time to get on with your life. But I worry that you have no life to get on with. You're a good man. And good men like you and me are destined to travel the lonely road. Goodbye. And good luck.

These men have an ongoing conversation throughout the film, making this form of doubling very different from what we saw in *Tightrope*. While the impetus for their relationship is Leary's projecting identification onto Horrigan, Horrigan has been so traumatized that he now shares Leary's pain: he does not know who he was before the government sunk its claws into him. As Sue Grand writes, trauma imposes loneliness, and indeed, throughout this film Leary often appears on camera alone—and we often see Horrigan alone with Leary as his only, silent witness. Leary entangles Horrigan in a bond created by his reminding Frank about his own past trauma, dangling it in front of him seductively, in order to draw him closer to the friendship that Leary desires. And, after all, Leary knows that only he can offer Horrigan what he really needs, the chance to redeem himself by playing the heroic role that he was previously denied. Their relationship leads them to engage in conversations that are truly man-to-man, not just hunter and hunted. Indeed, they recognize in one another a sense of honor lost on most government agents—agents who could be sent to kill their best friends. Because of this honor code between the two men, Horrigan is positive that Leary will, indeed, attend the fundraising dinner, and he passes this information on to Raines. Leary said he would attend, and Horrigan is sure he would never lie to him.

For government agents such as Horrigan and Leary, the ideals of masculinity that they share have become twisted through the government's betrayal of them. Leary knows Horrigan will identify with this betrayal, and it is through this identification that Horrigan will understand him. He is only asking for understanding; we should note that at no time does Leary seek any kind of mercy from Horrigan. For Leary, there is only one way out of this traumatic nightmare, in which he no longer knows who he is. He only knows the distorted life of a wetboy, a corrupted "not-him" image that he can never escape because it is all he has. Still, he retains a desire to be treated as a man, not merely a psychological case file. In fact, both men agree that, as Horrigan puts it, "A man's actions do not equal the sum of his psychological parts." Therefore, Leary does not want from Horrigan any pity that is premised on the life he has endured, on the causal factors that contribute to his apparent psychosis. He wants, as he puts it, respect and gratitude. He wants to find his way again, somehow, to being with a friend—and friendship has nothing at all to do with pity.

In this context we might interpret Leary's thoughtless killing of D'Andrea as a kind of jealousy. What is the basis of the erotic attachment? Leary sees in Horrigan a projected image of himself. In a certain sense, as in all classic cases of projected identification, they are one. Horrigan should have no independent identity on which he could reject him. Projective identification creates a twisted erotic bond because it is a love that obliterates otherness. Given the passion and the erotic connection that Leary feels to Horrigan, the realization of his plan only has room for the two of them; it would be disrupted by D'Andrea's constant presence at Horrigan's side. This rationale for D'Andrea's murder heightens Horrigan's profound guilt over the death of his friend, because he is not only complicit in the murder through his own inaction but is also drawn even more tightly into a friendlike relationship with the killer. Horrigan's opinion of Leary is never easily compartmentalized into categories of good or evil, highlighting his understanding that Leary is right about one thing: the ideals of our country have lost something important, and we only deceive ourselves by pretending that we can stand without contradiction against a flat moral conception of "evil."

The pathos of the film is that Horrigan is redeemed in his own self-image, because he does finally take the bullet, which stands in for the one he should have taken in Dallas. What does it mean, then, that Leary never meant to win the game, that winning for him was really all about saving Horrigan from himself? The game, in one sense, gave him his only way out of the catastrophic loneliness associated with trauma. His voice shakes when he feels that Horrigan does not understand him, when it seems that he has bought into the psychological reductionism that portrays him as a monster. To use Hannah Arendt's word, "evil" in this film is anything but banal.[12] At one point in his life, Leary was a loyal soldier who followed orders, but he never denies that what he did was terrible; he is forthright about the fact that he did "some pretty fucking horrible things for God and country." But where does remorse get you when at the end of the day your sins are protected secrets of state that cannot be admitted? Indeed, when a government that contradicts the wrongness of your sins will not prosecute them as crimes, but sets out to murder you, the one whom they hired to commit them in the first place? The contradictions of government-sanctioned violence piled up on this man as torments for which there could be no satisfactory relief.

The banality of evil, for Arendt, was that Adolf Eichmann, after being arrested in Buenos Aires for his crimes against humanity during World War II, was incapable of thinking from the position of the Other. It is Eichmann's thoughtlessness that makes his actions banal; he did the deeds, that's all, and any remorse seems shallow and untrue to his duty. Leary, on the other hand, is eaten up by the failure of the ideals that he thought he had been upholding on behalf of the government. He is obsessed by his own thoughts of how the country is failing. And in a very twisted way, Leary is only too careful to dig his claws into Horrigan's heart by getting at his traumatic past. Thus, Leary's final attack on a president who never played a significant role in his past is actually an attempt, in Sue Grand's meaning, to impress himself on Horrigan as a man whose masculinity is evidenced by his always playing fair and straight with Horrigan. Does he die with a smile, knowing that Horrigan has been redeemed? Does his identification with Horrigan allow him to believe that through Horrigan's vindication he has held on to the only part of himself that would be worth saving? Leary knows that death is coming to him for what he has done, but in losing the game he escapes the death of a monster and finds the death of a man. Honoring him by offering his hand, Horrigan treats Leary as a human being, if only as part of his job—an apt reversal of Leary's close friend who tried to kill him, though in that case it was also part of the job.

Both Leary and Horrigan resist psychological reductionism, and as a result both accept the principle of retribution. Leary accepts that he must die for what he has done, but he refuses to allow the government, which hired him only to betray him, to finally get away with his execution. Instead, he reinvests Frank with the ideals that they had both once believed the government stood for, until the government proved them wrong: it is not the job of a government agent to commit murder. The principles of justice that are betrayed in the very job description of a wet boy were themselves redeemed, insofar as Frank refuses revenge in favor of retribution, a legal concept. As Leary drops voluntarily to his death, he does so knowing that Horrigan—his "friend"—has succeeded where he failed. The last scene is a reenactment for both of them: Leary leads Horrigan in a carefully choreographed dance to redeem Horrigan's "pathetic little life," even as Leary accepts the death appropriate to the crimes he has committed.

It is the attachment with Leary, the passion for their shared ideals—and therefore for the relationship rather than the game—that takes us into the entanglement of the trauma and redemption of Horrigan, a redemption that demands the kind of tragic sacrifice of which Leary was clearly capable. Whatever remains of the Leary that existed before his life as a wet boy is invoked and redeemed in his death as a man. He leaves Horrigan behind to have a chance at the kind of life he could never have. By sacrificing himself willingly, he has pulled the darkness into himself so that it does not eat away at Horrigan anymore. This is a significant twist on the traditional end of the doppelganger film, in which the hero is freed by destroying the symbol of his own darkness. Here Leary takes responsibility for his own death, freeing Horrigan not by an act of vengeance but by accepting the retribution due him, which is death. By treating him as a man still within the law whose life he must save, Horrigan symbolically recognizes that Leary is not a monster.

Blood Work (2002)

Blood Work,[13] once again a film directed by Eastwood, opens with the renowned FBI agent Terry McCaleb (Eastwood) in pursuit of a serial killer who is clearly engaged with him and leaves him notes at the scene of each murder. Indeed, one of McCaleb's fellow agents jokes, "Another love note? The two of you should get a room." McCaleb is hot on the killer's trail, so hot that he has a heart attack while trying to climb the fence that the killer has successfully jumped. The incident effectively ends his career, because even though he is fortunate enough to get a heart transplant, his superiors do not think him fit to return to his duties.

But McCaleb's quiet retirement is very quickly interrupted. He has hardly recovered from his operation when Graciella Rivers (Wanda De Jesus), a young Chicana asks him to look into the murder of her sister, Gloria, who, as Rivers explains to his surprise and horror, was the donor of his new heart. Because her sister's heart saved McCaleb's life, Rivers believes he is obligated to at least look into the case, which the police have dropped with no leads. McCaleb cannot help but see some reason in her argument.

Because most police officers are reluctant to invite a high-profile FBI agent onto their turf, McCaleb seeks the help of Detective Jaye Winston (Tina Lifford), a young African American woman officer whom he helped to gain a promotion. Here we see, again, the Eastwood character relying on a woman, in this instance a black woman, whom he treats as an equal, as one who is worthy of sincere respect. He was, as Winston puts it, her "membership into this goddamn boys' club," and she agrees to reciprocate with whatever help she can in acquiring records on this murder. While she finds at least one other murder that may involve the same killer, McCaleb is unable to identify the relationship between the two murders, and he is in no position physically to pursue the investigation alone. Thus, he winds up soliciting his neighbor, Jasper "Buddy" Noone (Jeff Daniels), to act as his assistant and driver. Thrilled to be McCaleb's sidekick, Buddy eagerly accepts the opportunity.

Indeed, McCaleb needs all the help he can get. They follow a number of false leads, but even the fruitless search has such a great toll on McCaleb that his doctor threatens to stop treating him if he does not start looking after his health. But by this time he feels a deep ethical obligation to the woman whose heart he bears, and guilt over the reality that he wouldn't have received the heart if someone hadn't done this "evil hateful thing." Despite an unpromising absence of leads, he begins to believe that the heart inside him wants so badly to find the killer that he cannot stop. He relies on Rivers's advice: "You have Gloria's heart. She will guide you."

Gradually, McCaleb begins to realize that there are connections between his previous work and the murders under investigation now—including Gloria's, which he begins to believe was committed to provide him with the heart he needed to survive. In a related murder, the killer intentionally mouths "Happy Valentine's Day" into an ATM security camera, confirming McCaleb's theory about the rationale for the murders—but the man in that case died too quickly for doctors to harvest his organs, and the murderer had to try again. It becomes clear later on that he stayed by Gloria's side after killing her, tending to her until an ambulance could arrive and billing himself as a Good Samaritan who had discovered the scene. To McCaleb's horror, he realizes that both victims are dead because the love-note killer is back—and this time he has killed purely to put McCaleb back in the game. Indeed, McCaleb cannot back out now; he remarks, "I am alive because she is dead, and that cuts me into this in a big way." As he tells Winston, "He missed the action. Me and him. To get it back I needed a new heart. So Happy Valentine's Day." But now that McCaleb is back, the killer goes on a new killing spree, begging to be pursued, perhaps to be caught.

Meanwhile, McCaleb is drawn further into his relationship with Rivers, but as they move toward their first sexual encounter, he does not exhibit the self-assured, conquering attitude common in Hollywood men. Before they sleep together, we see McCaleb examining his deeply scarred body in the mirror, doubting his own attractiveness and desirability. This kind of self-critical gaze is usually associated more with women than with men. Nothing here resonates with the perfect, phallic male body—and McCaleb's body is not wholly masculine any longer, because it now contains a woman's heart.

As McCaleb continues to struggle with the realization that Gloria's death was a gift for him, he becomes even more terrified to discover that Rivers and Gloria's son have gone missing. Reflecting frantically on his investigation, he finally begins to piece things together, realizing at last that "Buddy"—who renamed himself Jasper Noone—was the serial killer all along. Rushing to Buddy's boat, he asks him to lift his shirt. Buddy does, revealing a bullet wound verifying that he is the man McCaleb shot the night he had the heart attack. Buddy, of course, wants McCaleb to be as excited as he is that they are now back in the game. They begin to struggle, but Buddy pulls a gun and tells McCaleb that if he ever wants to see Rivers and her nephew alive, he had better let him go, leaving them as they were and perpetuating the game of the chase. He tells McCaleb, "I've been a watchdog for you, getting you back to where you need to be. What did you say in the car the other day? You felt connected again? I almost *came* when you said that." He also reminds him, "I could have killed you if I wanted to, Terry (. . .). I gave you life."

Buddy continues, "I want you to live. I want me to live. I want all that battle again—me and you, Cain and Abel, Kennedy and Oswald. We're shit on the bottom of each other's shoes. I hope you think of me as often as I'll think of you." He intends these to be his parting words, but the two men struggle again and McCaleb gets off a shot into Buddy's leg. He demands that Buddy take him to Rivers and the boy. Buddy taunts him with his relationship to Rivers: "You think Gloria ever thought that her heart would be pumping blood in some guy who's banging her sister?" But he also reassures him that the hostages are safe, if only because the boy has the same blood type as McCaleb. It turns out that they are prisoners on the same boat, and when McCaleb finds them, he sends them away on a boat, hoping to protect them from his final battle with Buddy. Indeed, Buddy soon meets his end, falling into the water after struggling with McCaleb because he is in no shape to flee. McCaleb actually pushes him under, and Buddy's last words to him are, "I saved you." McCaleb's ironic response, as he pushes him under, is "Thanks, pal."

McCaleb has now inherited not just a relationship, but also a family. Indeed, when Winston, who has been so respectful of his avowed responsibility to Gloria, asks him how he will cope with the obligation to his newfound family, he says sincerely: "I have Gloria Rivers's heart. I'll probably just let that guide me."

Clearly this conclusion is a more traditional ending to a doubling film than we saw in *In the Line of Fire*; McCaleb kills Buddy in an all-too-familiar act of baptismal redemption and the double dies so that he can free him from a game rooted in projected identification. But as in *Tightrope*, the Eastwood character's relationship with his female counterpart forms an entirely different track or subplot to the film. It is that different track—not the death of the double—that completely disrupts any pretense of phallic wholeness restored after the death of the double. McCaleb's new family gives him a glimmer of hope for redemption. But before we return to his relationship to this new family, as well as to his own new heart, we need to look more closely at the erotic relationship between McCaleb and Buddy.

The eroticism we saw between Leary and Horrigan was much more understated in the form of Leary's passionate obsession with Horrigan's life and Frank's implicit hope that he can redeem himself by meeting Leary's challenge. But in *Blood Work* the erotic charge is perfectly explicit: Buddy's sexuality is entirely and consciously caught up in his relationship to McCaleb. His love of the game is not enough, because he cannot accept that anybody less / equal can play with him, not only McCaleb; that is why he takes extreme measures to ensure McCaleb's survival. Buddy has chosen him as his one true partner—and of course he expects McCaleb to embrace him, in his own way, in turn. Thus, although the double dies in that sentimental, baptismal way, the doubling relationship between the two men is as perverse as the one we saw in the last film. Buddy can only hang on to something of his own manhood through the clichés of good and evil played out as a crime drama. In this way he is a much more banal character than Leary and much more inclined to speak in cliché. Also, though we know details from Leary's past, we do not know anything about Buddy's past trauma, which in an important sense makes him a much less compelling antagonist. It is not surprising, therefore, that Eastwood never has us see the world through Buddy's eyes as we see the world through Leary's, except for a few brief moments when Buddy gazes lovingly at McCaleb. Although his story remains more ambiguous, Buddy's reaching out for McCaleb reminds us again that even the most shattered man seeks to salvage some of his masculinity through a projected identification with another man.

Of course, by arguing that both of these films portray strong erotic relationships between men, I do not intend to say that the subplot of these films implies some association between homosexuality and criminality. That would be far too simplistic. In *In the Line of Fire*, the traumatic subtext is made much more explicit; Leary's distorted friendship with Horrigan is his only way out of the trauma he endured as a wet boy. And in *Blood Work*, the eroticism of the game still upholds, if only as shattered remnants, the ideals of friendship in which men bolster the ideals of masculinity. Here a fractured masculinity has literally turned into fetishism as the Buddy claims a trophy to signify his conquest over each of his murder victims.

As in *Tightrope*, there is another track to *Blood Work*, in which McCaleb actually seeks a new life or a psychic rebirth after the trauma of his heart transplant. Shown in all his vulnerability when he examines his scarred body in the mirror, McCaleb dubiously tries to understand why Rivers could possibly still desire him. Again, these are not the actions of the macho Hollywood man. McCaleb behaves in a manner that is typically associated with female stereotypes as he attempts to reconstruct himself both psychically and physically. There is no simple assumption of phallic wholeness here. We are very far from the relationship between the masculine body and a projected ego ideal that purportedly gives us the image of a man absent of any form of vulnerability. To quote Anthony Easthope:

> The most important meanings that can attach to the idea of the masculine body are unity and permanence. . . . [T]he self finds its identity in its bodily image. Very clear in outline and firm in definition, the masculine image of the body appears to give a stronger sense of identity. From David to Tarzan and on to Superman, Captain Marvel, He-Man, Action Man, and Conan the Barbarian, the young male body is used to present not just the self as it is but as it would like to be. Not just the ego, but the ego ideal. The pleasure of the usual representation of the masculine body usually appeals to a narcissism in which images of the hard-trained body purportedly live up to the ego-ideal of a man who is dependent on no others, firm and whole in himself. These bodies, in other words, return to the male gaze a narcissistic fantasy of how the viewer would like to see himself.[14]

But McCaleb has to accept his vulnerability because of the reality that he is no longer whole. The physical condition of his body undermines any easy conflation of the ego-ideal. When we witness McCaleb in front of the mirror, we understand the integral connection between McCaleb's vulnerability and his metaphorical and literal embrace of the feminine other, which, now that McCaleb has a woman's heart, is literally a part of him.

Much has been written about how what human beings commonly understand as masculinity and femininity are in fact constructed roles that we play, roles that always fall apart when they come against the inarticulable ideals of who and what we are supposed to be.[15] But here Eastwood the director suggests that once a man's heart has been replaced by a woman's, the man's masculinity is by definition no longer whole, and the feminine other has been integrally woven into whatever wholeness the man can hope to reclaim. If we want to employ the popular belief that recognizes we are never completely male or female but are in fact transgendered, then McCaleb is no longer simply masculine in the fantasized sense of a body undergirded by an ego-ideal. He refers again and again to the idea that Gloria's heart will guide him—explicitly embracing the feminine within him.

The initial shock and guilt McCaleb experienced when he learned that his heart belonged to a murdered woman created in him the forceful obligation to pursue her murderer. He understands that, in a way, he was responsible for her murder. She died for him. But when he awakens to the possibility of new life and psychic rebirth by moving beyond the defensive belief that masculinity is everything that is not woman, his identity is radically shattered. In almost all schools of psychoanalysis, it is now commonplace to argue that masculinity forms in young children as an ideal inseparable from the refrain "I am not a woman"—so that everything feminine must be rejected and externalized in order to project a fully masculine presence. This reality underscores the significance of McCaleb's achievement in constructing a more wholesome masculinity, one that develops out of the integration, not the rejection, of the feminine other.

In one of his most provocative pieces of work, the thinker Jacques Derrida speaks of *lovance* as the opening up of one human being to the heartbeat of another.[16] *Blood Work* takes this metaphor to its highest degree of symbolic realization, implanting the heartbeat of a feminine other into a living male chest. That heart changes how McCaleb sees the world, how he feels about himself, and indeed how he feels about women. He can no longer see women as the mysterious abjected other, because he sees that a women has given him life—literally, as well as the possibility of love for another.

Sudden Impact (1983)

Sudden Impact[17] is the only *Dirty Harry* movie that Eastwood directed, and in many ways it follows the series formula. In spite of the film's formulaic aspects, it is different because, again, Eastwood explores the profound impact that a woman's trauma has on the male protagonist, shaking off, in the process, his easy convictions about the relationship between justice and retribution. As is often the case in *Dirty Harry* movies, Harry Callahan (Eastwood) has alienated his superiors by not following the exacting procedures of the legal system, taking it to the point where they send him to São Paulo for a while—a break from the hard streets of San Francisco. True to form, however, Dirty Harry has barely arrived in São Paulo when fate sends the criminal element his way: Callahan has to take down a robber by hijacking a bus full of senior citizens, ultimately saving a cop who will later help him with the case that drives the action of the film.

Indeed, something seems to chase Harry all the way to São Paulo, as he quickly discovers a murder very much like one that occurred in San Francisco just before he left. The police find a man shot twice, first in the genitals and then in the head; it seems all too obvious that this is the second in a chain of serial murders. Callahan cannot help but get involved. Meanwhile, the audience already knows the secret: an artist, Jennifer Spencer (Sondra Locke), is responsible for both murders and she will continue killing. She plans to track down each of the men who, years before, brutally raped her and her sister in São Paulo. She whispers her plan to her sister, Beth, who has been in a silent, vegetative state since the day of the rape. "It was like I was outside of myself," Jennifer says over her, "above me looking down. Then he touched me. And I killed him. Beth? I love you." Beth is unable to respond to her sister's dramatic revelation, but her speech serves to complicate the audience's straightforward moral understanding about right and wrong, good and evil.

Spencer's job in São Paulo has great symbolic significance. She paints old, decrepit hobbyhorses from a run-down fairground, refurbishing them for the carousel. The amusement park for which they are destined, moreover, was, years ago, the site of her rape. It was dilapidated and abandoned, but now she is participating in its restoration. The woman who hired her remarks, "It must give you great of satisfaction to make old, ugly things right again."

Furthermore, traditionally in English literature, the hobbyhorse is a symbol for the penis, suggesting even more symbolic irony: Spencer creatively reworks the penises of the men whose organs she destroys. Her own paintings, however, are more deeply colored with the trauma and anguish of her experience; she does not attend the opening of her own art show, because, though she can paint graphic representations of her trauma, she cannot face it directly. At this point, she can only take that anguish and turn it on its head, throwing it in the faces of those who caused it without giving them a moment's pity or remorse. When one rapist begs for his life, stressing he has moved on to a respectable life as a businessman since those events took place so long ago—making a thousand excuses about his drunkenness, his age, and peer pressure—she simply ignores his pleas. She shoots him, coldly, first in the genitals and then in the head.

Callahan first meets Spencer when, in an apparent coincidence, his dog knocks her off of her bicycle. Of course, he has no idea about her involvement in the murders, but as he explores São Paulo he begins to put together important pieces of the puzzle. He learns something about the gang rape that is the real beginning of the story, and he begins to suspect that important members of the town are involved in aa complex cover-up hiding the truth about what happened and who was involved. Moreover, it quickly becomes personal. When Callahan's friend Horace King (Albert Popwell), a black cop with whom he has worked many times, comes to visit, King is brutally murdered—but not, it would seem, by the serial killer. We later find out that he was killed by one of the rapists, and some of his criminal sidekicks, all related in one way or another to the group of men who committed the rape.

As anybody who has seen a *Dirty Harry* movie will know, Harry Callahan never has an easy relationship with justice as represented by most police departments and public prosecutors. Relating his endless troubles with his superiors to Spencer, he describes them as "questions of methods. Everybody wants results, but nobody wants to do what they have to do to get them done. I do what I have to do." Spencer replies sincerely, "I'm glad, Callahan. You are an endangered species. This is an age of lapsed responsibility and defeated justice. An eye for an eye means only if you get caught, and even then it's indefinite postponement—let's settle out of court. Does that sound profound, or just boring?" Callahan is clearly on her side, at least when it comes to a belief in lapsed responsibility and defeated justice. As he unknowingly relates his theory about the connection between the murders and the rape, Jennifer presses him about his understanding of revenge. "You don't approve?" she asks. Callahan responds simply, "Until it breaks the law."

Gradually unraveling the mysteries hidden by the town, Callahan finds a group photo that includes, he believes, the rapists and others connected to the rape. (The photograph belongs to the Chief Lester

Jannings (Pat Hingle), the chief of police, confirming Callahan's suspicions of corruption in the channels of local justice.) Tracking down the people in the photo, he comes to suspect that the next victim may be a woman named Ray Parkins (Audrie J. Neenan), who is possibly a lesbian but also clearly interested in Mick (Paul Drake), one of the leaders of the gang rape. Parkins taunts Callahan and calls him names, leading to a rather physical altercation with him; she also suggests tangentially that Spencer may somehow be implicated in the story. Indeed, Spencer murders Parkins not long after Harry leaves, and then she heads to the beach where she stares at the ocean, struggling with what she is doing.

Callahan finds Spencer at the beach and takes her home, where they begin a sexual relationship and he becomes more intimate with her distraught, pained artwork. He notices one of her paintings, a face in total anguish, and he also spots a shattered mirror, which was destroyed when Spencer attempted to paint her own anguished self-portrait. She quickly covers the work, remarking that she doesn't drink with her critics. But as Callahan examines the shattered mirror, his face exhibits a growing recognition that Jennifer Spencer is deeply troubled. The inability to see one's self after surviving a horrible trauma, such as gang rape, has been discussed time and time again. The familiar face in the mirror and the apparent wholeness of the body belie the psychic destruction that makes the victim feel like she has been torn to pieces inside. The seemingly normal face, the same face of the victim who was assaulted and damaged, seems to betray her because it refuses to reflect the horror that eats her up every minute. That face, ironically, prevents her healing because it will not admit that any damage has been done, hence Spencer's attempt to paint a self-portrait that speaks the truth about her inner torture. Callahan begins to confirm his suspicions about Spencer, checking the plate on her car as he leaves. He recognizes it as a vehicle he spotted outside Ray Parkins's place the night before. It must be clear to him now that Spencer is the murderer, but he does not immediately attempt to arrest her.

That same day, Spencer seeks out her next target, the police chief's son, and now we see how and why the rape was so effectively covered-up and ignored. She finds the son in a vegetative state, which is strikingly similar to the state in which her sister lives. At this moment, the Chief Jannings discovers her but does not move to capture her. Instead, he explains that his son could never live with what happened, that guilt over the rape had eaten him up inside, until one night he had deliberately crashed his car in a failed attempt at suicide. Jannings admits that he had done something terribly wrong when he tried to protect his son from the consequences of his crime let the other rapists go free. He is profoundly repentant for his wrongdoing, explaining that he had hoped to shield his son because the boy was all he had after his wife had died giving birth. Tragically, the chief's loving impulse had backfired against so many of those involved, perhaps most poignantly against his son, who had desperately wanted to pay the appropriate price for a crime that had no moral rationale. Spencer's exhaustion and the chief's sincere outpouring of grief and remorse seem to open her heart a little bit, to the point where she seems almost willing to walk away and end it all.

But at that moment Mick and his gang break in to violently drag Spencer away. Jannings tries to redeem himself by doing the right thing, pulling a gun on Mick in an attempt to save Spencer, but he is too slow and Mick kills him instead. The gang drags Spencer away to the amusement park that was the scene of her original trauma. Here, it is all too clear, she will be raped again; and this time Mick will surely kill her, finishing the job. Earlier that evening Mick and his sidekicks had attacked Callahan directly, beating him to unconsciousness and throwing him into the ocean where they left him for dead. Naturally, of course, Dirty Harry will not go down so easily: pulling himself to safety, he knows now that Mick will go for Spencer next; and he also understands the criminal mind of a man like Mick well enough to know that there is only one place he would take his victim for their final reckoning.

At the amusement park, Spencer struggles against her attackers, but Mick seems to be overtaking her just as Callahan shows up to save the day. This is, of course, one of those fantasy rescuer scenes that have made Dirty Harry movies notorious. The fog clears, and we see Harry's powerful form striding slowly out of the fog, aiming his mighty Magnum .44 at Spencer's assailants. Mick attempts to escape onto the roller coaster, holding Spencer as a hostage, but Callahan successfully gets him in his sights and—in a stereotypically mythic shot—takes him down. Mick meets an ironic ending, falling off the coaster to be impaled on the shaft of a carousel horse. Perhaps there is no more fitting end for a man who thought, stupidly, that his penis was invested with the phallic power that could make him invincible, beyond the reach of the law and morality alike.

Callahan has called in backup, and the police arrive on the scene to clean up and continue the investigation. Spencer challenges Callahan: "What happens now?" He begins, "I guess now I have to"—but she interrupts him with a furious tirade.

Read me my rights? And what exactly are my rights? Where was all this concern for my rights when I was being beaten and mauled? And what about my sister's rights, when she was brutalized? There is this thing called justice—and was it justice when they all just walked away? You'd never understand, Callahan.

But perhaps he does understand. Harry's young cop friend walks over with Spencer's gun, which Mick stole and which the police found in his hand when he died. Callahan is faced with an existential decision, and he tells the officer that if he checks out the gun, he will find that it was used in all of the serial killings; Callahan makes Mick culpable for the murders that really happened because of him. "So it's over?" the officer asks. Callahan replies, "Yeah. It's over."

As Callahan leads Spencer away by the elbow, she is obviously stunned by what he has done. Her shock is significant; it emphasizes that the Callahan did not make the decision based on his personal affection for her. Indeed, the real contrast of this scene is between an ethic of retribution and an ethic of mercy. Spencer has systematically carried out her own brand of retribution, while as a character, Dirty Harry has always stood for the value of retributive justice against a system that is lenient and caught up in procedural snags—though up until now, it has not been portrayed as decidedly corrupt or backward. The outcome of this film, however, puts a deeply philosophical slant on our understanding of justice; According to Eastwood, retribution is necessarily based on a respect for a person's ability to do the right thing, even against difficult circumstances and profoundly traumatic events. Even more importantly, true mercy is based on the same kind of respect.

As we have seen, the police chief's son had genuinely desired that retribution be exacted against him for his crimes. He knows that he has committed a terrible crime, and he can only accept his father's protection from justice by denying his own dignity as a moral human being. He can no longer live with himself, and he can no longer live with his father because the man refuses to offer him the respect of allowing him to willingly accept the blame for his crime. For this reason, his son can only exist in a sort of living death. Indeed, by denying his son the respect he desires—a kind of recognition, in Benjamin's sense—Jannings deprives him of the sense that he is a moral subject who can decide his own way in the world. He traps his son in a moral riddle that transforms his assertions of agency into a self-hating masochism that can only lead to suicide.

Retribution and Revenge

The German philosopher Immanuel Kant has written eloquently on retribution,[18] and his ideas might explain the reasons why someone like Jannings's son would actually desire retribution as an expression of his self-respect mediated through the respect he expects from others. For Kant, our dignity hinges on the possibility that we can imagine ourselves capable of doing the next right thing, no matter how tragic our circumstances and no matter how profound our trauma. Leary demands this same sort of dignity, as we saw in *In the Line of Fire*; in that he does not want to be reduced to a psychological profile, to a sum of psychological parts. Corrigan's respect for Leary means that Corrigan can understand that his complex assassination plot is an attempt to bring the punishment he deserves down upon himself. The same respect makes it impossible to understand Leary's fall into the elevator shaft as a pitiable act of suicide. Leary does not want anyone's pity, least of all Corrigan's, even though he is very forthright about how traumatized and damaged he has become as a result of his life as a wet boy.

It is important to note that Kant does not believe we can theoretically or empirically prove that we have free will. Indeed, quite the opposite is true: we cannot know with any certainty that we are free, and, just as significantly, we can never know ourselves as wholly determined. Free will, for Kant, remains a choice that we must decide whether to act on, a choice left open to each of us because we can never be reduced to any particular theory about ourselves. We can always decide what to do next, and we can always take ourselves as free in making that decision. Thus, to reduce someone to a causal explanation, even an explanation that purports to "understand" that person—as Chief Jannings restricts his son's response to his crime—is for Kant deeply disrespectful, because it denies that person the sense of agency that we ascribe to ourselves and expect others to respect. In Kant's view, we all possess a propensity for evil, because it is integrally tied to the possible freedom of moral action. Each one of us, then, because we can act as if we were free—and the *as if* here is crucial—can also imagine what it would mean *not* to do the next right thing.

Of course, Kant also recognizes human frailty, which is one of the reasons why, as phenomenal creatures, we do not always do the right thing, even when we know very clearly what it is. Chief Jannings's frailty in *Sudden Impact* is actualized through his love for his son. He knows that retribution demands that he turn his son over to the courts for judgment, but he cannot bring himself to go through with it. Tragically, his effort to save his son from retribution is turned on its head when his son punish himself on his own—and the punishment he chooses is in all likelihood far worse than what a jury would have mandated.

Mercy, according to Kant, is often associated with our common understanding that we are all vulnerable to evil, but if we do not allow mercy to devolve into pity, then it too must be grounded in our respect for the person's capacity to do right.[19] But even though we know our-selves as creatures who are free to obey the moral law, we fail to do the right thing because we are frail and because, according to Kant, our perversity of heart leads us to sometimes deliberately defy the moral law. Directed by these impulses, In the Line of Fire's Leary knows exactly what he is doing and wants Corrigan to recognize that he does it freely, out of perversity of heart rather than out of a determined psychology, because, paradoxically, his deliberate violation of moral law allows him to reclaim a fragment of his self-respect against the various medical analyses that turn him into nothing more than a subject of psychological analysis. In this sense, Leary defies the possibility of a mercy based in pity or understanding by insisting throughout that he *wants* to do wrong, he *wants* to defy the very ideals that have betrayed him.

Leary resists the common understanding of mercy, which supposes that the more we understand about a person, the more we know about his life history and the trauma he has experienced, the more we can understand his transgressions as a natural outgrowth of his past. We can put ourselves in his shoes, adopting what Martha Nussbaum has called "the equitable attitude," in which we come to see ourselves in his posi-tion and are compelled to admit that in similar circumstances we might have reacted the same way. Nussbaum writes:

> Mercy also involves identification. If I see Oedipus as one whom I might be, I will be concerned to understand how and why his predicament came about; I will focus on all those features of motive and agency, those aspects of the unfortunate operations of chance that I would judge important were I in a similar plight myself. I would ask how and why all this came about—and ask not from a vantage point of lofty superiority, but seeing his tragedy as some-thing such as might happen in human life, in my own life. Tragedy is thus a school of equity, and therefore of mercy.[20]

By point of comparison, others have argued that retributive justice is mitigated by understanding because certain objective circumstances undermine the exercise of free will, seeing it as a naturalized concept, as an agency contingent upon circumstances favorable to its development and actualization.[21] Although a full discussion of this argument is beyond the scope of this chapter, I have consistently rejected a naturalized conception of free will, arguing instead that Kant's position should be read as an interpretation of the limits of theoretical knowledge about human beings. We simply cannot believe that a person's actions are reducible to the result of causal chains that can effectively predict whether or not he will, in fact, do the next right thing, even when those chains are rooted in trauma. In other words, we can always see ourselves as capable of making a decision, or else we must see ourselves as incapable of any decision at all, and it is the latter perspective that Kant rejects as inherently disrespectful for ethical reasons.[22]

Interestingly enough, if we follow Kant's concept of understanding, in *Sudden Impact* Callahan never attempts to "understand" Spencer. He does not create his own psychological explanation to deny her ferocious insistence that she freely acted to exact vengeance for a crime never punished by the official channels of the law. Indeed, her challenge to Callahan both recreates and inverts Leary's assertion of agency from *In the Line of Fire*—where Leary intentionally assaulted the ideals he had at one time upheld, where he does wrong because he cannot meaningfully do right. Spencer invests her murders with a moral rightness that flies in the face of justice gone wrong. But Callahan's merciful silence about her actions arises not out of understanding, but rather out of a respect for her assertion of rightness in the context of what he *cannot* understand. Moreover, because Spencer takes responsibility for her actions, and because they have a moral rather than a natural cause, he can regard her as a human being who is not simply "prone," in some psychological sense, to violence. What he "understands" is that she has taken responsibility for her trauma and she has seen it through to a resolution. Therefore, he need not fear that she will kill again.

In a sense, then, Callahan's proclaiming "It's over" both recognizes the fact that Spencer has achieved closure and asserts his own moral claim, which he holds against Spencer as the single condition for his mercy. She must continue to take responsibility for what she has done, and she must live her life in a way that makes her retributive killing spree meaningful. As a consequence, she must also close off her claim to independence from the law. As Callahan told her earlier, revenge that breaks the law is morally unacceptable; but he has also listened carefully to her angry tirade against "justice" and "rights" as they are commonly understood—and he has perhaps realized that the very system of justice that he upholds retains a profound masculine bias. To quote Paul Smith,

> Although this may seem like another traditional Hollywood move to find a higher law that goes against the written law, it is irreducible precisely because of Callahan's understanding that her rights have indeed not been recognized. Rather, I want to point out how the alliance with the woman necessitates a particular kind of recognition, that the law that Callahan has been enforcing is indeed a matter amongst men and that it normally excludes women and their interests. . . . This is of course a critical moment and a radical one in that it marks a kind of problematic disjuncture between, on the one hand, the law; and the man's heroic service-man relationship to it; and on the other hand a femininity that demands a satisfaction that cannot be given legally.[23]

The radicalism here lies in Callahan's recognition that the law does not have the moral authority to exact retribution against a woman, precisely because it is too closely related to a masculine imaginary—what Smith calls the "amongst men"—that tragically trivializes rape. Thus, Callahan and Spencer meet at the limits of a theoretical system of law, a point to which the law simply does not reach; here they meet as two moral individuals who respect that they are both independent agents of a moral law that we all participate in creating.

Callahan does not trivialize Spencer as a woman who was raped and has played out the inevitable consequence of that event, and he does not have the hubris to claim that he can identify with her, as if he could, as a man, understand what it means for a woman to be brutally raped. Instead, his act of mercy has the character of humility, but a humility strikingly different from the one Nussbaum described, for this is not the humility of a man who claims to understand but rather the humility of a man who knows he can *never* understand. His humility comes out of his critical recognition that the law commonly functions as a matter amongst men, so it falters systematically when it attempts to encompass the rights and agency of women.

In each of these films, Eastwood recognizes of the problems that derive from a man's alliance with femininity and feminism against the limits of law. In *The Gauntlet* (1977), an earlier film about a failed cop who escorts a prostitute to testify against a mafia boss, Eastwood first began exploring this theme in a much more indirect way than in *Tightrope*, *Blood Work* or *Sudden Impact*. The female protagonist, Gus Mally (Sandra Locke), who chooses to go by a masculine nickname, takes up her own tirade against the complete corruption of the police, including the police officer who is driving her and Ben Shockley (Eastwood) into a setup. She suggests that most cops are a lot like prostitutes, but less honest because they sell themselves to the Man while pretending to have integrity. She attacks the driver's sexuality, railing against what she sees as a generalizable masculine imaginary—and in every way Mally's tirade breaks up the fantasized phallic male point of view by disrupting it from a woman's perspective, through a woman's voice. In *Sudden Impact* Spencer's abrupt interruption of Callahan when he begins to read her Miranda rights has a similar but much more profound effect; it shatters his fantasized masculine point of view from the perspective of authority and undermines the idealized self-image of the upstanding serviceman of the law.[24]

In all of these films, masculine sexual violence is pervasive, transcending even boundaries of class. In *Tightrope*, as well, sexual aggression and sadistic sexual behavior are profoundly related to the masculine unconscious. The struggle to realign this masculinity so that it is not a threat to women haunts all of these films, but especially *Tightrope*. Still, Paul Smith in his study of the production work of Clint Eastwood is frustrated by the ending of *Tightrope*, because it seems to suggest an all-too-easy narrative out from what has otherwise been portrayed as a deep dilemma surrounding how masculinity becomes integrated with sexual violence. I disagree with his reading of the final scene, however, because it is not the kind of happy ending that Smith sees in it; instead, it offers only the barest glimmer of hope in the form of a newly available, shared symbolic space in which Block *might* reconfigure his relationship to his own sexuality. As I have applied Benjamin's point, the only way to break up an imaginary that leads men to defend against their feminine side by ruthlessly pushing it out and brutalizing its reflection in others—particularly women—is to offer to share that psychic conflict in a mutual symbolic space. Therefore, it is neither a coincidence nor a cinematic distraction that Thibodeaux is an active feminist, because it is only through her feminism that she can help Block to free himself from frozen gender stereotypes by giving him the chance to safely play with his own sexuality. While there are many kinds of feminisms, Thibodeaux's feminism—and certainly my own—is as much about freeing men as it is about freeing women.[25]

But we have also seen in these films a profound exploration of the erotic, if twisted, bond between fellow men who are desperately holding on to the ruins of masculine ideals. This eroticism is most profoundly depicted in Leary's relationship to Corrigan, a relationship in which he not only demands respect and recognition but also the confirmation from Corrigan that Leary actually cares about him, because the two have shared the ideals that should have underscored their friendship—ideals that have, instead, led them to become enemies, at least in name. But, of course, Leary is at no time Frank's enemy in a conventional sense, because we know that the restoration of Frank's own masculine self-assurance is Leary's central goal, even though he knows no restoration or redemption is possible for his own shattered life. It is an act of profound identification that makes him go after a president that he considers worthless, a crime he undertakes only so that Corrigan can have the chance to redeem himself. This gives back to Leary the only semblance of meaning in manhood that he can possibly find.

Although Buddy is not a strong character and we do not find an elaboration of his traumatic past—which would give him an opportunity to speak in the clichés that Hannah Arendt has associated with the banality of evil—he too has a profound identification with his antagonist, Terry McCaleb. Indeed, he cannot find meaning in his life without McCaleb and "the game," as McCaleb calls it. So for the game to go on, Buddy must find McCaleb a heart. The real surprise, of course, is that the heart changes McCaleb in ways that Buddy cannot possibly imagine: the feminine, for McCaleb, ceases to appear as a projected other, becoming internalized both literally and metaphorically. By embracing his heart, McCaleb accepts his own feminine side, thereby posing a challenge to the simplified masculine ideals for which Buddy has admired him—and perhaps this is the reason why Buddy must finally escalate their game toward its inevitable conclusion. He knows he will not have any fun with an adversary who has become a family man, a nurturer rather than a fighter.

In these films, simplified phallic notions of masculinity are challenged in at least two categories: First, we have seen the ideals of masculinity that have been utterly corrupted by a government that holds them up only to abuse and degrade them. It is not, of course, that the ideals themselves are corrupt, but when they are left in ruins, they can only be revived through erotic connections doomed to devolve into violence. Second, masculinity is examined as an imaginary ideal that turns to violence when it leads men to defensively reject everything associated with the feminine. To take in the heart of a woman, as a metaphor, undermines the very notion of masculine wholeness, and it exposes an illusion that is dangerously associated with the trivialization of crimes that are as violent and psychically destructive as rape. Perhaps Eastwood's struggle as a director to critically engage the very masculine personas with which he has been popularly associated—particularly from his early days as a cowboy—that has led him so profoundly to envision another kind of masculinity. Even so, he seems to have been dissatisfied with the apparent one-sidedness of his vision, pushing himself to take an even more surprising step by shooting an entire movie, *Bridges over Madison County*, from the perspective of a female protagonist. We turn in the next chapter to examine this new directorial turn.

3
Ties That Bind:
The Legacy of a Mother's Love

The *Bridges of Madison County* (1995) is Eastwood's only mature film in the romance genre.[1] Early in his directorial career he made *Breezy* (1973), the story of a May-December relationship.[2] *Breezy* moves through a story line that is quite typical for Hollywood romances, and it was released long before Eastwood has cinematically explored the significance of a man's taking in a woman's heart as he did in *Blood Work*. But since this early romance, he has advanced in other directions as well, as exhibited by his shooting *Bridges* almost entirely from a woman's perspective. The film follows the female protagonist's erotic gaze as she openly lusts after her male love object, and the film's narrative is essentially hers.

Interestingly, Robert James Waller's novel takes the opposite position, relating the conflicts of a male journalist who is a loner struggling to come to terms with the ways in which the first woman to grab his heart disrupts every idea he has of himself and his position in the world.[3] The novel works well through the familiar themes of Hollywood romance. Consider, for example, the recent film *Something's Gotta Give* (2003), in which a wealthy sixty-three-year-old man finally learns what it truly means to love—and (my God!) the object of his affection is at last older than the twenty-two-year-olds he usually goes for; a fine film as far as it goes.[4] Yet this twist does absolutely nothing to disrupt the fundamental diegetic reality (to use Paul Smith's phrase) of how the construction of the romance genre is integrally tied into an imagined reality and all of the possibilities therein. Telling the same story but turning it on head by reorienting it from the point of view of the desiring woman, Francesca Johnson (Meryl Streep), Eastwood begins, as we have seen elsewhere, within the conventions of the genre, only to later twist them to bring into question the cultural foundations that support the genre's stereotypic reality. A woman's desire, recorded in loving detail as the camera brings the audience into her world, challenges not only the Hollywood romance genre; it also resists one of the most powerful psychic under-tows of our stubbornly sexist culture. As the writer and philosopher Susan Bordo eloquently reminds us,

> It is not only those with a religious agenda, however, who censor purposefully or not the sexual subjectivity of women. All feminists know in theory that Hollywood rarely plays to the female gaze. But sometimes you only truly realize—viscerally—what's been for-bidden when it is finally permitted. Clint Eastwood—who began his career as a "screw you" action hero and wound up directing and starring in one of the best "women's movies" of all time improved vastly on *The Bridges of Madison County* by telling the story of the affair almost entirely from the heroine's (Meryl Streep's) point of view, focusing on her desires, conflicts, and anxi-eties, rather than the hero's as was the case in the book. Eastwood's film was the exception that made me aware of what I'd been missing.[5]

Meanwhile, Eastwood's film also foregrounds the lessons learned by each of the children within their own lives, as each of them comes to terms with their mother's life and identity through her retelling. The film's narration unfolds retrospectively as Johnson's children, Caroline and Michael, read from journals that their mother left for them. These recount her sexual affair in such vivid detail that Caroline remarks to her brother in shock, "And now I find out that in between the bake sales my mother was Anaïs Nin." The account is even harder on Michael, who struggles to come to terms with the fact that his mother's journal violates the safe stereotype through which he had always understood her. Indeed, Johnson had not shared her story when she was alive because she was deeply afraid about how her family would respond, and she under-stood that even in death the truth would be difficult for Michael, willing the letter and key leading to the journal's discovery to her daughter Car-oline. She explains in the letter that as a person gets older, her fear sub-sides and it becomes increasingly more important that the truth be told.

"How sad it seems to me to leave this earth without those you love the most ever really knowing who you were." After death, she asserts herself at last by giving her family a chance to know her as a woman who claimed her desire and followed her heart, contradicting the images they had of her.

The story of Johnson's affair begins when her husband takes the children to the state fair to show Caroline's prize steer, leaving Johnson alone for four days. Eager for the reprieve from raising the children and maintaining a busy household, Johnson is distracted and impatient at the last dinner before her family leaves. She goes through the motions of a caring wife and mother, reminding her husband not to smoke and checking that his suitcase is packed, but her relief is palpable when her family finally departs. Left to herself she is restless; she tries to listen to opera but is clearly unsure of what to do with herself outside her daily routine.

Robert Kincaid (Eastwood) enters her life the next day; he is trying to locate the covered bridges that he wants to shoot for *National Geographic*, but he has gotten lost. We do not know at first whether she is attracted to this stranger or to the adventure of driving off with him, but her fascination with him rapidly increases, particularly when he tells a romantic story about getting off the train for an unplanned visit to her hometown in Italy simply because he thought it was pretty. His life is so different from hers, and she is clearly drawn to him because he reawakens her sense of adventure. When he reaches for the radio, the camera focuses on his hands as they brush against her and, through a shot-countershot technique, we watch through her eyes as he tests the lighting for photographs he will take in the morning. Eastwood's direction communicates Johnson's curiosity and desire as she peers through cracks and around corners at him, irresistibly drawn to him but afraid to let him see her looking. When he sends her to his truck to look for a drink, she works her hands through his things with palpably erotic interest in the man who owns them, who touches them every day.

Kincaid returns her interest, giving her flowers and responding with a sincere, appreciative smile when she jokes that they are poisonous. Johnson nearly walks away from the possibility held out by his flirtation, with the camera clearly recording the hesitation in her expression as she decides, finally, to invite him in for iced tea. Tea turns into dinner, dinner into a walk, and a walk into a nightcap. Periodically, the camera steps back to show Johnson's enjoyment of Kincaid's enthusiastic storytelling, but it is his ability to understand and relate to her ambivalence about her

life in Iowa—her restlessness before the dreams she has lost—that ultimately draws her closer to him. Indeed, when he unwittingly hurts her
by turning down her offer to tell a story—"You're asking a man if he is
too tired to talk about himself? You don't get out much, do you?"—he
understands that he has caused her pain by being insensitive to how it
feels to be trapped in Iowa. But she is pleasantly surprised when he apologizes sincerely for his remark; she sees that he is paying attention to her
feelings in a way to which she is not accustomed.

While this may seem like a minor incident, it is actually very significant because it shows the development of what Jessica Benjamin calls
"the third" within Kincaid and Johnson's relationship. The third for
Benjamin is not something outside the bounds of the relationship, nor is
it a symbolic embodiment, such as legal marriage, that bestows a kind of
social or legal legitimacy upon the couple.[6] Rather, the third grows out
of mutual recognition of each other and, in turn, feeds and deepens this
recognition as the couple finds in each other, through the creation of a
shared world, imagined double meanings that belong only to them—
and, of course, sexual involvement with all its fantasies and promises of
intimacy. The third represents what it means to find each other through
the struggles of discord and harmony, to understand how to both lead
and follow the other. Benjamin's third is not static; on the contrary, the
movement itself brings the two people together in a relationship
expressed as an ever-changing dance. Over time, within the safety of
genuine intimacy, one of the partners may playfully revise or change the
steps of the dance, transforming the shared language of mutual fantasy.
When Kincaid asks Johnson if she wants to leave her husband, he risks
disrupting the conception of the third between them by misreading the
subtext and stepping too quickly; but he also leaves on a note that registers his commitment to listening to her: "Don't kid yourself," he tells
her, "You're anything but a simple woman." Here Eastwood pays careful
attention to the dance between them, moving the camera back and forth
to record their reactions to each other and closing in on Johnson's growing fascination, even as the camera steps back for the occasional third-
person angle that celebrates the engagement and intimacy between the
two. Eastwood portrays falling in love not as an irrational attraction but
as an ever-deepening recognition, in Benjamin's complex sense of the
word.

After Kincaid leaves that first night, Johnson twice opens her robe to
the night air—at first only to be eaten by mosquitoes, then again to treat
her wounds. As she applies ointment to the mosquito bites, she examines

herself in the mirror, stroking her skin and wondering—hoping—that she still has what it takes to be attractive to a man. Anxious but willing to take a risk, she composes a note for Kincaid, in which she quotes Yeats—for whom they share a mutual appreciation that has become a part of their third—and leaves it nailed to the edge of the bridge in the middle of the night. Despite her anxiety Johnson is beginning to reclaim her own desire, and her initiative certainly undermines the overused Hollywood stereotype of the manic lovestruck woman, who is, in the worst case, a person to be explicitly avoided. We have come a long way, indeed, from Eastwood's portrayal of Evelyn Draper, the relentlessly aggressive woman of *Play Misty for Me.*

While Johnson is clearly not the irrational female lover of so many Hollywood films, Eastwood leaves no doubt that it is her simultaneous desire and refusal to relinquish the same that drive the development of a natural sexual relationship between Johnson and Kincaid. Kincaid, after meeting Lucy Redfield (Michelle Benes), another woman who has been shunned by the town as an adulteress, offers to tame or even call off the pending affair, leaving the decision in Johnson's hands. But at this point in the film, she has put so much energy into taking a chance to be with him that she refuses to give up the opportunity, even though there will be consequences. She describes in her journal the profoundly erotic thoughts she experienced as she lay in a bath in which he had showered, preparing herself for the impending initiation of an eagerly awaited sexual relationship. "I was lying where the water had run down his body, and I found that intensely erotic. But everything about Robert Kincaid had begun to feel erotic to me." Susan Bordo aptly describes how the camera brings out the sexual lust in Meryl Streep's performance of the scene:

> From her kitchen window, fanning her face, growing restless and disturbed, Streep watches shirtless Eastwood in the yard (the fact that his chest is frankly aging, sagging makes the scene all the more erotic; in an era of plastic beauty, Clint was real flesh—and so was Streep, zaftig for the role). Later in the bathtub, she is transfixed by the drops of water coming from the showerhead that has just recently poured onto his body. That touched you, we imagine her thinking, your body was here, where mine is now.[7]

Eastwood brings the camera to bear on all angles of her experience of the water dripping on her hands, looking up at the dripping shower, where he stood. The careful camera work brings us into her imagination; we see her and we see her imagining him, imagining feeling him. This is a middle-aged woman hot, hot, hot for her man and expressing herself, no holds barred. No, we do not see this kind of lustful female subject in the movies, unless of course she is or becomes a crazy monster, as in *Fatal Attraction*. It is only at the moment of her entrance that we see her through Robert's gaze. We see him bowled over by how stunning she is, "running around the block howling." But the camera does not linger on Robert. When the phone rings she touches him, letting her intentions to him be known. It is a subtle and gentle first move but it is indeed a first move:

> After she's had her bath and dressed—and it's still clear between them what's going to happen—she places her hand on his shoulder during a phone call. That's all—a hand on his shoulder. But the film has been so finely tuned to her as a sexual subject—except for him telling her she looks "stunning," it never focuses on his reactions to her body, always on her reactions to his—that the erotic charge of the gesture is almost unbearable.
>
> My sister and I, watching the movie, gasped in unison. I felt as though I had put *my* hand on Clint's shoulder. My body was visited by memories of *that* moment in my own life—that moment when a gesture, a look, a meeting of eyes, a brush of the skin, makes what what's going to happen clear and unalterable.[8]

Their dance prolongs the tension, but Bordo has it right: the first touch sealed their fate.

This is not the aerobic passion of twenty-year-olds that is so often idealized in today's films—super-agile men and women jumping on top of each other while balancing on a washing machine—this is real intimacy. Eastwood uses lighting and angles to heighten the intensity of their desire for one another, shooting one position and then returning from an angle that emphasizes the mutuality of their embrace. Sex deepens their private language. When they are lying together afterward, Johnson asks Kincaid to take her somewhere—to Bali, to Africa—to share more of himself with her, everything he has been. She is asking to be erotically transported, using travel as a metaphor. As her daughter Caroline reads her mother's journal, she reflects on her own disappointing sex life—her husband certainly had never taken her to "Africa." This turns us again to Benjamin's discussion of the third. The couple's "own" language of sex becomes part of a third that pulls the audience into a growing relationship of its own.

The next day as Johnson and Kincaid listen to jazz at a bar, Kincaid breaks down: "I can't do this. . . . Try and live a lifetime before Friday. Cram it all in." Again, Eastwood reverses the stereotyped gender roles: it is Kincaid who becomes clingy and vulnerable, who cannot bear the impermanence of the relationship. Eastwood the actor allows the anguish to take over his face, playing "the woman." When one of the neighbors stops in, Kincaid is forced to hide, and when Johnson finally finds him, he is immobilized by his sorrow at the hidden, contained nature of their relationship. She comforts him, though she shares his grief over their impending separation. A grief that she expresses the next morning not through weeping or sobbing, but through anger: she accuses Kincaid of routinely sleeping with women and leaving them as he travels the world. But he declares his love boldly, unable to endure her accusations: "It seems right now that all I've ever done in my life is make my way here to you." He hugs her, tears in his eyes, praying that their affair should not end and that they should build a life together.

Alone in her room, packing, Johnson looks with sorrow upon the familiar furnishings and architecture of her home, and it becomes increasingly clear that though she has packed she will not be able to leave. As the night wears on, Kincaid also becomes aware that their hopes of a life together will not be realized: Johnson cannot simply begin a new life with him, because it would be wrong. Ultimately, she cannot step out of her life with her family that has defined who she has become over all the years. The obligations of the life she had made limit her options for herself. Her husband's farm has been in the family for generations, and given the smallness of the community, he would be humiliated by her leaving him. Also, she would be leaving a house that only became a home through her labors. In a sense, she identifies herself through what she has done to make their house a home. Indeed, the house and her place within it represents the past that has made her who she is, and she cannot leave that part of her behind or simply cut it out: "No matter how much distance we put between us and this house, I bring it with me." Her recognition that her life's choices have turned her into a woman who lives with this husband and these children, and that she cannot simply remove the time that has passed, makes her understand sorrowfully that she cannot start anew and still be herself. Johnson's revelation leads her to the conclusion that their love would be undermined by her leaving her family, contaminating their third with bitterness and resentment.

Johnson thinks of her daughter at the vulnerable age of sixteen, who is struggling to come to terms with her sexual difference. And her son too is involved with his Oedipal fantasy that his mother is the one for him. The abrupt disruption that would be caused by their losing the maternal figure as a stable object in their lives seems to be too cruel for her to ignore, because her investment in her life as a mother is not peripheral to how she identifies herself. One could read this as a classical female sacrifice, where a woman must give up her dreams for the sake of her family but Johnson's realization is more subtle. At another point in her life, she might have been a different person; but now she has become a mother who has built up a life that is inseparable from who she is. It is a profound recognition of finitude: we can't simply make ourselves up from scratch and step out of time. Johnson's love for Kincaid has put her in touch with the woman she could be, but she is too honest to believe that this new woman could eclipse the life she has created for the woman she is now in Iowa. To simply deny who she is would itself be a form of traumatic dissociation, and she knows that very dissociation would return with a vengeance to destroy the relationship.

Kincaid, on the other hand, does not have the same sort of obligations that are inseparable from himself. The right thing for him, then, is to follow his desire and his love for Johnson, but of course there is no risk of dissociation for him. Kincaid tries to convince her to leave with him; indeed, he almost pleads with her that what they have found is too unique and valuable so they must be together: "Some people search their whole lives for it and wind up alone. Most people don't even think it exists and you're going to tell me that giving it up is the right thing to do?" But for Johnson, as we've seen, it is too late to leave the life she has made. "We are the choices we've made. . . . No one [understands] when a woman makes a choice to marry to have children—in one way her life begins, but in another way it stops. You build a life of details. You become a mother, a wife, and you stop and stay steady so that your children can move." Here again Eastwood reverses the gender stereotype: Johnson decides for both of them, while Kincaid pleads with her to put off her decision. He puts his head in her lap; he bows down in submission. He pushes her close to going with him, but she ultimately decides she must stay. As he leaves, Johnson runs through the door after him, but she does not call out for him to return.

The next day, her family returns and she falls back into her past life. Her two lives—one with Kincaid, another with her family—are so different from each other that being with her family again makes her intense desire for Kincaid more bearable: life with him no longer seems a realistic possibility. Soon after her return to normalcy, she sees Kincaid's truck in town when she is running errands with her husband, Richard. Richard is in the store when Kincaid gets out of the truck, getting soaked by the pouring rain as he, stands there, smiling, awaiting her acknowledgment. But he does not approach her. This is an excellent example of the trope that Katja Silverman has described as the subversive power of a man who deliberately casts himself in the role of masochist. The scene is so emotionally powerful because, as Silverman writes, this kind of absolute laying bare before the Other deliberately disrupts the foundational fantasy of masculinity—the premise that the man has the phallus, that independent of all others he stands alone. For Silverman the male masochist

> acts out in an insistent and exaggerated way the basic conditions of cultural subjectivity. . . . He loudly proclaims that his meaning comes from the Other, prostates himself before the gaze even as he solicits it, exhibits his castration for all to see, and revels in the sacrificial basis of the social contract. The male masochist magnifies the losses and divisions upon which cultural identity is based, refusing to be sutured or recompensed. In short, he radiates a negativity inimical to the social order.[9]

Silverman's description of the male masochist highlights the disruptive force of Eastwood's performance: he bares himself before her, totally captured by her gaze, leaving it to her to come to him if she will. All he can do is show himself in all his vulnerability, because only she has the power to make a move. His face is filled with love, and with the pain of losing her.

As Kincaid drives away, we see him only from behind—again from Johnson's perspective—as he takes his gift from Johnson, a medal from her grandmother, and hangs it from his rearview mirror. Then we see her husband, Richard, as she sees him, his anxiety mounting as he begins to understand something is wrong. Kincaid lingers at the traffic light, hoping against hope, and Johnson's hand actually reaches to open her car door and run to him, but she restrains herself. Kincaid finally makes the turn after Richard persistently honks the car horn. As Richard drives her home, Johnson finally weeps and her husband attempts to comfort her, asking, "You feeling better, Franny?" Much of the film's significance lies in its dramatic details, and here we see that, even though Richard is a good man and Francesca respects him as a father and a husband, he does not really understand her as Kincaid does—a shortcoming reflected when he calls her by an Americanized bastardization of her Italian first name. And she does not try to make him understand. He loves her, but his love is inseparable from her role as wife and mother. He cannot love her in the other way, the one that creates a more playful and creative third, which would ultimately give her an expansive, symbolic space in which to move.

Johnson relates in her journal that Kincaid ultimately respected her decision. He writes her one letter and buys a subscription to *National Geographic*, but then he falls silent. He does not press himself on her. Only after her husband's death does Johnson look for him, but by then he has left *National Geographic*. She learns that he left all of his belongings to her, including a book about the four days they spent together. His ashes were scattered off the Rosamunde Bridge, which formed such an important part of their third.

Romantic affairs that break the social contracts governing gender conventions often end in suicide. Indeed, there is a long and proud history in drama upholding suicide as the only way out for a couple doomed by law, convention, or social conflict. Yet neither of the lovers in this film needs to die to make sense of their relationship. Johnson's decision to stay with her family is not merely a capitulation to convention; it represents instead her profound recognition that "we are the choices we have made"—and thus, as finite creatures, we cannot simply deny the past and the commitments to which we are bound without conceding to an even deeper denial of ourselves. Significantly, Johnson reaches out to Lucy Redfield, who later becomes Lucy Delaney, a woman who chose the forbidden alternative by disrupting her first marriage and taking up a new life with another man. Many years into their friendship, Johnson confesses her own affair, and through her confession the secret becomes an intersubjective reality rather than merely a fading memory, a fantasy in her own mind. Just as importantly, her identification with Redfield preserves her relationship with Kincaid as a meaningful love—a *could-have-been* that emphasizes the reality of Francesca's decision qua choice rather than an inevitable defeat. While the suicide romance celebrates a tragic commitment to love that cannot be realized, an attachment to a third that cannot exist in the real world, Johnson's ethical commitment to her family transforms her return to life with them into a livable alternative.

It is livable because it is hers, and it is hers because for her there was no viable alternative.

Kincaid respects Johnson as an ethical being who has done what she believes to be right for her life. Integral to his love for her is this respect for her otherness, including her otherness to his own desire: she is not just a woman to him, but a singular Other. And she asks her children to respect that singularity as well, a respect she asks them to realize by throwing her ashes from the Rosamunde Bridge where she can, symbolically, rejoin the only true love of her life. "We were as bound together as tightly as two people can be. . . . I gave my life to my family. I wish to give Robert what is left of me." After intense psychic struggle, they concede to her wish. Their struggle to come to terms with their mother's desire and her unrepentant subjectivity has a profound impact on them by undoing their own fantasies. Michael struggles with his anger at his mother, feeling betrayed and storming out to get drunk enough to attempt, again, to touch that enormous taboo, his mother's sexuality. He reacts with a classic commentary on his own fantasy resolution of his Oedipal conflict, which was no resolution at all, because it continues to deny his mother her subjective otherness: "I feel really weird. Like she cheated on me, not Dad. . . . Being the only son, you're sort of made to feel like you're the prince of the kingdom, ya know? And in the back of your mind, you kind of think your mother doesn't need sex anymore because she has you."

Returning to his wife after a long night away without explanation, he interrupts her anger by asking, "Do I make you happy?" He realizes now that a conventional "resolution" of the Oedipal conflict is not enough, because it is not enough to step into his father's shoes by getting a job and handing a paycheck over to his wife. To truly be a man and a husband, he must open himself up emotionally and intellectually to the person he has married. Oedipal complimentarity—"You play the girl, I'll play the boy, and everybody knows the rules of the game"—is too closed to the possibilities for play, for creativity in the third.

Caroline's life with her husband, meanwhile, is no longer workable. In her struggle to come to terms with her mother's subjectivity, she has blown apart her accustomed excuses; she can no longer believe that her marriage is as good as life can get. Kissing the dress her mother wore on her first night with Robert Kincaid—fondling of clothes is a gesture that Eastwood uses throughout the film as a sign of intimacy—Caroline expresses a new kind of identification with her mother, a desire to be like her, to follow through on her mother's fantasies for herself. It should be noted that though it is an important part of the film, the children's struggle with their Oedipal crises does not appear in the novel. Yet the unfolding of the narrative as presented in the film is inseparable from this subtext. Johnson, unable to fully claim her love for Kincaid while she was alive, projects her ideals of romance and erotic fulfillment into the lives of her children, enabling Michael to become the kind of lover an independent woman desires (and deserves) and encouraging Caroline to reach for new possibilities in her own life.

An ominous "they" haunts this film, which stands for the expectations of society. With its imposed gender roles, the very law of Oedipal complimentarity its acceptance become a kind of living death for all too many couples. The psychoanalytic theorist Jacques Lacan explains this "they" as a part of the social contract, the shared symbolic order that we must accept if we are going to have culture at all. The idea of this order serves as a starting point in our efforts to reconcile with both the impersonal nature of "they" and our unconscious stake in maintaining this position. Lacan helps us to understand the cruelty faced by Lucy Redfield when she breaks the bonds of the social contract; for Lacan, to break this symbolic order is to threaten everything we understand to be civilization. Of course, the cruel treatment of Redfield after her affair also highlights the paradox at the heart of a civilization that is based on imposed orders of sexual difference, a social order that we enter symbolically when we become sexually differentiated. It is something imposed on us, not something that we create.[10]

At times Lacan maintains that the law of separation, which he calls symbolic castration and which differentiates us as individuals, must take a certain form of sexual difference. It also enforces a particular kind of sexual differentiation, in which we are either masculine or feminine, man or woman—however, these classifications do not directly correlate with our biological sex. In Lacanian terminology, we are identified—and thus come to identify ourselves—either as the one who has the phallus or the one who *is* the phallus. The two positions, however, are not symmetrical. According to Lacan, there is a symbolic referent for the masculine position: the man can identify as the one who has the phallus. This identification is a fantasy, however, because no one in fact has the phallus; it is the ultimate fantasy that underlies masculinity. To put it simply, the phallus is what a man thinks he must have to be a man; the penis is his actual biological body part. This fantasy association allows little boys to place themselves in the line of paternal descent, relating to the male identity to gain him a compass with which to direct himself as an active subject. He can imagine himself in his father's place. To urge a man to "do the right thing" is comprehensible as a command, simply, to be a man. "Stand up and be a man," we say, and this alone seems to contain every ethical standard, every ideal of strength and success, that an individual should need to assert his place in the world. The connection between "standing up" as an active subject and being a "man" seems so natural that it is almost tautological.

In this Lacanian story, can a woman tell her daughter to "stand up and be a woman"? Is this not a mixed metaphor, a contradiction in terms? Does a woman "stand up" by identifying with the masculine? What meaning could the command to be a "woman" entail? Be compassionate, Dress attractively, Make yourself up to be sexually appealing, Stand by your man, Don't follow your heart, Reduce your life to the details, Be a good wife and mother—are all ideals that could be associated with the directive "to be a woman." When Lacan writes that Woman is the symptom of Man, he means Woman is only representable to Man as the object of his desire: Man desires, hence there must be some object of his desire.

We must deconstruct Lacan if there is to be any way out of this nightmare of gender difference that simultaneously makes heterosexual love impossible while enforcing heterosexuality. The law with which Redfield and Johnson clash cannot be reduced to their trepidation before the stronghold of convention; they are up against a crisis of femininity that precludes a woman's self-assertion outside of fulfilling the masculine fantasy, where she is relegated to the limiting roles of whore or mother. The power of *The Bridges of Madison County* lies largely in its sensitivity to the fact that the answers to ethical questions of love and commitment take women to a cultural crisis surrounding the question of what it means to be a woman.

If Lacan can help us understand the law that prohibits Johnson from claiming a life with Kincaid, he cannot help us understand how to overcome it or why Johnson's confession to her children helps them heal. But feminist Lacanian clinicians have made great progress in deconstructing the limits of his theory. By rethinking the Lacanian concept of *jouissance*, the feminist Lacanian Judith Gurewich[11] has argued that the Oedipal myth is an effect rather than a cause of human subjectivity. According to Lacan, the mirror stage is a structural moment in which the child comes to see himself as the beloved object of his mother. Viewing himself through the Other's eye, the child creates an image of himself, which in turn shapes the ego-ideal that directs the child's aspirations toward what he might become one day. But the experience of the mother's love carries another message as well, one that conveys that the mother is *fulfilled by* the child. As long as the child maintains the fantasy that he is the heart of her mother's life, he is spared the experience of her mother's *jouissance*; while the child remains the center of attention, his mother's desire is not threatening to him. But mothers are not *only* mothers, as Caroline and Michael learn in *Bridges*—a mother may well have a secret life as Anaïs Nin.

Running up against signifiers of the mother's real desire, which is much broader than her desire for the child, the child formulates a retroactive fantasy in which he is the only one for his mother. Michael still lingers in that fantasy space. The mother's desire, successfully articulated, should prevent the child from retreating to the safety of that fantasy, but as we have seen, Lacan explains why it is so difficult for women to articulate their desire and claim it as theirs. Thus, the mother always appears to be slipping away, to be lacking something that cannot be replenished by the child, and so he sets off on the trail toward understanding her desire, wondering, *What does she want that is not me?* In a patriarchal society, of course, we are likely to find a father at the end of this trail—but not necessarily. Indeed, for Johnson it was not truly the husband/father at the end of the trail, but someone else offering her something different.

At the beginning of the film, both Johnson children are trapped in deadening relationships, and Gurewich's reading of Lacan helps us to understand why. If the mother's desire remains something mysterious, which is seemingly empty but for shallow clichés of femininity, the child cannot separate from the mother as an individual subject. The mother's desire must have a symbolic referent beyond the child, one that the child can understand and even respect. Thus, the child does not necessarily need the fearsome father to enforce the incest taboo and ensure separation from the mother; what he or she needs is the symbolization of the mother's desire itself. The father may play this role if he fulfills the mother's desire; otherwise, his mere presence cannot be enough because he does not fill the mysterious vaccuum of the mother's desire. This is why Gurewich says that the Oedipal fantasy is an effect of our desire to escape a position in which we are forever hooked into the wants and whims of our first love. We wish for a law that promises the possibility of separation, of selfhood, and that law is expressed as the Oedipal myth when the father stands in for mother's desire. But the conventional Oedipal complementarity still leaves us caught in the fantasy.

The work of analysis, for Gurewich, means freeing the patient from this fantasy so that she can actively create a life as a desiring being. Crucially, for Gurewich, when the confrontation with the mother's desire occurs, the child must be able to find signifiers for what the mother truly wants, so that he or she can avoid the trauma of remaining caught up in the fantasized world of the imaginary mother of early infancy. The hold of the Oedipal myth with its rigid gender roles must be dispelled, not reinforced—only then can we have the possibility to be ourselves. Once we read this Oedipal myth as effect rather than cause, we obliterate the appeal to civilization as a block against the woman's desire and free both the individual woman and the culture itself for a more meaningful, more creative life. We do not need the image of the father as the law to endure individuation and separation as cultural and institutional realities.[12]

By exploring their mother's desire through her journal, Caroline and Michael free themselves to see that they have both lived fantasies that have constrained their perceived options in the world. Ironically, against Johnson's assertion that a mother must hold firm so that her children can move, it is only when Caroline and Michael learn that their mother did indeed move after what she desired that they too can move in their own lives. Michael now wants to move into a shared symbolic space with his wife, in which he can come to know her true self beyond his stereotypes of womanhood, which derived from his attachment to an Oedipal fantasy. Caroline decides to proceed with her divorce.

Why do so many women take for granted that the worst thing that can happen is to become like our mothers? Why don't we cheer for the possibility? Here we see that Johnson's journal opens up her life, so women can lead meaningful lives outside the strictures of Oedipal complementarity. She gives her daughter a mother who can embrace her own desire, and hence her daughter understands that she is capable of doing the same. Caroline kisses the dress that signifies her mother's break with her feminine stereotypes. Identifying with her mother, she puts the dress on. Johnson showed that she loved her children in many ways. But in the end, her final gift to her children was her greatest gift of all: she gave them a mother who claimed her own personhood. She stole the image, which came from their Oedipal fantasy, of a mother who was always theirs, who needed only them, and in its place she gave them her complicated self with all its struggles. In this way, she undermined the Oedipal myth's hold on them and opens up the possibility that they may both lead richer lives than they had been able to lead before reading her journal.

4

Psychic Scars: Transformative Relationships and Moral Repair

Is it possible for one person to intervene in another's traumatic past, to change the course of a life's path through love or responsiveness? Trauma is often defined as an experience that falls beneath the reach of memory, belies articulation, consumes the traumatized victim in symptoms beyond her or his control. But is the victim fated to a prison unreachable by others because it cannot be expressed? Is she inevitably, irrevocably isolated in despair before her own inability to reach out to others with words capable of truly expressing the interiority of her soul? Are the tragedies of acting out symptomatically the only expressions remaining to a victim? Is she bound to forever play out her own internal dualism, either by becoming the perpetrator or by playing the perpetually abused?[1]

The question of whether the scars of trauma can heal sufficiently well to free the victim to reach out for healthy, genuine contact with others haunts in one way or another almost all of the films we have discussed so far. But in this chapter we turn to a series of films in which Eastwood deals more directly with the complex issues at the heart of moral repair: *A Perfect World*, *Absolute Power*, and *Million Dollar Baby*. Certainly in *Absolute Power* and *Million Dollar Baby* the theme of failed fatherhood is grappled with explicitly. Yet what makes these movies so interesting is that the failure here is not portrayed in any simple way as a man's inadequacy before traditional Oedipal complementarity. The Eastwood model is the opposite from the stereotypic good father who knows best; he is a father who is desperate to restore some sort of relationship with his female children by admitting to his failure and apologizing for it. In a sense, as we saw in the previous chapter, these fathers are admitting symbolic castration as part of what it means to be ethical men and, yes, fathers who might even be able to find ways to reconnect with their daughters.

A Perfect World (1993)

A Perfect World[2] opens with a fading sun as seen through the eyes of a dying man, Butch Haynes (Kevin Costner), who is bleeding out from multiple bullet wounds. A large bird—a hawk, possibly a buzzard or vulture—flies momentarily across the sun. A helicopter hovers overhead. Butch's expression is gentle, seemingly full of love as his life passes from him. The scene blacks out.

In a far different scene, boisterous children trick-or-treat in the streets of a small town. At one house, a woman appears at the door to explain that her family does not participate in Halloween: she does not give treats, and her children may not dress up to play with the others, because they are Jehovah's Witnesses and do not believe in celebrating the holiday. Her son, however, gazes longingly through the window, even as the children hurl eggs at it to retaliate against his mother's not offering them treats. We learn that his mother is a single mother. We fade to black again and begin elsewhere. One senses, perhaps, that the director could not easily decide where first to take hold of the painful events he has elected to relate.

Next we see two prisoners making a daring escape from prison. Taking a guard hostage, they force him to drive them through the prison gates; one of the prisoners seems mad with excitement, or just plain psychotic, as he wildly brandishes his gun. Shortly we find them, now without the guard, driving into a neighborhood familiar to us from the earlier trick-or-treating scene. The stark moral differences between the two fugitives are quickly made clear when they break into the Jehovah's Witnesses' house. One of them strikes both Gladys Perry (Jennifer Griffin) and her son, Phillip (T.J. Lowther), simply to get at their bacon and eggs, only to have his partner intervene, furious at the his unruly behavior. In the ensuing struggle the gun falls to the floor, and we see Phillip lingering in the doorway, frightened and uncertain about what to do. Here the gentler of the men, whom we will come to know as Robert "Butch" Haynes speaks softly to Phillip, turning the terrifying situation into a game: "Pick [the gun] up. . . . Now say 'Stick 'em up!' " By now, however, the disturbance has wakened a neighbor, who comes bursting in with a shotgun to save the day. Butch grabs Phillip as a shield, telling the older man to put his weapon down before something happens to the child. Of course, by now other neighbors have risen as well, and Butch has no choice but to flee with the young boy as a hostage. The elderly neighbor has tried to come to the rescue of Gladys, a woman on her own, and he is taunted by Butch's partner as the old man struggles to shoot out a tire or otherwise impede the escape.

We are then somewhat abruptly taken to another central character. Texas Ranger Red Garnett (Eastwood) carefully examines the fugitives' case files, preparing to lead the manhunt. Sally Gerber (Laura Dern) enters the room, and the rangers immediately mistake her for a new secretary, joking that they hope "this one" will not start drinking until noon. Gerber earnestly explains that she is actually a criminologist working for the state prison system who has been sent to work with Garnett on this "penal situation"—a remark that does nothing to impress the men. Garnett corrects her usage: this is not a penal situation, but a manhunt. She is clearly unused to this kind of fieldwork and fumbles with her books and files, nearly missing out on the chase as the rangers prepare to depart—in a fancy new trailer courtesy of the campaign-trail governor, a man who is prepared to put on a big show to capture Butch quickly and not to hurt his chances at reelection.

The relationship that develops between Garnett and Gerber should be familiar to the reader by now because it follows the same pattern we witnessed in the other Eastwood films. Garnett is openly sexist as well as anti-intellectual; he is suspicious of Gerber not only because she is a woman but also because she expects—foolishly, he believes—to track Butch down with books and files, profiles and statistics. But Gerber stands up for herself—"You think I'm what? Some dumb school girl who wandered into the boy's locker room?"—and Red is almost immediately impressed by her feistiness and her refusal to be cowed. As we have seen elsewhere, Eastwood depicts sexism in his heroes only to have it answered—effectively—by the talents and the force of will of a strong (often explicitly feminist) woman. Of course, Garnett's over-the-top sexism might be read as the setup for a heavy-handed message, but even so I find little reason to complain. After all, can we really be reminded too many times that sexism is not only frighteningly pervasive but also emotionally shallow and shortsighted? Impressed with her commitment Garnett encourages Sally to speak up, saying, "Might not agree, but [he'll] listen." Garnett is clearly determined to find Butch, and Gerber shares that determination. Yet as she sadly remarks, "In a perfect world, things like this wouldn't happen in the first place."

Returning to the fugitives, we find that Butch's partner continues to behave erratically toward their hostage, despite Butch's efforts to keep him in check. Butch finally punches him and takes the gun, which he gives to Phillip with instructions to shoot the other man if he so much as moves. Meanwhile, Butch shops for provisions. Phillip, of course, has no experience with weapons, and as a result the other prisoner easily escapes into a nearby cornfield—followed by the boy, who has decided not to give up his charge. Butch, returning from the store, finds the car empty and quickly follows the two into the field. Discovering Phillip first, he quietly retrieves the gun and motions the child back toward the car. The camera focuses on Butch's face as he aims the gun at his comrade. Phillip, running from the field, only hears the shot.

With the shopkeeper alarmed at the sound of gunfire, Butch knows he needs to make a hasty exit but does not force Phillip to come with him. Instead, he asks the boy if he is coming and waits respectfully for an answer. Phillip shakes his head at first, but finally nods. By now it is clear that while Butch is a criminal, a man who would kill his partner even, he is not wrapped up in the same kind of deep psychosis as the other man was. He does not kill for enjoyment, and he does not kill with indifference. Perhaps more importantly, even though he was the one who kidnapped the child to begin with, he paradoxically will not keep the boy against his will.

Butch turns their flight into a game: the car is a kind of time machine, with Butch as the captain and Phillip as the navigator. The gas pushes them steadily into the future, while the brake can take them back into the past. Indeed, they are pretending for a moment to be moving toward a more perfect future, and all the while we see genuine love gradually unfolding between them. Butch tries to play the father Phillip never had; he tries to imagine what a fun, loving father would be like; and Phillip increasingly falls in love with Butch and his world—a pretend world. In this world, Phillip plays games and explores, and he is rewarded for his success by Butch's appreciative congratulations. Their relationship deepens as their shared fantasy takes on its own history, expressing itself both in play and in hardship—with the lines never quite clear between the two. In one moment, Phillip plays the Indian scout who successfully locates the keys for a new vehicle; seconds later the owner of the car tries to intervene, but when Butch reaches for his gun, Phillip bites the man's hand instead. The man is forced to relent, and they get away without another shooting—and now Phillip is playing an active, positive role in what has become an adventure.

As Butch and his hostage grow closer, Butch learns that Phillip was named after his father, who left when Phillip was so young that he does not even remember him. Phillip repeats his mother's assurances that his father will one day return. Butch exposes the lie, explaining that men like Phillip and himself must face the reality that they have to go on alone. "You and me have a lot in common. Both of us are handsome devils, we both like RC Cola, and we both have old men who aren't worth a damn." This is the first we hear of Butch's own traumatic past, and it helps to explain his deepening identification with Phillip. Playing the father, Butch purchases some new pants for the boy, and at this point he asks the child to pick a nickname for himself—clearly because a boy named "Phillip" will be all over the news, but it is also a way to distance the child from his missing namesake by giving him the option to define himself differently. Phillip decides to call himself "Buzz."

By now the shopping trip has cost them their anonymity; an officer has recognized the car and a store manager hears word of the kidnapping on the news. Leaving Phillip in the store, Butch manages to escape, and with some expert driving he eludes the local police and circles back around for Phillip. Here he makes his position on the boy's freedom perfectly clear: "It's up to you, boy." Phillip runs to get into the car.

As Phillip slips into his new pants, Butch notices another package under his shirt, a Casper the Ghost costume that Phillip had admired in the store. Attempting to teach a moral lesson—as he feels any good father should—Butch explains to Phillip that stealing is wrong, but he is willing to allow some exceptions to the rule. Still, Phillip is reluctant to don his stolen prize, and Butch quickly understands why, guessing that Phillip is afraid that Butch will see his "pecker." Indeed, Phillip admits that he is embarrassed about his puny equipment, but Butch insists on verifying the boy's assessment. Butch strongly disagrees, reassuring the boy, "Hell no, Phillip! It's a good size for a boy your age." Phillip, delighted, gives the man a big smile for delivering that welcome news. Here Butch struggles to live up to a traditional Oedipal role in which his reassurance underscores the identification of the penis with the phallus, so that ultimately Phillip will be able to take his place in a man's world. Of course this attempt at Oedipal complementarity is undermined by Butch's position as a wanted fugitive with very little chance of escape, and Butch's own masculinity is at stake in his attempt to run away with Phillip into a fantasy world where there really is such a thing as a good father who knows best.

Meanwhile, the authorities continue to pursue the fugitives. Sally Gerber demonstrates the usefulness of her research and tries to understand Robert "Butch" Haynes by playacting an account of his life, reciting significant events in the first person so in order to better identify with her subject. We learn that Butch was born in Amarillo, Texas, but grew up in the French Quarter of New Orleans. At the age of eight, he had already killed a man. Garnett becomes intrigued by Gerber's first-person approach, joining in the game. "How did you kill him?" he asks, learning that Butch shot the man with "a thirty-eight special." The victim was a john abusing Butch's mother, and therefore the killing was covered up.

After that, according to Gerber's narrative, went well for Butch until, when he was twelve, his mother died and his now paroled father turned up again. Garnett pushes Gerber here, and we later discover that he is right to expect more: Butch's mother eventually hanged herself, and his father was a brutal child-abuser who beat his son regularly. For now, Gerber skips ahead to an incident involving a joyride in a stolen car, which resulted in a surprisingly harsh sentence, four years in juvenile detention with hard labor. Garnett and Gerber exchange a glance, suggesting that they both know her research is on to something important: there was something seriously amiss with that sentence.

At that moment, Butch and Phillip drive by the marshals' headquarters, engaged in another game. Gerber catches a glimpse of Phillip—an eyewitness reported that he was now in a Casper costume—and points out to the rest of the team that the fugitives they are pursuing just drove by. The team tries to quickly turn the unwieldy trailer around to chase them, but disaster quickly results when the driver tries to push the vehicle to its limits. They ultimately rip the modern crime trailer away from the truck that tows it along. The trailer crashes and, although none of the team are hurt, it is clear that they are not going anywhere until the trailer is fixed or some other means of transportation is offered to them. Escaping yet again, the fugitives discuss what they need to do in order to make it to Alaska where Butch hopes, despite everything we have already learned about his past, to reunite with his father. Although the audience knows about the brutality of Butch's father from Gerber's narrative, and we know that Butch has condemned his father for "not being worth a damn," there is clearly a longing in Butch to restore something he never had. Here again as we saw in the last chapter, Oedipal complementarity, which is the fantasy effect of the struggle of individuation, is portrayed as an ideal but always one that has already failed.

Deciding that they need provisions, Butch suggests playfully that they should get them by trick-or-treating. Phillip is wearing a Casper costume, after all. Even though the boy knows he is not permitted to trick-or-treat according to the tenets of his mother's faith, Butch insists on empowering Phillip's will: "I am asking you, Phillip. I ain't asking yer mother, and I ain't askin' Jehovah. Do you wanna to go trick-or-treating or not?" We see here what was at stake in Judith Gurewich's revision of Lacan's analysis of the Oedipal myth: If the Oedipal myth is the effect of the desire for separation, and a myth that ultimately must be dispelled to achieve separation, then Butch does not allow Phillip to idealize him as a father, not even for a moment. Instead, he shows him to listen to his own voice, which is independent of all adult authorities. Trick-or-treating eventually involves holding up a woman at gunpoint—because, of course, she does not understand that it is still Halloween in Butch and Phillip's fantasy—but Butch is careful to conceal the gun from his young partner. As far as Phillip is concerned, he gets the treats for the sake of his costume as any child his age would on Halloween.

Next, they need another new car—and their only option is to steal one. Butch is friendly to the victim and even admires of him openly to Phillip. He commends Bob for making the wise decision not to resist them. "Bob's a fine family man and that's about the best thing a fella can hope to be." Butch tries again and again to set a good example for Phillip, who is struggling to live up to an Oedipal ideal that constantly eludes him. Even when Butch is seduced by a waitress at a roadside restaurant and Phillip sneaks out after them to peek at their intimate activities, Butch runs out after the distressed little boy to explain that he loved the waitress and it wasn't meaningless sex: "Kissed her butt didn't I?" In this pretend Oedipal situation, he tries to present a good example of what a man should be. And of course part of the complexity of the movie is its subtle engagement with how an idealized Oedipal masculinity is always pretend.

Stranded back in the trailer, Garnett and Gerber end up discussing Garnett's relationship to Butch. And now we come to understand why Garnett seems so intent on Gerber's rendition of Butch's past: he has run into Butch before. Garnett played a central role in Butch's life by saving Butch from his own father and his abusiveness, which he thought was the right thing to do. When young Butch got himself in trouble with a stolen car, Garnett actually brokered the deal that sent him to juvenile detention with such a harsh sentence; he claims that it was the best way to get the boy away from his father and that many young men actually benefit from spending time in juvenile detention. Under his breath Garnett mutters that one boy whom he sent away for a few years wound up becoming a priest. Yet for all his attempts to justify himself, we can see that doubt clouds his features, belying his words and underscoring his special interest in the case. And here again we see Eastwood shooting the complexity of so-called masculine Oedipal ideals; the very harshness of the sentence that Garnett claims can make a man into a man, this time underscored Butch's hopelessness and ultimately did exactly the opposite of what Garnett had hope it would do.

The movie moves back and forth between the chase and our exploring Garnett's guilt that doing what he thought was the right thing turned against Butch's chances at leading a moral life as an upstanding citizen. Butch knows he is in a desperate situation. Yet he and Phillip are having the time of their lives. One night when they go to sleep in a cornfield, an African American farmhand finds them and invites them into his home. Together, they sleep peacefully with Butch's arm wrapped protectively around the boy he is treating as his son. In the morning they have a hearty breakfast and Phillip plays with a new friend, the farmhand's grandson. Meanwhile Butch shows off his dancing skills, performing for the farmhand's wife. But it cannot last: Butch becomes increasingly agitated when he realizes that the farmhand has been listening to the radio, and though he tries to recapture the feeling of family joy by playfully flipping about Phillip and his new friend, it is already too late. The farmhand grabs his grandson to pull him away and then slaps him when he resists, causing Butch to lose his temper. The show of violence releases his own anger as a traumatized child; now grown up, he can at least fantasize that he can act out the role of the protector who was not there for him. But, once unleashed, his rage is is identical to the rage pent up over the years in the heart of an abused child. He punches the farmhand and attempts, obsessively, to continue playing with the child. But he has been sent back to a deep world of inner pain, and for the first time he yells at Phillip, demanding that he fetch rope from the car so that he can bind the man. Despite himself, as he seeks to position himself as the ideal protector, he is becoming the abuser. Brandishing a gun in his face, Butch instructs his host to tell his grandson that he loves him—and he had better mean it. Phillip weeps, understanding that the Butch he loves is no longer himself but having no idea how to reach him. Where has his ideal father gone? Butch only gives him one sign that he is still the caring one who has spent all this time with him: Butch gives Phillip the option to stay with him for what he's going to do next, or to go wait in the car. But Butch has encouraged Phillip to be his own person and make his own decisions. The gun falls to the floor as Butch works with the ropes and duct tape, using the duct tape to silence the grandmother's prayer. Phillip, trembling, picks up the gun. He refuses to give it to Butch and then shoots him, tears running down his face.

The shock of being shot breaks Butch out of the traumatic repetition in which the ideal of the masculine protector elides into the masculine abuser. The elision is presented when Butch, in a non-stereotypic masculine way, tries to get the grandfather to say that he loves his grandson. Butch runs after Phillip, handing the family a knife with which to cut themselves free and thanking them for their hospitality. Badly wounded, Butch only intends to prove to the boy that he is not angry, that he wants them to stay together. He calls to Phillip. "You're a hero. Prolly be all in all the papers tomorrow, how you saved those folks!" He also tries to save himself in Phillip's eyes: "Truth is, I don't think I woulda killed 'em." He explains that he has only killed two men: one for abusing his mother and, as we saw earlier, his fellow prisoner. Phillip climbs into a tree to escape from Butch, but when Butch reads him a postcard from Butch's father, Phillip finally climbs down to be with his friend. He weeps while he listens to Butch's fantasy that they might still make it to Alaska to find his father; they might still escape in their "time machine." Butch drifts into unconsciousness, but Phillip wakes him up to make sure that he is holding onto the life that is slowly escaping from him. Even as the police arrive, Phillip struggles to help Butch to get up and Butch reassures the boy that he is not upset at him for the shooting: "Truth is, if it had to happen, I'm glad it was you. As opposed to someone I don't know, I mean. All things considered, I feel pretty good."

As the police arrive, Butch initially keeps up the act that Phillip is his hostage, shouting to Garnett that he will shoot the boy if anyone approaches. But when Phillip looks up at him in horror, Butch takes back his threat and makes two demands to the police: he tells Garnett to gather some candy, and he orders that Phillip's mother do everything on a wish list that the boy prepared for Butch as they lay in the cornfield the night before. Phillip's mother has been flown to the scene by helicopter, and as Garnett scrambles to find candy, she agrees to do everything on the wish list. Butch tells Phillip to don his mask and to go trick-or-treating with the officers. Butch heralds his departure: "Make way for Casper the Friendly Ghost!" But Phillip only makes it half way before he turns and runs back, much to Butch's surprise. "Personally, I thought we negotiated a pretty fair deal. But if there's somethin' else you want . . ." Phillip responds, "Do they want to shoot you?" Phillip helps him up and the two stagger forward together; Garnett responds that now he has seen everything. Walking forward unarmed, he hopes to end the incident without further violence. Butch appears to recognize him, but Garnett responds that no, he doesn't know him, "not really."

Butch knows he is in bad shape, and he wants to give the boy his wish list before he falls unconscious. When he reaches into his pocket, the agents think he is going for a gun and against Garnett's explicit instructions, they open fire. The camera focuses on Garnett's horrified expression, then on Garber's. She screams for them to stop, but it is too late. Butch is fatally wounded, and Phillip struggles to stay with him as the police attempt to pull him away. Garnett punches the federal agent responsible for the shooting, and Garber kicks him in the groin; but what is done cannot be undone. Butch is dying, his senses fading so that he can no longer hear or make sense of what goes on around him. His last vision is of Phillip looking down on him in grief and sorrow, desperately grasping his wish list in one hand. We have come full circle to the beginning of the movie where we see Butch lying in the field, but now we know why the smile lingers on his face. Butch is smiling at Phillip.

The story has come full circle in other respects as well: now another man has been shot by an eight-year-old boy, only this time man and boy have loved each other, and continue to love each other. Twice Garnett tried to intervene in Butch's life, and twice now he has failed to make the story right. The film ends with Gerber reassuring Garnett that he "should know" that he did his best, and Garnett's total despair echoes in his answer to her: "Don't know nuthin'. Not a damn thing." Garnett is no longer the same cocky character we met at the beginning of the film. There is certainly a hint of the connection between the hubris inherent in certain ideals of Oedipal masculine identity and Garnett's former cockiness, even if driven by guilt that he could not make it right this time. He could not save Butch by providing him a meaningful relationship between men of different generations; instead Butch had this intergenerational relationship with Phillip. But there is no way out of the horror that has transpired. Eastwood does not even provide the usual secondary narrative track of a romance with Gerber to give us some sense of fulfillment. Even though Garnett has come to respect her, they have not engaged each other romantically in any sense. It is, indeed, one of his saddest films but also one that questions Oedipal ideals of masculinity because they promote violence in the very effort to live up to them. The camera rises and the scene fades, to an Irish song of mourning. The mourning here is not for an Oedipal ideal gone wrong. The mourning is for a man's life, lost unnecessarily because of the harsh notion of manhood connected to Oedipal ideals, which are particularly evident when we see Butch allowing Phillip the ultimate separation to leave him and to follow his dreams.

Absolute Power (1997)

Absolute Power[3] tells a more optimistic tale of moral repair in the context of a father-daughter relationship gone sour as a consequence of the father's life as a professional thief. Because Luther Whitney (Eastwood) was in prison when his daughter, Kate Whitney (Laura Linney), was growing up, his daughter spent her formative years living with her mother. Reluctantly, his wife forced herself to become distant from him. Since Whitney was released from prison, he has not openly visited his daughter, and the last time he saw her was at her mother's funeral.

Luther Whitney is a sophisticated professional thief; he regards his profession as a kind of artistry, a skilled occupation with its own set of standards and mores. Indeed, at the start of the film, we find Whitney drawing sketches in a museum. Impressed, a young woman sketching at his side takes note of his work, commenting ironically (and all too accurately) that he must "work with his hands." Whitney has been inactive for years, but he has finally decided to do one last job—a big one—to set himself up for the rest of his life. As Whitney breaks into the home of one of the wealthiest men in the country, everything goes smoothly until a drunken couple interrupts his work. Hiding in a strange closet equipped with a one-way mirror, Whitney has little choice but to watch the couple engage in sexual intercourse. What he sees appears at first to be rough but consensual play. Soon, however, the man's aggression transforms the encounter into rape: he strikes the woman violently in a manner that she clearly did not invite. Finally, she pulls a letter opener on him as he strangles her, but just then two men break into the room and shoot her in the back.

Throughout the battle, the camera repeatedly returns to Whitney's horrified, guilty expression. He has chosen his own safety over the dangers of intervening, but he is clearly ambivalent about the decision. Though he has made a career of breaking the law, he has never used

violence in his thefts and can only watch in horror at the crimes unfolding before him. And it gets worse. The attempted rapist was the president
of the United States, Allen Richmond (Gene Hackman), who was having an affair with the wife of his friend, and the armed men who saved
him were members of the Secret Service. Waiting for the scene to clear,
Whitney listens as the chief of staff discusses plans to cover up the mess:
the official story will be that the house was robbed and the victim killed
in the commission of the crime.

When he thinks everyone has left, Whitney leaves his hiding place,
picking up the letter opener as he goes. When the president's staff realizes
that they have neglected to take important evidence, Secret Service
agents return to collect it and Whitney must make a hasty escape. When
they discover that the evidence has gone missing and find Whitney's
rope hanging out the window, the agents are dismayed indeed to realize
that there has been a witness to the terrible crimes they intend to cover
up.

Whitney knows the agents will come after him, and he plans to leave
the country. Indeed, the president's staff quickly decides that the only
way to solve their problem is to kill the only witness. Meanwhile, the
police do not buy the story sold to them by the White House. A strong
black female officer points out the many defects in the story: nothing
about the crime scene fits the claim of a robbery gone too far. Still,
Officer Mike McCarty (Richard Jenkins) decides to approach Whitney
directly, concluding that he is one of only two living thieves who could
have successfully invaded the home. He does not believe that Whitney
is a killer, however, and merely hopes to learn more about the real story
by talking to him. He finds Whitney at the museum working on his
sketches, and Whitney gives nothing away. After not getting anywhere
with Whitney in his first encounter with him, the officer decides that
Whitney won't crack without some further motivation; he reasons that
an appeal from the man's estranged daughter may help.

After discovering that an officer is already on his trail, Whitney is all
the more eager to leave the country as quickly as possible. But he cannot
bear to leave the country without seeing his daughter one last time. It is
here that we know how carefully he has watched over her since his
release, because he knows exactly where she will take her morning run.
He hides in the bushes along her jogging route and confronts her as she
passes by to tell her that he is leaving the country for a long, long time.
From his behavior Kate guesses right away that he is active again and she
is enraged that he has included her in it. But she also berates him for his

absolute failure as a father. This little show is of no interest to her because he has already disappointed her so much in the past. She runs away from him, but despite his sadness he is determined to follow through with leaving the country. At the airport, however, Whitney sits at the bar while the president appears on television at a press conference with his widowed "best friend," vowing to bring his wife's murderer to justice and breaking down in tears in a skillful performance. Deciding that he cannot let this kind of deep moral hypocrisy and abuse of power stand, Whitney determines to risk his own life to bring the president down. He knows he is taking a risk but does not yet understand the full range of forces arrayed against him. He is well aware that the Secret Service is after him, but he doesn't know that the victim's husband has also hired an assassin to kill him.

Here we have an interesting portrayal of the thief as the one who is outside the conventional symbolic order of masculinity. He regularly sketches in the museum, a pastime that is degraded as feminine unless one is extraordinarily successful at it. In his sketches he mimics the world around him, and a mimicry over assertiveness has long been considered a feminine virtue. For certain psychoanalytic theorists, femininity is a kind of masquerade, a playing at being something, but according to Lacanian analysis, there is nothing in a women's being for her to be.[4] So, positioned outside the law, the thief is almost feminized by being in a place from which he is not allowed to fully enter the symbolic law of phallic authority.

Meanwhile, Officer McCarty has located Whitney's daughter, Kate, who has become a successful prosecutor and does not care to think about her father one way or the other. Here again we have an interesting portrayal of a woman who enters law in order to distance herself from a traumatized father who has refused to perform the duties associated with Oedipal complementarity. Desperate for her help, McCarty takes her to Whitney's house, which turns out to be a kind of museum of her. Whitney has a picture of her at every major milestone in her life: her high school graduation, law school commencement, sitting on the courthouse steps after her first trial. Amazed, Kate admits that she often felt a presence in her life, a loving watchful presence that she could not name. In spite of herself, she is moved. She agrees to set up a meeting with her father. Her father is thrilled at the idea that he may be able to find a way to reconnect with her and at least seek her forgiveness, even if he cannot reestablish a relationship. Unfortunately, their first attempt at a meeting is disrupted by the hitman and Secret Service agents, who manage to track him despite his attempts at disguise. They open fire almost as soon as Whitney arrives. He makes sure that his daughter is safe before he flees again. Whitney's primary concern is his daughter's safety, even as he skillfully manages to escape the scene in the disguise of a policeman. The law here has become a masquerade for Whitney.

McCarty takes Kate home. He is obviously interested in her romantically and wants to ensure her safety. She offers him a glass of water, mentioning that she keeps very little in her refrigerator, but when she opens the door to find the refrigerator fully stocked, she realizes her father is in her home. She pushes McCarty out and calls out to her father that she knows he is there. He reveals himself and levels with her: he explains that he is not a murderer and he plans to expose the president.

Unbeknownst to him, the Secret Service has been ordered by the president's chief of staff to kill Kate as well, because they are afraid that she may know what happened. An older agent, already disgusted with himself for taking part in the cover-up, will ultimately kill himself out of guilt for his role in the events. His younger partner, however, nearly succeeds in killing Whitney's daughter, following her to a remote location where she likes to jog and pushing her car over the edge of a cliff. Knowing her routine, her father understands the danger of something happening to her during her run in an isolated area. Unfortunately, he arrives too late and we see his horror when he understands that there is some truth in her accusation that he is either absent or too late. However, he calls the ambulance to come to her aid and she ultimately survives (barely).

Whitney is convinced that the agent is determined to finish the job, given what is at stake for the president of the United States. The agent disguises himself as a doctor, planning to give Kate a fatal injection, but Whitney tackles him to the ground at the last moment. The self-righteous agent says that he must protect the president, right or wrong, and Whitney retorts that no one should be protected "right or wrong." Here Eastwood returns to a theme he has addressed throughout his work, and which we have explored throughout this book, namely the danger of a phallic assertiveness that assumes it can control the world—an assertiveness that aspires to a position of absolute power. The profound abuse of executive power, and even more profoundly the self-assured and arrogant manner in which cover-ups and executions are ordered in the president's name—to save his "ass" (and I use the term very deliberately)—make this film very timely indeed. Significantly for Eastwood, it is ethical, not political, disgust that leads Whitney to expose the president. Moreover, his love for his daughter strengthens his commitment to stand for principles that can make her truly respect him. As a director Eastwood often returns to how ethical commitments, and in turn those associated with sincere repentance can bring his masculine characters out of a state of dissociation, in which one cannot live out family connections but—as we see in this film—instead revives them through photos that hold a memory of what might have been different.

At this point, Whitney goes on the offensive once again, using his ability to mimic roles and disguise himself. He stands in for the widowed Walter Sullivan's chauffeur. When Sullivan (E.G. Marshall) discovers the subterfuge, he flies into a rage at the man he still believes to be his wife's murderer. Gradually, however, he comes to accept Whitney's story, which accords to a certain extent with what Sullivan already knows: he explains that he installed the secret closet with the one-way mirror as a way to take part in his wife's infidelities, including her encounters with the president, his friend, even though he could not satisfy her himself because he is impotent. While he admits that he never loved her as he did his first wife of forty-seven years, he insists he had a kind of love for her; thus, losing her led him to seek revenge on her killer. Here again we return to a profound theme in Eastwood's oeuvre as a director: masculine rage, often rooted in the exposure of impotence, fortifies itself as revenge. Believing Whitney, Sullivan lets him go but he of course still has to deal with the fact that he confessed his impotence, thereby undermining his class status as an extremely wealthy man. He never expected to be so thoroughly betrayed by the president, and that very night he goes to confront his friend with what he has learned. The last we see of Sullivan is when he enters the president's office, where he is always welcomed in as one of the president's wealthiest supporters.

Later, Whitney is at his daughter's bedside when the media broadcasts news of the president's suicide. Reporters interview Sullivan, who describes his attempts to talk his friend out of his gruesome self-destruction, but we never know what really happened and strongly suspect that Sullivan killed the president himself. Again we are left with a contrast between the last two scenes of the movie, which results from the fact that Sullivan himself is still caught up with a phallic assertiveness as the only way to settle scores between men. However, we are left to imagine the scene and to draw our own conclusions.

In the next scene, we see that Whitney's profound commitment to morally repair his relationship with Kate and to go straight permanently if that is what is necessary to prove his metamorphosis to his daughter.

Kate wakes up in the hospital to find her father sketching at her side. She asks him to reassure her that she is going to be fine; instead he affirms that "we" are going to be fine, making it evident that he intends to build a relationship with her. Thus, the film ends on a more optimistic note than *A Perfect World* does. Perhaps that is in part because in *A Perfect World* Garnett does not give up his masculine ideal of control, wanting to be the one to save the other until it is already too late and Butch is dying. There are different risks at stake here: in a conventional sense Garnett risks his life by facing Butch unarmed, even though he may be armed and willing to kill. Whitney also risks his life by deciding to take on the president combined and to stay close to his daughter to save her from being the hapless victim of his own crusade against absolute power. There is an interesting twist and difference between the two movies: Garnett's hubris in insisting that he can bring Butch back into the law and into safety has to be undone. Whitney on the other hand accepts that he must live within the law if he is to have a relationship with his daughter and that his purported escape from being an ordinary man is what led him to lose the relationship in the first place. He realized he valued his daughter more than the so-called freedom that he had escaped in his many disguises from conventional masculinity. We have seen that genuine moral repair always involves considerable psychic risks that go beyond the literal danger of putting your life on the line, and ironically they may be more dangerous to pretenses of masculinity.

Whitney's taking moral responsibility as a witness—his putting himself into the action rather than remaining in the background as a spectator—also opens him up to imagining what it would be like to act as a father who does more than lurk in the shadows collecting photographs of his daughter's success. The fantasy that he can be a father without being involved is an extension of the fantasy that he can get away with anything; in part because it allows disassociation from true engagement with his daughter, replacing it instead with the distanced eye, a protected male gaze that shields him from the pitfalls of deep emotional attachment. When he accepts responsibility, he opens himself to the vulnerability that comes with love—vulnerability to the danger that we can lose the ones we care for. We observe utter horror in his expression when he sees Kate's totaled car and learns that she has been critically injured. Shattered by her near death, he can no longer hold on to the narcissistic fantasy in which nothing can affect him. And on that note, let us turn to Eastwood's masterpiece *Million Dollar Baby*, the very heartbeat of which is the theme of the risks taken on by opening oneself to the possibility of love.

Million Dollar Baby (2004)

The screenplay for *Million Dollar Baby*[5] was written by Paul Haggis, who incorporated a number of stories and characters from a collection by Jerry Boyd (writing under the pen name F. X. Toole), who was a fight manager and cutman. Haggis deserves a great deal of credit for the success of the film, because he was the one who put Morgan Freeman's character, Eddie "Scrap-Iron" Dupris, into the story, creating the retrospective voice through which the story of Frankie Dunn (Eastwood) and Maggie Fitzgerald (Hillary Swank) unfolds. Moreover, the screenplay remains true to the magic of boxing that inspired Jerry Boyd as a fighter and later as a writer.

Hillary Swank trained extensively with a championship boxer whom Eastwood then cast as her deadly opponent in the film, because she needed to become a boxer in order to understand the fear and the taste for violence, as well as the self-respect and sense of power that come with facing down the terror of a grueling physical match—all themes of which Boyd writes so eloquently. Where human beings instinctively run from pain, a boxer runs headlong into it, revels in it, and learns to find something profound in it.

> It's magic of the mind as well, because each thing they do, with their whole heart and soul, takes them to a new level of understanding. The higher they climb, the wider the horizon. And they begin to see and understand combinations they have never dreamed of. Like the writer, the more the fighter knows his game the greater the magic for him and for us.[6]

This "magic" takes the fighter over and keeps him going against all odds, even against the most excruciating pain. It is transformative. "Magic: that's why I am in it. For the voodoo."[7]

Dunn and Dupris go way back, to the days when Dupris was a fighter and Dunn his cutman. We learn that they have been friends through hard times, such as in one fight when Dupris was beaten so badly that he lost an eye—Dunn was only the cutman, not Dupris's manager, so he had no authority to call the fight. Still, Dunn maintains a close lifelong friendship with Dupris, at least in part because he cannot escape the feeling that somehow he failed him in that fateful fight. He has taken an important lesson from that night: beware the risks you take with your fighter. Now, Dupris maintains the gym that Dunn runs, and because of his blindness in one eye he is unable to play a larger role in the sport he still loves. Indeed, he rues the fact that Dunn continues to hold back with his fighters because of what happened to him, and he tries to convince Dunn that he is making a huge mistake in refusing to take Big Willie Little (Mike Colter), his prizefighter, to the championship. Dunn thinks he is protecting his charge, but Dupris and Big Willie both fear that if Willie does not take his shot at the championship now, his chance will never come around again. Finally Big Willie leaves Dunn for another manager and, as Dupris predicted, he does win the championship fight.

Meanwhile, Fitzgerald is desperate to train with Dunn, waiting to talk to him after Willie's earlier fights and determinedly trying to train herself in boxing at his gym. Dunn is immediately very clear that he does not train "girls," but Fitzgerald refuses to give up. Dupris sees Fitzgerald's great boxing potential long before Dunn does. If Dunn ever deigns to notice her at all, it is to complain that Dupris should tell her to give up and leave the gym. Finally, when Dunn loses Willie, Dupris intervenes more forcefully. Night after night, Fitzgerald has done her best without a trainer, without anyone at all in her corner. As Dupris narrates retrospectively, "She grew up knowing one thing: she was trash." Indeed, she sustains herself on leftovers, scraps left by the patrons at the tables she waits to make a very meager living. And in that gym at night, alone, Maggie sustains herself on the hope that she can become a fighter. She fights for her life, lashing out at the pull of her past that would send her back to a trailer park in Missouri. To quote the great American poet Samuel Menasche, Maggie's life is already at stake "In the Ring":

Knock yourself out
Shadowboxing—
Skull numb, mouth dry—
Blind the mind's eye[8]

Finally taking matters into his own hands, Dupris comes out one night and gives Dunn's speed bag to Fitzgerald so she can practice her punches. He knows this will get Dunn's attention, but Dunn's initial reaction is to tell Fitzgerald what he believes to be the hard truth: she is too old to become a fighter. He leaves her with the punching bag after that first encounter only because he is afraid that otherwise she will break down in tears—something that he can't stand—but he still refuses to train her. Another night, after Dunn and Dupris have it out about Dunn's mistake with Willie, and Dunn retorts by claiming that Dupris cannot bear what has become of his life after losing his eye, Dunn returns late in the evening with cheeseburgers to make peace with his friend. Fitzgerald is still at the gym, with a speed bag of her own that she bought having saved every penny she made waitressing.

It happens to be Fitzgerald's birthday. When Dunn tries again to convince her of the realities of her age, repeating his belief that she will never be a fighter, she counters with the brutal truths of her own life: "Truth is, my brother's in prison, my sister is on welfare, pretending one of her babies is still alive. My daddy's dead and my mama weighs three hundred and twelve pounds. . . . If I'm too old for this, then I got nothing. Is that enough truth to see you?" Hearing the reality of her situation, Dunn agrees reluctantly to teach her a few things before he turns her over to another manager. He also gives her his cardinal rule: "Protect yourself at all times."

Now we see Fitzgerald training in earnest, jumping rope, doing crunches, and running on the beach at four o'clock in the morning—tireless, working herself to the bone. As she works closely with Dunn, she tries to get to know him better, even as the viewer learns more and more about his inner pain. Fitzgerald asks him about his family, and he will only tell her that he has a daughter—and at least at one time she was athletic. After revealing this to Fitzgerald, he gazes into the distance. What the audience already knows is that he bears an immense burden of guilt when it comes to his daughter. We know that he writes to her frequently, but that the letters always come back, marked "Return to Sender." We also know that he dutifully, tenderly places each of the returned letters into a special box. So the audience knows why Fitzgerald's question seems to pain him so, even if she does not.

Ultimately Dunn decides that Fitzgerald is ready for a fight, but brutally keeping to his statement that he does not train women, he turns her over to another manager. Still, he cannot keep himself away from her first fight, and ultimately he cannot even keep himself from intervening. Finally her manager suggests in frustration that Dunn should just take over if he cannot leave well enough alone. At last Dunn utters the words that Fitzgerald has been waiting to hear: he tells the referee, "Yeah, this is my fighter." And Fitzgerald wins the fight. Afterward, she challenges him to stand up for his own rule about putting protection first. "You gave me away. How is that protecting me?" Then she asks him straight out, "Are you ever going to leave me again?" He makes a promise with one word: "Never."

As Fitzgerald trains with Dunn, the pair discovers that while Maggie is a superb fighter, she has a fatal weakness from a business perspective. Because she tends to knock her opponents out in the first round, no manager will allow a fighter to face her because they do not want to risk total humiliation. But Fitzgerald can only put everything she has into a fight; she doesn't know how to pull back just to make it a good show. Dunn has to pay managers under the table to get her any fights at all. Finally, he makes the difficult decision to take a risk (violating his own rule) by pushing her up a class, where she will face much stiffer competition. Her first fight in the new class is rough indeed, so rough that the other fighter breaks her nose. Not surprisingly, Dunn wants to call the fight, but Fitzgerald won't let him. She insists that he do his best to fix it so that she can go on. He literally smashes her nose back into place. While she is in agony but almost cheerful about it because she won her fight, her manager and cutman Frank endures an agony all his own. As Toole brilliantly situations like these,

> There's magic that breaks your heart. You've got a kid with a bloody nose. If it's broken, forget it. It's going to keep bleeding. But just a bloody nose you can usually stop. So you wipe the boy's face clean, shove a swab soggy with adrenaline into the nostril that's bleeding. You work the swab around, and you close the nostril with your thumb. You tell the boy to inhale so the adrenaline will flood the broken tissue and constrict the vein and widen the blowhole. But the boy doesn't inhale. You say, "Inhale." Nothing. You say it again. Goddamn it! Time is running out, and then you see the boy looking at you as if you had been speaking Gaelic or Hebrew. So then you understand. "Breathe in." . . . Blood is pumping in your neck because you almost didn't stop the blood. But part of you has traveled to a place where the boy lives, to a place where no one uses the word inhale. That's magic too, but it's the kind that hurts you, the kind that makes you better for hurting.

Of course, Fitzgerald's nose is not just bleeding—it's broken. In the emergency room, Dunn is a nervous wreck. He tries to think about the

Irish poets that he loves, like Yeats, but he cannot concentrate on anything besides Fitzgerald and her injury.

In only a year Fitzgerald's success has surpassed any of their wildest
dreams. On her next birthday Dupris takes her out for a frank discussion
of her manager's past, explaining that his excessive concern for his fighters may prevent him from taking Fitzgerald to the championship. Indeed,
at that moment, the manager who stole Willie away from Dunn comes
in—an apparent coincidence that Dupris may or may not have set up.
But Fitzgerald makes her position clear: because Dunn promised never
to leave her, she will never abandon him. Surprisingly, Dunn seems to
support her aspirations as he takes yet another risk by putting her on tour
in Europe. There he gives her a gift of a robe with the Irish words *Mo
Cuishle* printed on it, but he tells her he isn't sure what it means. The
tour is an incredible success, but the time is approaching when Dunn
must make his most difficult decision of all: whether to put Fitzgerald up
for the championship.

Meanwhile, Fitzgerald has taken Dunn's more practical advice, building a nest egg and purchasing a small house—not for herself, as it happens, but for her poverty-stricken family in Missouri. Fitzgerald asks
Dunn to join her in a surprise for her family, and, overjoyed, she presents
them with the house, only to have her joy almost instantly deflated when
her family arrives. They fail to appreciate the gift of a free house, and
they actually berate Fitzgerald for putting their welfare checks at risk.
Her mother tells her, "I know you didn't mean nothing hurtful by this.
It's just that sometimes you don't think things through." Dunn watches
the scene with sadness, even as Fitzgerald still desperately seeks her family's approval. Not only do they fail to offer support or gratitude, but they
actually mock her profession, teasing her about the very idea of a "girl"
fighter. Her mother advises: "Find a man. Marry him. Live proper.
When people hear what you do, they laugh. They laugh at you."

As she and Dunn drive away from the house, Fitzgerald's despair sinks
into an agonizing silence, which she finally breaks to tell Dunn about
her father's love for his favorite dog, Axle. When Axle's arthritis became
too severe for the dog to walk properly, her father took him out back
and ended his life himself. For Maggie, that was love: to put the dog
down himself, to be there with it to the end, and to personally give it a
more dignified end than it would have had wasting away from arthritis.
Sadly, already foreshadowing her end, she tells Dunn, "I've got nobody
but you, Frankie." And Dunn responds: "You have me." There is no

question now that he will always be in her corner, and he decides to let her go for the championship.

On the day of the big fight, Fitzgerald faces a "dirty" fighter, and the fight is tough indeed. Still, she fights through it, and in the end it seems like she might win—until, when her opponent is apparently down, she turns her back and never sees the attack coming at her from behind. The world seems to stop for Dunn, who is horrified as Fitzgerald falls and he frantically tries to reach her. We then see the world momentarily from Fitzgerald's perspective as consciousness fades; the lights swirl, dim, and fade out.

As Fitzgerald lies in a hospital bed, the film marks the passing of time through a series of fade-in/fade-out shots as she slips in and out of unconsciousness. Each time, Dunn is there. Finally, she wakes up and struggles to stay awake while Dupris explains jokingly that Dunn has only left for a moment to tell the doctors how to do their job. But soon we learn the truth: there is nothing they can do. Fitzgerald will have no use of her arms or legs at all, and she cannot even move her head. Dunn is furious, clearly at himself, but with no one to attack but his friend Dupris. He hurls accusations at him: "It's your fault, yeah it's your fault she's laying in there like that, you kept at me until I trained her, I knew I shouldn't have done it, her being a girl and all, everything kept telling me not to, everything but you." He gives Dupris no space to answer, because he is so eaten up by despair. Again, to quote the poet Samuel Menasche, who so movingly records the overwhelming trauma of viewing someone you love in such a horrifying situation:

> Pain finds its place
> Invades each vein
> Whose lines trace
> You in pain

Dupris understands there is no way to break in to his self-accusation, knowing how deep the instinct runs in his friend.

Dunn finds Fitzgerald the best rehabilitation center available, where she is treated kindly. Each day, in a grueling four-hour session, she is dressed and waits for her family to visit her. Dunn stays with her all the while. Finally, her family arrives, dressed in T-shirts that show how they have been spending their time in southern California: seeing the sights, Disneyland among others. Dunn pleads with them to change into decent clothes, ones that will not so glaringly mock Fitzgerald's immobility and inability to go places that she will now never see. They refuse to change, and things only get worse. Fitzgerald wants to see her family alone, still holding out hope for the love she has never received. She wants her mother to know that she almost won the fight . . . but all they can see is that she lost. Worse still, her mother wants her to sign papers relinquishing her assets to the family and absolving them of any responsibility for her care, even though she has already assured them that the boxing association will handle her medical expenses. They shove a pencil into her mouth, and finally she has had enough. She spits it back at them, telling them to leave and never return. Dunn can hardly think of anything to say to mitigate the terrible disappointment of realizing that, at her most desperate moment, her family would never give her the love or even the acknowledgement of how she has helped them.

Fitzgerald's state continues to degenerate. The doctors need to amputate her leg, and Dunn waits outside the operating room, totally stricken by grief. He accepts the devastating responsibility of telling Fitzgerald that her leg is gone. When he returns home, things get worse for him: he finds yet another letter returned, unopened, from his daughter's address. Frozen in anguish, his motionless form seems almost to mimic Fitzgerald's immobilized body. Helpless as Fitzgerald's immobility threatens one limb after the other, he is even more helpless before a woman, his own daughter, who will not forgive him. He seems, indeed, frozen by a pain that "invades each vein."

Still, Dunn hides his personal anguish from Fitzgerald as he desperately searches for a way for her to go on, even without her leg. His best idea is community college: using a straw to write, she could get an education, improve herself, and find a way to go on in the world. But Fitzgerald has something else on her mind: "Remember what Daddy did for Axle," she asks. In response, Dunn barely chokes out the words, "Don't even think about it." Yet Fitzgerald insists, as she always has.

People chanted my name—the names you gave me, too. But they were chanting for me. The magazines . . . Do you think I ever dreamed that would happen? I've earned my way out. That's all I want to do, Frankie. I've got to go before they take it away. I don't want to live until I don't hear those people chanting no more.

He pleads with her. "Please, don't ask me." But she will not let him off the hook. "I am asking," she insists.

The philosopher Emmanuel Levinas has written that we enter a genuine ethical relationship only when we open ourselves fully to the Other as a person who makes real demands on us.[9] Here Dunn faces what may be the ultimate ethical crisis. On the one hand, ethical arguments often make a powerful case in opposition to a suicide, and a priest tells Dunn straightly that if he concedes to her demand his own soul will be lost. Indeed this priest has almost been a comic character throughout the movie, because Dunn is always bugging him about questions about Catholic concepts, such as the Immaculate Conception, but his constant presence at church—he goes to mass every day—shows his deep feelings of guilt and repentance. But this priest is the only one Dunn can ask whether he should end Fitzgerald's life. The priest takes the classical Catholic position that suicide is always wrong and that only God can decide who dies and when they die. Yet in Levinas's terms, we never confront God directly. Rather we are powerfully confronted by the ethical demand put on us by the face of the Other who calls out to us for help. An anguished Dunn explains to the priest, after the clergyman explains that it is best to leave her in the hands of God: "She's not asking for God's help. She's asking mine."

That night, Fitzgerald takes things into her own hands, attempting to kill herself by biting her tongue. Stitched up, she tries to do it again. By the time Dunn arrives, she is barely herself at all, barely able to focus. He is losing her—and worse yet, he is watching her lose herself. He cannot bear the sight, and finally he is called, tragically, to take a stand against it, in spite of his continuing hesitation.

Returning to the gym, Dunn apologizes to his friend for his tirade against him: it was never Dupris's fault. Dupris, however, not only forgives Dunn for berating him but tries to explain to Dunn everything he gave Fitzgerald by using the pretext of why Frankie should forgive him: "I found you a fighter, and you made her the best fighter she could be." "And then I killed her," Dunn concludes. But Dupris will not let go:

When Maggie walked in here, she had no chance in the world to be what she needed to be. A year and a half later she was fighting for the championship of the world. You gave her that. People die every day mopping floors and washing dishes. You know what their last thought is? *I never got my shot.* Because of you, Maggie got her shot. If she dies today, you know what her last thought will be? *I did pretty good.* I know I could live with that.

Even Dupris's words can't comfort him in his despair over what he must do. As he enters her room again, he finally confesses that *Mo Cuishle* means "My darling . . . my blood." He kisses her cheek, caresses her hair, and tells her that when he takes her off the respirator she will simply go to sleep. Then he will give her an injection . . . and she will stay asleep.

As Dunn fulfills his tragic task, the viewer gets a close-up of Dupris, hiding in the darkness but nevertheless present for his friend as he feels he needs to be. As the film closes, we realize at last that Dupris has been narrating the story not so much for our benefit in the abstract; rather, we hear what Dupris writes to Dunn's daughter. The letter of course is a way of Dupris coming to terms with the fact that no one has seen or heard from Dunn after he killed Fitzgerald. Indeed Dupris speculates that that last action broke him completely. He tries to comfort himself that Dunn might have gone to his daughter to seek forgiveness, or he might have opened a diner somewhere. But this is just Dupris hoping against hope. His last act of friendship to Dunn is to tell his daughter the kind of man that he was. We have been hearing the story from his perspective all along.

Eastwood does not give us a clean ending nor does he ever define the relationship between Fitzgerald and Dunn. Is it a romance? A father-daughter relationship? Both? More? Eastwood is not a cinematic realist, in the sense that he prefers to allow room for play in the imagination of the viewer. What we do know is that theirs was an abiding love; and we know that their love created an ethical obligation for Dunn that he could not refuse, even as it exposed him to the most painfully searing grief. Again, I leave it to Menasche to describe such agony. It far exceeds the capacity of mere prose.

Disbelief
To begin with
Later, grief
Taking root
Grapples me
Wherever I am
Branches ram
Me in my bed
You are dead[10]

Love always carries within it the possibility of being shredded by grief, but if these movies tell us anything it is that love also opens us to what is of enduring value in human life. What makes these films so extraordinary is the connection they draw between learning how to be a good man and learning to accept the risks of love beyond the conventions of Oedipal complementarity and the fantasized rebellion against that complementarity through traumatic dissociation from attachment. Despite the profoundly sad ending of *A Perfect World*, Butch does give Phillip a glimpse of the father-son relationship that Butch never had. Butch undoubtedly puts himself in danger because he has allowed himself to become close to his hostage, and he would do anything to keep it from degenerating into the kind of (non)relationship he had with his own father. In *Absolute Power* Luther Whitney gets a second chance only when he turns his back on the easy way out and stays to confront "absolute power"—even to show up for his daughter knowing full well that he is walking into a trap.

Moral repair may be possible, but not without some acknowledgment of what has gone wrong. Whitney must let his daughter know how much he regrets wronging her in the past, and he must also show a determination to make a different future. He is no longer running. Nothing Dunn can do will ever give Fitzgerald a loving family, but by being in her corner he gives her the chance to think of herself as the kind of fighter she can respect. It is indeed a huge risk to give her a shot. But perhaps in a way love is like boxing: we have to dare to run toward the pain. Through his attachment to Fitzgerald and his belief and support of her, Dunn gets a kind of second chance, even though it demands the most difficult of ethical commitments: to kill the one you love. The relevance of Eastwood's portrayal of the complex struggle with moral repair, particularly for men who mistakenly believe they can avoid the ultimate dangers of attachment and love, is not to assure us that we can find such repair, but to remind us how difficult it is and what it demands of us. Yet without the hope of restoring a meaningful ethical or love relationship; we may be left with nothing but violence and revenge.

5
Parables of Revenge and Masculinity in *Mystic River*

Roger Berkowitz and Drucilla Cornell

I n this essay, we read Clint Eastwood's *Mystic River*[1] as an insightful exploration of the seductions and dangers of revenge and the relation of vengeance to violence and masculinity. What revenge offers in response to trauma and loss is the fantasy of control. The "value of vindictiveness," to use Karen Horney's suggestive phrase, is that revenge offers a "safety-valve" that protects a victim against the self-destructive impulses that accompany the act of being injured or insulted.[2] Confronted by a traumatic injury, all people feel a "natural propensity" to hit back that, according to Horney, has its reason in the impulse to defend one's ideal image of oneself; failure to respond to an injury threatens to show the injured party as either physically or psychologically incapable, which can lead to feelings of self-hatred so extreme that they "constitute a real danger for the individual."[3] By externalizing harm as a result not of one's own weakness but of another's wrong, the avenging victim both restores his injured pride and steels himself from self-blame and self-destruction.

Beyond the value of vengeance itself, Horney's article "The Value of Vindictiveness" identifies two alternatives to revenge: neurosis and "becoming more human." Neurotic capitulation, either from physical or moral incapacity to act upon vengeful impulses, leads the traumatized

The authors thank Jenny Lyn Bader, Sara Murphy, and two anonymous reviewers for reading and providing helpful comments on earlier drafts of this essay. This chapter originally appeared in *Law, Culture and the Humanities* 1 (2005), pp. 316–32.

victim to see himself "as a helpless jellyfish, a prey to anybody who chooses to step on him and a prey also to his own self-contempt." Becoming human, on the other hand, means abandoning his idealized vision of his own grandeur; by disowning his prideful belief in his uniqueness and his masterful control, the human victim becomes an "ordinary human being like everybody," and thus "part of the swarming mass of humanity he so despises." The goal of Horney's therapeutic response to vindictiveness is to reverse the valuation of prideful vindication so that "'becoming human' will feel like the most desirable goal toward which to strive."[4]

Horney's tripartite understanding of the vindictive responses to traumatic injury offers a helpful frame within which to view *Mystic River* (2003). In *Mystic River*, three men are confronted with proof of their powerlessness; unable to prevent an injury to themselves or their loved ones, the men respond in different ways. Their choices, human in every way, are parables for three fundamental human responses to trauma. Dave Boyle (Tim Robbins) is so overcome by trauma that he can only articulate a mere stuttering of his loss in speeches that remain incomprehensible even to those closest to him. Jimmy Markum (Sean Penn), on the other hand, refuses to admit his vulnerability to trauma. In striving to overcome the forces buffeting him and in powerfully seeking to control his life, Jimmy rebels against the finite and limited nature of his humanity. His effort to avenge his daughter's murder is a desperate struggle to understand and thereby to master a universe gone mad. Sean Devine (Kevin Bacon) neither succumbs to his traumatic experience of his wife's leaving him nor, however, does he deny her power over him. Rather, Sean comes gradually to humbly accept the limitation on his power and control that marks the humanity of his masculinity.

Together, these three responses to trauma—collapse, rebellion through vengeance, and upright acceptance of finitude—comprise the structuring triad of *Mystic River*. Whereas Dave is consumed by his neurotic response to trauma, Jimmy and Sean present two meaningful responses to the impulse to respond to injury with revenge. Jimmy's act of vengeance is driven by an idealized fantasy of superhuman power and control. Sean, however, comes to embrace the very limited nature of humanity that Jimmy rejects. Sean's heroism, his decision to become more human, is a powerful counterweight to Jimmy's more traditional masculine heroism, one that is located in the need to stand upright as a man who recognizes he is inevitably shaped by forces beyond his control.

Precisely because *Mystic River* leaves the conflict between Jimmy's avenging hero and Sean's upright hero unresolved, it offers an insightful glimpse into the psychological foundations both of vengeance and the overcoming of vengeance. Jimmy may indeed strive to uphold an idealized image of himself as a proud and powerful person; moreover, Jimmy's identification as a king, one with the natural authority to rule and to avenge that is denied to mere men, is, at least on one level, positively figured as the natural and noble striving of man for justice. It is this fantastic claim of kingship that *Mystic River* suggests can gird—if not justify—Jimmy's act of vengeance. And yet, insofar as avengers rebel against their human limitations, they fail in the profound calling that makes us human: namely, the thoughtful embrace of finitude.

Mystic River and Revenge: Breaking the Mold

Mystic River, on one level, is a classic example of the genre of revenge movies. It begins with the murder of the nineteen-year-old daughter of Jimmy Markum. Jimmy is one of a trio of childhood friends who have grown apart, the film's main characters. Suspicion quickly settles upon another of the three, Dave Boyle. The investigation is led by the third of the childhood friends, Sean Devine, now a detective. Although Dave's own wife, Celeste (Marcia Gay Harden), comes to believe that he is the murderer, Sean remains skeptical and releases him from custody. Jimmy, distrustful of what he sees as the bureaucratic and laggard police, takes Dave out to a secluded bank of the Mystic River, forces him to confess, and executes him. By the final scene, Jimmy is perched on his front stoop surrounded by the followers of his former criminal gang, his wife, and remaining daughters; while he may still mourn the loss of his favorite girl, the traditional scene of familial bliss suggests that Jimmy has—through his revenge—asserted his power over the loss and chaos that threatened to consume him. At least on one reading of the film, the violence against Jimmy—and even the world itself—has been made right.

Or so it appears. For underneath the conventional waters, *Mystic River* is a decidedly unconventional exploration of revenge as a response to trauma. In a bold break from the norms of contemporary American moviemaking, *Mystic River* never resolves the conflict between Jimmy and Sean. The movie's strength is its incredible sympathy for each of its main characters.

This generosity of perspective is evident in Eastwood's filming itself. *Mystic River* forsakes the usual Hollywood practice of presenting the story of revenge from an omniscient point of view in sympathy with the avenger.[5] American revenge movies typically depend on the solitary male father figure, the "John Wayne figure," who, like God and the Father, "embodies the fantasy of a man who makes himself out of nothing and who is therefore purely masculine, a hard man all through."[6] For this reason, revenge movies traditionally are filmed realistically from one central perspective that presents the hero's world as simple fact.[7] Instead, Eastwood films from the perspective of the character who is central to the resolution of the drama particular to each scene. We see Dave sink into his nightmare world; shot in near darkness in a room without any visible doors or windows, the scene pictures the claustrophobia of Dave's internal world. Sean, too, is filmed from his own perspective. When he speaks to his wife over the phone, he is pictured through his own experience of isolation and disarray. We see Sean on the streets as a cop trying to assert some kind of hold on the trauma that is always haunting him. He is oftentimes filmed from the back or the side, speaking out to a reality that continually threatens his sense of control. Finally, Jimmy, in the scenes he dominates, is shown struggling to control himself and his world, and Eastwood's filming focuses on the ferocity of his struggle. In one extraordinary scene, Eastwood shoots Jimmy's frantic effort to break free from the police from above, showing Jimmy's struggle to free himself as he is nearly crucified by his own anguish.

Beyond its merely filmic qualities, *Mystic River* also has a plot that separates it from traditional Hollywood revenge films. Most importantly, the act of revenge in *Mystic River* gets the wrong man. When Jimmy kills Dave, he kills an old friend, one whom life has profoundly scarred. While Dave did enact his own vengeance by killing a pedophile he caught raping a young boy, he did not kill Jimmy's daughter. Dave may be troubled and pitiable, but he is also deeply innocent.

Because Jimmy avenges his daughter against the wrong man, *Mystic River* does not follow the well-worn path of revenge films that William Ian Miller describes as the journey from "pity and fear to catharsis"; there is no "sense of satisfaction of having the wrong righted on the body of the wrongdoer."[8] In the genre of revenge films, the avenging hero must be made not only palatable, but also noble. The avenger must be shown to be a man or a woman of justice, even if he or she is acting beyond the law. More precisely, it is the avenger's claim to be doing justice beyond the obstacles and niceties of the law that underlies his or her appeal.[9] In *Mystic River*, however, the usual sense of cathartic justice from an act of revenge well taken cannot emerge because Jimmy kills an innocent man.

An act of revenge against an innocent man might be made palatable if it were accompanied by the arrest and downfall of the errant avenger. Such a predictable result would have fit *Mystic River* neatly into the genre of anti-revenge films that portray the dangers and horrors of emotional revenge freed from the constraints of procedural legalism. Indeed, the undoing of a mistaken avenger might provide its own catharsis, insofar as it reinforces our faith in the justice and wisdom of our liberal legal system. A film in which the wrong man is killed in an act of revenge offers up revenge as an easy target of moral outrage.

Eastwood, however, resists the temptation of facile critique. The provocation underlying *Mystic River* is that Jimmy—along with Sean—is to remain one of the film's two sympathetic heroes, despite his errant vengeance. Eastwood's challenge, therefore, is to defend Jimmy's vengeance without ceding to him the moral high ground typically accorded to cinematic avengers.

It is to overcome this difficulty that revenge movies generally share one premise: the avenging hero gets it right. In fact, revenge stories are rarely whodunits. In *The Searchers* (1956), it is expected that Ethan Edwards (John Wayne) will spend years tracking down and eventually killing the Indian Chief, Scar (Henry Brandon), because we know that Scar killed Ethan's family as well as his true love. Similarly, we accept that Michael Corleone (Al Pacino), thrust into the title role of *The Godfather* (1972), will go on a killing rampage because we understand he is driven to it by the murder of his father. And we can understand why Myrl Redding (John Cusack) in *The Jack Bull* (1999)—based on the great Heinrich von Kleist story *Michael Kohlhaas*—will burn towns and sacrifice his life in order to avenge the injury that Henry Ballard (L. Q. Jones) has done to his honor. Indeed, in nearly every Hollywood revenge movie, the film's omniscient viewpoint subdues the fear of unjust revenge with the promise that the heroic avenger will get the right man.[10] Whatever ethical problems with revenge might remain, the question of the need for due process is rendered mute by the moral clarity of the final act of justice.[11]

Against the facility with which Hollywood eases the justification of vengeance, Eastwood's *Mystic River* stands out as the rare film willing to present revenge as a defensible urge and, simultaneously, as a terrifying danger. Our aim in turning to *Mystic River* is neither to justify nor to vilify revenge, but to understand why it continues to so fascinate and seduce. To this end, *Mystic River* offers a nuanced canvas. Because *Mystic River* so radically breaks with the tradition of killing the right man that is embedded in "revenge movies," it offers an especially rich way to focus on the question of the claim to justice in the activity of vengeance itself, apart from its consequences. For this reason alone, *Mystic River* stands out as worthy of serious attention.

Mystic River: A Revenge Tale with Three Men

The movie starts with the three boys who, after playing a street game, decide to mark their initials into the wet cement of a nearby sidewalk. Suddenly, a man pretending to be a police officer orders Dave into his car for having defaced public property. Confused, the other two boys reluctantly allow Dave to get into the car. What is done to Dave by his kidnappers is the sort of trauma that reveals the very real vulnerability of men to an act of penetration. Dave, therefore, experiences the shattering of the ultimate heteronormative fantasy that conflates masculinity with impenetrability.

Mystic River revolves around three male characters, each of whom reacts differently to traumatic experiences of loss that challenge both their masculinity and their power to impose order on their worlds. While Dave is broken by his ordeal, Jimmy and Sean confront their traumas in very different ways. Jimmy, the avenging hero, acts from the prerogative of right. A man's man, he is a king in his own house. The literal and repeated identification of Jimmy as a king—as one with the natural authority to order a world—works to justify Jimmy's refusal to give in to trauma as well as his decision to forcefully resist it. Sean, on the contrary, neither succumbs to trauma nor masters it. Instead, Sean—when confronted by his wife's challenge to his masculine control and with the fact of Jimmy's lawless and unjust vengeance—responds by admitting his vulnerability and indeed identifies with Dave Boyle. In all of his actions, Sean remains faithful—to his wife, who has left him, and to the law, which he faithfully upholds. He is an upright man struggling to balance his masculinity with the reality of his tragic limitations, and his willingness to accept his finitude is set against Jimmy's rebellious insistence on maintaining his fantasy of superhuman strength.

Dave

After Dave escapes his kidnappers, we see him only as a shadowy figure. We see the two boys looking up at their recently escaped friend behind a bedroom window only to have his mother quickly shut the shade, as if to hide Dave from the world and himself. Dave, as he will say later, survived but not as himself; as he puts it, whoever got out of that basement was not Dave Boyle.

Later in the movie, an adult version of Dave Boyle returns one night from a neighborhood bar covered in blood with a stab wound. His story to his wife was that he was robbed and had to defend himself against the mugger. He is completely undone by the violent act he has undertaken, sputtering in horror about what it felt like to hurt another human being. We only later find out that Dave had caught a pedophile in the act of raping a young boy and beat the perpetrator to death. Yet the closest Dave comes to revealing this truth to his wife is through cryptic confessions telling his wife how he feels like a monster, an admission that tells us more about how Dave feels haunted by his trauma then it does anything about his incoherent efforts to communicate to his wife what he has done. But in a deeper sense, why was Dave unable to tell his wife what happened that night?

Here we are returned to the wordlessness and unspeakability related to traumatic events. Dave feels like a monster before his own vengeful act, an act that takes him back to the traumatic scene where he acts out, but is unable to come to terms with, what he did and what happened to him. The act is unplanned on the deepest level. Dave is horrified by the nightmare scene that he is once again returned to, even if now as the perpetrator. In the deepest sense, the nightmare that was his life in the basement of his kidnappers completely takes him over as he beats the pedophile to death. But this death cannot bring peace; it only brings the nightmare fully to life again. As Dave tries to express his sense of being a character in an ugly alternate universe, his wife tragically comes to identify him along these lines and suspects him to be the murderer of the daughter of his childhood friend Jimmy. The more he tries to speak from his understanding of his reality, the more he takes his nightmare to be a reality. He is desperately trying to explain how he has been ensnared by the original trauma. There are no words to describe the subterranean world Dave Boyle remains trapped in; his incapacity to express himself only furthers his identification with a monster with no means to represent himself. Of course, when Jimmy falsely accuses Dave at gunpoint and demands an explanation for his recent strangeness, Dave is unable to communicate the truth: he murdered the pedophile and not the daughter of his childhood friend.

Jimmy

Jimmy was one of the three boys who were at the scene of the initial kidnapping; he grew up to be the leader of a neighborhood gang and was briefly imprisoned. Jimmy had a partner in crime named Ray Harris, whose sons are important to this story. While in prison, Jimmy learns that he was betrayed by Ray. Jimmy kills Ray for his transgression. However, Jimmy does not leave the tragedy behind him, because he continues to support Ray's two children: Brendan (Tom Guiry) and Silent Ray (Spencer Treat Clark), Brendan's supposedly mute younger brother. We meet Jimmy as a struggling adult trying to leave the criminal world behind and make it in a small legitimate business. His daughter Katie (Emmy Rossum) falls in love with Brendan, but Jimmy will not allow the relationship to go forward because Brendan is the son of the man he murdered. Katie and Brendan decide to run off to get married, but she is murdered the night before their escape. Jimmy is drawn to the murder scene as he exits from the church where another of his daughters is taking her First Communion. The haunting image of him being restrained by a gaggle of Boston police as he screams to Sean and to heaven, "Is that my daughter in there?" is among the most harrowing portrayals of emotional despair ever on the silver screen. And yet as overwrought as Jimmy is over the loss of his daughter, he quickly pulls himself together. His old gang members Nick and Kevin Savage (Adam Nelson and Robert Wahlberg) show up, and Jimmy immediately starts giving orders.

In the next scene, Jimmy is sitting with his wife, Annabeth (Laura Linney), and talking with Sean and Sean's partner, Whitey Powers (Laurence Fishburne). Jimmy asks Sean: "Did you ever think about how just one little choice can change your whole life? I heard Hitler's mother wanted to abort him. At the last minute she changed her mind. See what I mean." Jimmy continues:

> What if you or I had gotten into that car instead of David Boyle? . . . If I had gotten into that car that day, my life would've been a different thing. My first wife, Marina, Katie's mother, she was a beautiful woman, regal, Latin women are and she knew it. You had to have balls just to go near her and I did. Eighteen years old. Two of us. She was carrying Katie. Here's the thing, Sean. If I'd have gotten into the car that day, I'd have been a basket case and I never would've had the juice to go near her. Katie never would have been born, and she never would have been murdered, you know.

Even as Jimmy considers whether it would have been better had Katie never been born, we learn something about the mettle of his character. Dave was destroyed by his kidnapping and molestation. Jimmy, however, escaped. And for Jimmy, this is no mere accident. Even when they were young, it was Jimmy who was the leader of their gang. And as a man, Jimmy remains a leader, both of his criminal gang and, more recently, of his community. It is not a coincidence, therefore, that Jimmy refers to his first wife as regal. She was a queen, and, by implication, Jimmy is a king.

It is precisely Jimmy's claim of royal prerogative that is the lynchpin of Eastwood's attempt to give meaning to Jimmy's wrongful execution of Dave. The movie's penultimate scene opens with Jimmy silhouetted in front of his bedroom window. He is naked from the waist up, and we see, for the first time, the tattooed cross that fills his back. Religion, however, plays an ambiguous role in *Mystic River*. There is the suggestion from his ring that one of the men who abducted Dave in the opening scene was a bishop. Jimmy, a practicing Catholic, attends his daughter's First Communion. Given that Jimmy has just learned that he has taken revenge on an innocent man, and on his former friend, it might be thought that the cross on his back signifies the burden that Jimmy must bear. Indeed, as he hears his wife step lightly into the room behind him, Jimmy confesses: "I killed Dave. I killed him and I threw him in the Mystic. But I killed the wrong man. That's what I've done. And I can't undo it." But the scene of Catholic repentance that this opening promises quickly veers in an altogether different and more secular direction.

In response to Jimmy's confession of sin and powerlessness, Annabeth responds by cooing, "Shhhhh, Jimmy, shhhhh." She will hear nothing of his confession, weakness, and doubt. Instead, as the devoted wife, she offers a speech of belief and power. Annabeth believes in Jimmy, in his goodness, his strength, and his nobility. As she comes up and embraces him from behind, she strokes him, caressing his ego, and whispers into his ear. She says:

> I wanna feel your heart. Last night when I put the girls to bed I told them how big your heart was. I told them how much you loved Katie, because you created her, and sometimes your love for her was so big it felt like your heart was going to explode. . . . I told them their daddy loved them that much too. And he had four hearts. And they were all filled up and aching with love for them and they would never have to worry. And that their daddy would

do whatever he had to for those he loved. And that is never wrong. That could never be wrong. No matter what their daddy had to do. And those girls fell asleep in peace.

There is a vision of wifehood here that is explicitly contrasted with the other two wives in the movie. Whereas Celeste, Dave's wife, becomes convinced that Dave killed Katie and rats on him to Jimmy, and Laura, Sean's wife, demands equal standing in her marriage—so much so that she leaves pregnant (a traditionally vulnerable position)—it is Annabeth who plays the dutiful and adoring wife. She knows that a man's job is to protect his women, and Jimmy is a master at protection. He has four hearts, one for each of his girls, and he will do whatever it takes to make sure that they are safe. And when that is not possible, he will seek to make those who hurt them pay. That is his job. Annabeth's role is to keep her husband standing erect.

This familial fantasy of a wife who supports her husband and of a man possessed of a love so strong that it will require and justify any violence is at the core of *Mystic River*'s exploration of revenge. From this perspective, revenge is not merely a paternal right; it is a duty of love and obligation. Just as Sethe's love for her children in *Beloved* redeemed even her tragic killing of her children, so here are we asked to understand, if not forgive, Jimmy's transgression borne out of a love too strong to be harnessed within legal bounds. Similarly, one of the authors of this essay grew up with a father who repeated, throughout her adolescence, that if anyone ever harmed his children, he would seek them out and tear them apart. Recently, prompted by a viewing of *Mystic River*, he reiterated that he would have truly acted on his promise to kill someone who had harmed his children. We tell this story because children are not the only ones who may be terrorized and thrilled by such a fantasy of paternal love; as adults, movies like *Mystic River* enable us to, at the very least, understand Annabeth's boast that her children fell asleep in peace. The fascination with Eastwood's movies is, in part, an attraction to characters like Jimmy, who has a heart so big that he will make the world safe. Vengeance borne of love, in other words, comes to buttress a rhetorical demand for safety that trumps all competing conceptions of justice.[12]

Love alone, however, cannot authorize Jimmy's revenge. If love were the only ground for Jimmy's killing, it might work to justify his taking revenge against Katie's killers; but, Jimmy made a mistake, one that, as he understands, he cannot undo. While an act of violence in the name of love might suffice when the outcome is considered correct, Jimmy's love for Katie does not explain *Mystic River*'s at least grudging acceptance of Jimmy's vengeance.

Eastwood refuses to condemn Jimmy for mistakenly killing Dave. Instead of abandoning the avenger who gets it wrong, *Mystic River* takes seriously the claim that the rightness of revenge, insofar as it is just, is independent of whether the outcome is correct. By dramatically presenting the deep psychic appeal of Jimmy's willingness to act whatever the consequences, *Mystic River* necessarily forces open the question of revenge in a radical way. Beyond the question of a successful outcome, it asks: what is the original source of the ancient and seemingly irrepressible recognition of the justice of revenge?

While it is possible to make a legal argument defending Jimmy based on *mens rea*, that argument would only provide Jimmy with an excuse; the strong claim that Annabeth makes in the movie is that Jimmy acted justly.[13] Whether or not Jimmy's revenge was correct, legal, or justifiable, it is Annabeth who makes the claim that it was right. And in spite of the ambivalence of the film's final scene, which we will discuss below, it is impossible to read the respect and honor accorded to Jimmy out of *Mystic River*. Instead, we believe it is important to take seriously the way in which Eastwood's film grapples with what is perhaps the cinema's most subtle and powerful defense of vengeance.

Within *Mystic River*, the claim of rightful vengeance can only be grounded in the right of the one who takes it. It is a claim of natural right that attaches to the person of the actor. And here is where *Mystic River* offers its ultimate defense of Jimmy's revenge. His act is not a mere emotional reaction; rather, it must be seen as the act of a loving king. As Annabeth says,

> I told the girls: Your daddy's a king, and a king knows what to do and does it, even when it's hard. And their daddy will do anything he has to for those he loves. And that's all that matters. Because everyone is weak, Jimmy, everyone but us. We'll never be weak. And you? You could rule this town. [*They begin to have sex.*] And after, Jimmy. Let's take the girls down to the parade. Katie would've liked that. [*Cut to parade.*]

Here Jimmy is figured as a king, and his murder of Dave is sanctified as a kingly act grounded in love. In order to understand one of the many viewpoints about revenge present in *Mystic River*, the ideas of noble rule and royal prerogative must be further explored.

To say that revenge is a right of kings sounds strange at a time when all privileges, including revenge, are seen as the equal right of all people. But it may be, as Goethe once wrote of Hamlet, that some people are not equal to the task of revenge.[14] Indeed, the very thought that any mere mortal would assume the right of vengeance flies in the face of the entirety of Judeo-Christian morality: "'Vengeance is mine,' saith the Lord."[15] And there is something about revenge that, as Shai Lavi argues, exceeds any attempt at human justification.[16] God's divine right of revenge, his destruction of Sodom and Gomorrah, for example, is just even though—and in fact precisely because—it is not justifiable according to any utilitarian or ethical calculus. Similarly, in every act of mortal revenge, there is a partial claim that one acts justly above and beyond any need for rational justification. Revenge, in other words, partakes in the hubristic claim to act like a god.[17]

Given the intimate connection between revenge and divinity, it should not be surprising that kings would come to be accorded the right of taking vengeance.[18] The great German historian of kingship, Percy Ernst Schramm, spent a lifetime exploring the way in which the institution of kingship relies upon and is infused with religious, mythic, and magical power. Early Germanic kings carried a standard ("*Standart*") representing the tree of life ("*Weltenbaum*"); throughout the Middle Ages, French kings, after being anointed with the holy oil and crowned in Reims, traveled to the little village of Saint Marcouf where they healed the sick; European peasants would travel to the funerals of their kings to lay seeds on the coffin in order to guarantee that they yield better fruit; and German Emperors from Konrad II (990–1039) to Otto I wore miters under their crowns, draped themselves in carpets adorned with the zodiac, and carried bells, all to associate themselves with the high priests of the Old Testament.[19] The Greek word for "king," *basileus*, denotes the highest cult officer in the polis, and early Greek states divided governance between *basileus* and an archon who was responsible for the day-to-day administration of the polis.[20] The king, as Ernst Kantorowicz has shown, has two bodies; beyond the earthly flesh, the king also has a political, mythical, and spiritual body.[21]

The irrepressible connection between secular and divine rule requires a rejection of any theory of sovereignty that is founded upon simply the sovereign's formal power to decide on the exception.[22] That is why Michel Foucault—who preserves the traditional distinction within kingship in a way that Giorgio Agamben does not—structures his account of the political nature of sovereignty around an analysis of Plato's discussion of the question of whether the king of a community is like a shepherd.[23] A shepherd, Foucault argues, has a number of characteristic tasks which include: to supply his herd with food; to care for them when they are sick; to entertain them and guide them; to aid in their procreation and the rearing of the young; and finally to be at the head of the flock as the leader. The politician, however, isn't concerned with "feeding, nursing, and breeding." Instead, the politician's task is to bind a people together: "The royal art of ruling consisted in gathering lives together 'into a community based upon concord and friendship.' "[24] Kings—as politicians—are engaged with the problem of unifying what might always already be unified and governing a (already) bounded multiplicity. The king, as the person charged with speaking the law of the community, articulates and rearticulates the law that unifies the community.[25] It is this legal–political realm that the king governs. The legal and political ideal of kingship that Foucault illustrates cannot be reduced to mere juridical governance; even in his role as judge and avenger, the king is more than the formal seat of the power to decide. Rather, the essence of kingship is the political and legal relation—the unifying and bonding relation—par excellence.

Jimmy's claim to kingship is neither hereditary nor economic; instead, it is "natural": a sign of his God-given gift of (supposedly) superior masculinity. Even as a child, Jimmy was the leader of his gang. As an adult, he inspires admiration and fidelity from his friends and neighbors. The Savage brothers, Jimmy's praetorian guard, follow him blindly out of nothing but love and respect. Celeste, Dave's wife, goes to Jimmy with her suspicions that Dave killed his daughter rather than to the police. Jimmy's first wife, a "Latin Queen," chose him when she could have had any man in the neighborhood. And then, in the film's final scene, a parade passes right in front of Jimmy and Annabeth's front stoop. While Celeste scurries around the parade grounds and Sean stands amidst the throng, newly reunited with his wife and daughter, Jimmy strolls gallantly out onto his stoop, surveying the parade from above. Surrounded by his wife, two daughters, the Savage brothers, and a coterie of friends, it does appear that Annabeth is right: Jimmy can rule this town.

Mystic River does not necessarily suggest that Jimmy's killing of Dave is justified, nor does the film condemn it. As a kingly figure, Jimmy acts not out of a theory of justified punishment, but from his natural and elemental right. Importantly, he resists crying for his daughter. Tears are not his medium of grief. A king does not cry; he acts. And his power comes from his nature.

The natural source of Jimmy's power is most clearly evidenced in the scene in which Annabeth names him a king. As she does so, she seduces him to sex, first climbing atop him, and then allowing him to turn her over and mount her from above. "You could rule this town," Annabeth tells Jimmy. Then they have sex, followed by the horns and ecstasy of a parade. The conjugation of sex and parade is nothing if not an orgasm, which literally means "what rises from earth." The Greek word also has an intimate connection with the anger that swells as a natural response to wrong and leads to the justification of punishment.[26] Similarly, Jimmy's claim to kingship and his arrogation of the right of revenge are grounded in nothing but his elemental and orgasmic fertility. It is a right he has as the man he is.[27]

Sean

Sean, the last of the three childhood friends, has become a detective. He is, importantly, a man of the law. In contrast to Jimmy, who claims to be a hero of absolute kingship, Sean is a hero of fortitude and fidelity to law.[28] He seeks to be an upright man whose commitment to justice is tempered by the recognition that no "man" gains from lawlessness. We first meet the adult Sean at a crime scene. He is silent, until he wanders to the edge of a bridge and looks longingly at his past. "What are you looking at, Devine?" asks his partner. "The old neighborhood," he replies. Sean at first appears as a melancholic figure holding on to a lost childhood and standards of morality that have lost their ground. Only Sean, the one of the three male characters who has moved up and out of the old neighborhood, flips through pictures of the childhood he has lost. But as Eastwood unfolds Sean's character in *Mystic River*, we see his commitment to the real world beyond himself and to actual institutions such as law and marriage. Pulling himself away from melancholia into an acknowledgement of vulnerability and love, Sean allows himself to remain open to a radical transformation of who he has become—a transformation unavailable to Jimmy, who remains snared as he is in the fantasy that he can be king.

If Jimmy deviates from our idea of the stereotypical avenger by getting the wrong man, Sean's upright detective also departs from the usual image of the detective. Sean is neither a corrupt cop nor a Dirty Harry–type rebel. When his police chief asks him where the investigation stands, Sean responds, in a whispering and breaking voice: "We'll get the guy, sir." Not a hotshot, he is nevertheless a dedicated officer who believes in the promise of the law and acts upon his belief.

The law, however, is not the only object of Sean's fidelity. Sean's wife, Lauren (Tory Devine), left him while she was pregnant. In the months since she left, their baby was born, but Sean doesn't even know its name or sex. Lauren calls, but not once does she speak. These calls pierce the movie with their silence, as Sean struggles to find the words to bring his wife to speak with him. He clearly does not understand what his wife expects of him, and yet he insists upon being faithful to her. Early on in the movie we see Sean turn down a good-looking female police officer who is clearly seeking a casual sexual relationship with him. His colleague teases him, saying: "So the wife left you what six months ago . . . The girl just wants to bed you, she doesn't want to wed you. You don't even blink. She wants to worship at the temple of Sean Devine." Sean's response is to simply confirm that he is married.

Eastwood has been long interested in the promise of fidelity as a way in which the masculine persona resists the notion of the exchangeability of women. In the movie *Unforgiven* Bill Munny remains faithful to his dead wife. In *Mystic River*, Sean's promise of fidelity is portrayed as one way a man can articulate a masculinity that does not have to define itself upon treating women as exchangeable objects.

Throughout the movie, Eastwood films Lauren as a classic fetishistic object. We see her only from Sean's viewpoint and as she appears in his imagination. We hear her breathing and see her mouth. The shots of her mouth, silhouetted against a white background or painted bright red in scintillating close-ups, are some of the most arresting of the whole movie. Lauren is portrayed as the infinitely desirable mouth that engulfs Sean in its silence. We see nothing else but the mouth. The beautiful, perfectly made-up lips tempt him, but Sean has no idea what she wants him to do in order to break the silence.

In order to understand the significance of Sean's obsession with his wife's mouth, we have to proceed through how Freud understands the nature of the "sexual drive." For Freud there is no "sexual drive" per se (which is why we put it in quotation marks). Instead drives are always partial in two senses. First, the sexual drive is partial insofar as it focuses not on a person but only on parts of a body—for example, the genitalia, mouth, eye, or ear. The mouth, Sean's particular obsession, is also the object that represents dependency in that it needs and desires the mother's breast, which it is always in danger of losing. The mouth is the child's own projected identification with the breast as an object that can be taken away. Sean's infatuation with his wife's mouth, therefore, is a symbol of his fear and insecurity in relationship to the goal of sex and reproduction.[29]

The second reason the drives are partial is the object of the sexual drive, which is always one's own self; the sexual drive, in other words, is autoerotic. From this point of view, a sexual partner is always a means and never an end in him or herself. The supposedly loved Other serves merely as a partial object as a means of achieving a goal of self-satisfaction. Hence, what is focused on in the objectified person of the Other is the partial fantasized object that can always be exchanged with another object—the mouth of a lover that serves as the goal of the sexual drive can then be replaced by any other mouth; any woman's mouth will do.

The stalemate between Sean and his wife extends so far that he cannot see her or hear her as she is to herself. Her silence is the resistance to this reduction of her self as the object of Sean's partial drive. That is why she waits for him to speak to her as a gesture acknowledging that she is a person to him and not an object of his fantasy. Although Sean is unable, throughout most of the movie, to speak to her, he is in an internal struggle with himself against the vision that both drives him to her and keeps him from seeing her; instead, he is captured by the vision of her as the scary, infinitely desirable made-up lips. His resistance to domination by his own partial drive takes the form of a promise of fidelity only to her.

Sean's promise to a woman he can't actually see as a woman is the necessary first step in his coming to resist the seduction of the partial drive. What stops him from seeing Lauren as a whole woman, within Freudian psychology, is the repressed fear of what the female body represents—the fantasized possibility of castration that symbolizes his inability to control his world. And yet, Sean's absolute pledge of fidelity opens a space for the possibility of transformation.[30] This space not only offers to women the possibility of an imaginary domain—that "moral space" where women are freed to dream themselves independently from their roles in the partial drives of men—but also allows men to learn to care for women free from the psychic fear of femininity as the general unease of Otherness itself.[31]

Within *Mystic River*, the fear of castration that would destroy sovereignty is palpably represented by the rape and kidnapping of Dave Boyle. Having seen his friend subjected to the ultimate male terror, Sean is aware that he too can be penetrated, reduced to a powerless object to be "fucked" on the basis of nothing more then the whim of the Other. It is as an example of an upright confrontation with femininity as a threat to his masculine fantasy of control, mastery, and even kingship that Sean stands opposed to Jimmy in *Mystic River*. Sean's fortitude is his struggle to let Lauren be the person who she is, an allowance that demands he accept his finitude and relinquish the drive for sovereignty.[32]

Sean only faces his fear in the movie's climactic scene, when he seeks out Jimmy to tell him that the murderers have been caught. Jimmy is sitting on the curb after a drunken night trying to drown his own grief and sorrow. Sean realizes that Jimmy might have already acted against Dave. It is at this point that the two are standing exactly where they were when Dave was so brutally kidnapped, and when the two failed in their minds as men because they did not try to rescue their friend, even though they were only children. Sean fully confronts his trauma and speaks it to the extent he can by suggesting to Jimmy that "we are still eleven-year-old boys locked in a cellar, imagining what our lives would be like if we escaped." By bringing the unspeakable to speech, Sean comes to terms with how his own most profound relationships have been shaped by the traumatic wound that undid David Boyle.

Having faced down the fear of castration, Sean is finally able to speak to his wife and risk confronting her as her own person. Immediately after the scene with Jimmy, Sean's phone rings. It is Lauren, and her luscious red lips fill the screen with silent reproach. Yet, having faced the trauma he can now face the wound of his own inability to speak to her. He dares to speak first, saying, "I know I pushed you away and I am sorry." At this point the mouth finally responds, "You have a daughter," and the fetishistic object now turns into a living woman. Sean tells her that the house is just as she left it and waiting for her return, allowing the conversation to end on the hope for their reconciliation.

Here is where Eastwood points us toward the hope for the end of the cycle of violence unleashed by the traumatic event caught in the kidnapping of Dave Boyle. When Sean reaches out to his wife, asking for a true connection with her, he risks making himself vulnerable to her rejection, but she is finally able to appear to him as a fully embodied women. Scary, yes, but someone he can dare to face. He is the one who ends up with a wife and a living daughter.

In the final scene, standing together at a parade, Sean and Lauren are awkward and strained, but they are together as a family with their daughter. It is in the acknowledgement that he is sorry, even if he does not know for what, that opens Sean to the possibility for contact with a woman who is not simply a fetishistic object. Eastwood is not a Lacanian, so he would not put it this way, but by accepting his vulnerability, and thus his symbolic castration, Sean can now relate to a woman as a human being and as a full person.[33] This is precisely the hope that is left open when Sean breaks the silence and risks that his apology may not be heard or accepted by his wife.

Conclusion

In Sean and Jimmy, *Mystic River* gives us two very different versions of masculinity and also of the response to a criminal trauma. For Jimmy, the attack calls for a response that reestablishes his sovereign personal identity as well as the claim of vengeful justice. Even though the act of revenge killed the wrong man, it is justified—or at least underpinned—by the higher need for recognition that underlies the psychoanalytic theory of the sovereign self as well as liberal political thinking regarding the sovereign state. Jimmy's embrace of kingship and the arrogation of the right of revenge serves to "deflect the experience of finitude."[34] In doing so, however, it offers a powerful critique of the very idea of sovereignty embodied in the liberal legal state. As an absolute and unjustifiable arrogation of the right to avenge, Jimmy's claim goes far beyond the usual effort to excuse vengeance on the grounds that otherwise justice would never be done. As a royal prerogative, Jimmy's revenge is a right of nature; it sounds, therefore, in a register fully antithetical to the liberal idea of law as the justified act of a sovereign power.

Sean, on the other hand, counters Jimmy's justification for identity-giving vengeance. Instead of responding vengefully to his pregnant wife's departure, he struggles to open a space in which she and he can relate as friends. In doing so, Sean gestures toward an Aristotelian ideal of friendship that, as described by Jill Frank in her book *A Democracy of Distinction*, both preserves his own identity while also offering to others the space to be themselves. Such an understanding of friendship that, as Aristotle suggests, gives to each their own, is built upon an ideal of the self that can forego the fantasy of identity that revenge so powerfully supports. Indeed, Sean comes to accept his finitude and thus to seek a relation with his wife that is based on friendship rather than exclusion.

6

Militarized Manhood: Shattered Images and the Trauma of War

The Outlaw Josey Wales (1976)

While Eastwood has recently gained attention as the director of two profoundly antiwar masterpieces, *Flags of Our Fathers* and *Letters from Iwo Jima*, his first true antiwar movie came much earlier in *The Outlaw Josey Wales*.[1] The film makes a powerful statement about the lasting trauma of war for people on both sides of the battle lines, regardless of which side wins. It was released in theaters shortly after the end of the Vietnam War when our country was just starting to realize the full devastation of that war not only in Vietnam but also one in the profound traumas of the young American soldiers who fought for the United States.

The movie opens quietly with Josey Wales (Eastwood) peacefully plowing a field with his son (Kyle Eastwood). His wife (Cissie Wellman) calls them both to dinner, and he sends his son ahead while he completes their chores. But he hears an unusual sound and looks up to see men on horses pounding through the trees near his farm—then he notices thick smoke rising from the direction of his family's home.

Frantically Wales runs to the burning house only to watch helplessly as Union soldiers drag his wife from the building; his son must still be inside. Wales struggles with the soldiers to protect his wife, but he is overpowered and hit in the face with a sword hilt, knocking him unconscious. Chaotic violence engulfs him as he falls. Everything is turned upside down in a rapid series of disorienting camera angles, a technique Eastwood frequently employs to undermine the steady viewpoint of the audience, bringing viewers directly into the shattered world of human violence.

When Wales wakes, his wife and son are dead. After he tenderly buries their bodies, he falls to pieces as while erecting a cross where he can pray at his wife's fresh grave. He bursts into tears, literally falling over from the weighty reality of all he has lost. Enraged, he recovers a rifle from the ashes of his home and he desperately practices his aim.

Shortly thereafter a group of Confederate soldiers approaches Wales, asking him to join them in the war against the Union. Like him, they have had their lands destroyed, their wives raped, and their children killed, and they have taken up the rebellion more as a quest for revenge than out of any particular loyalty to the aims and ideals of the Confederacy. Though poorly armed, they manage successfully to surprise several Union camps; indeed, their attacks become almost repetitive, routine— even boring. This is a reality of war: the same violent acts repeated over and over, men shooting and being shot, writhing on the ground in pain trying to save themselves, sometimes punching and shooting at the wind as much as at each other. In the blur of bodies, it becomes uncertain who is fighting whom—or why. Indeed, by this time the Confederacy is not only losing, but the war is essentially over. These battles continue only through a kind of mechanical inertia that has not yet slowed to the beat of history.

Wales has joined up with these men purely to revenge himself on the soldiers who committed the atrocities he witnessed on his farm, not because he aligns himself politically with the South. Thus, when the de facto leader of Wales's band, Fletcher (John Vernon), offers to negotiate a deal with the Union troops, only Wales refuses the possibility of surrender, which would be a meaningless gesture for him. He hardly cares to save his own life, and he has yet to find the men who destroyed his life and his family. But his comrades have tired of war, and they agree to surrender their weapons and swear their allegiance to the United States on the condition that they will be allowed to return to their homes safely. Wales watches the surrender from some distance, and he only learns of the treachery behind it when it is too late: Fletcher had been paid by Union officers to turn over his unit, and no sooner have the men finished their oath of loyalty than a Gatling gun opens fire. Rushing into the slaughter, Wales manages to save only one terribly wounded boy who survived the initial onslaught.

For his attempt to save the men who only sought peace, Wales becomes the Outlaw: Fletcher and the Union officers put a steep price on his head. Realizing that he will not be safe in any "civilized" area, Wales flees toward territories controlled by Indian nations, believing that he may find help and respite among people who also have no reason to trust either of the warring governments. The boy soon dies of his wounds—yet another loss for Wales—and he buys precious time by sending the boy's body off on his horse to confuse the Unionists, who at first think it is the slumped-over form of Wales riding past them.

Nearby, a Cherokee Indian attempts to shoot at the dead man, falling for the trap and thinking that it if it is Wales, he can collect the bounty. Wales stealthily approaches the Cherokee man, surprising him and then joking that he thought Indians were the only ones who could so successfully sneak up on a man. Introducing himself as Lone Watie (Chief Dan George), the man provides a sad commentary on the so-called civilizing process of his own life. Thoughtfully, he tells Wales,

> Here in the nation we are called the "civilized tribe." They call us civilized because we are easy to sneak up on. White men have been sneaking up on us for years. They were sneaking up on us and telling us that we wouldn't be happy here on our own land. So they took away our land and sent us here. I had a family—a fine woman and two sons. But they all died on the Trail of Tears. And now a white man is sneaking up on me again.

Watie is happy enough to give up on the bounty for Wales, and Wales in turn holds no grudge against him for trying in the first place. They camp together that night.

Wales wakes the next morning to find that the Cherokee chief has burned his civilized clothes, the suit and tall hat of the white man. Having decided to start a new life, he convinces Wales that they should head for Mexico, where they both might have a chance for a more peaceful existence. Wales is uncertain, but he agrees at least to escort Watie to a trading post so he can procure a horse. As Wales prepares to broker a deal at the trading post, however, he finds two men raping a young Cheyenne woman, one of the trader's employees; they have told the trader that she is among the goods they wish to buy. Wales shoots the men, and the young woman, Little Moonlight (Geraldine Kearns), joins his growing entourage to which he has become somewhat bemusedly resigned.

After they continue on their way to Mexico, they encounter Grandma Sarah (Paula Trueman) and her granddaughter; they are surrounded by bandits who have robbed them and killed Granny's husband. The bandits also capture Watie when he accidentally reveals his position, and they tie him up along with the women to be led across the desert—leading, of course, to a classic cowboy-style rescue in which Wales single-handedly takes out the bandits and adopts the women into his party. As it turns out, Granny is a committed Unionist who believes that her soldiering son died for a noble purpose, but Wales makes it clear that her stance should cause no quarrel between them. He fights not for the Confederacy but for vengeance in the name of his slaughtered family.

Granny's son had a ranch in Texas, and the group decides to make that their new home. The nearby town has more ghosts than residents, most people having left when the silver mines dried up. Wales manages to procure some whiskey, and with liberal handouts he befriends the handful of people remaining in the town. But his troubles have followed him, and shortly several bounty hunters come looking for Wales, leading to another gun battle. Still, eventually everyone begins to settle in to their new home. Wales, however, remains tortured by the traumatic memories of his burning farm and his dead family; he is still too eaten up by such psychological torments to believe that it is possible to begin again, to call a new place home.

Two men from town, who had worked on the ranch for Granny's son, offer to help them get the place in running order by corralling some cattle, but in the process they are captured by the Comanche who control most of the surrounding territory. Wales instructs the party as best he can about how to defend their home should the need arise, but he also plans to ride out alone to reach a settlement with the Comanche. He finds the two workers buried up to their necks, but they are hardly relieved that he has come to their rescue. Instead, they worry how one man can possibly save them from the mighty Ten Bears (Will Sampson), who has proven himself in bitter battle against the Union army, gaining a reputation for his skills in his battle as well as his refusal to move his people again.

The exchange between Wales and Ten Bears is truly remarkable among Hollywood depictions of dialogue between white men and Native Americans. When Ten Bears tells Wales to simply "go in peace," Wales responds, "I reckon not. I have nowhere to go." Somewhat reluctantly the chief replies, "Then you must die." Wales acknowledges a profound truth in his response. "I came here to die with you—dying isn't hard for men like you and me. It's living that's hard, when all we really care about has been brutalized and raped. I came here to show you that my word of death is true, and my word of life is true."

Wales assures the Comanche chief that if they allow him and his friends to stay, they will live by the basic tenets of life as understood by the Comanches: they will hunt only for their own subsistence, not to profit by trading pelts. "They all live here, the antelope and the Comanche, and so will we," says Wales. They will share their cattle and they will provide whatever assistance they can, since they are asking for the Comanche's hospitality. Wales seals his terms with a promise: "The sign of the Comanche will be on our lodge. That's my word of life."

Ten Bears explains to Wales that he can only offer things that they already have, and Wales agrees that he cannot offer a proper contract or an exchange—that is indeed asking for hospitality. Wales responds, "That's true. I ain't promising you nothing extra. I'm just giving you life and you're giving me life. And I'm saying that men can live together without butchering one another." He makes it clear that if they do fight, it will be a fair fight according to rules acceptable to both; if a conflict is unavoidable, then he will fight with honor. Indeed, in a sense, honor is all Wales can promise. He will not behave as the governments of the states and the Union have done, promising treaty lines only to push them back farther and farther; surrounding the Comanche in the night when they are unaware and unable to defend themselves; outnumbering them by amassing armies that no Comanche war party could meet—certainly not after so many have been murdered already.

Ten Bears is impressed. "There's iron in your word of death for all of the Comanche to see, and there is iron in your words of life. No signed paper can hold the iron. It must come from men. The words of Ten Bears carries the same iron of life and death. It is good that warriors such as we meet in the struggle of life . . . or death." Finally, quietly, he adds, "It shall be life." Cutting his hand, Ten Bears extends it to Wales in a sign of friendship. Wales cuts his own hand to grasp the Comanche's extended palm, making them blood brothers between whom there can be no thought of war.

In many ways *Josey Wales* echoes the John Wayne film *The Searchers* (1956), directed by John Ford, but it presents several important ethical reversals on the themes of that film. Let me be clear that I am not attempting to offer here a full cinematic discussion of *The Searchers* as a film, nor am I attempting to give an overall interpretation of the complex and brilliant directorial work of John Ford. I want to emphasize instead how Eastwood, as we have seen throughout this book, works within traditional genres so that the imaginary that gives the films its seeming sense of shared meaning is both challenged and made explicit. In *The Searchers* John Wayne plays a Confederate general who, deeply committed to the politics and commitments of the Southern states, has returned after several years of war to what remains of his family. Ethan Edwards (Wayne) too lives in Comanche territory, but his hatred of the Native Americans (he contemptuously calls them "Comanch") is intensely palpable. In a classic cowboy-and-Indian story line—and I insist that it is one—members of Edwards's extended family are brutally murdered in a Comanche raid, and the Native Americans also kidnap one child. The family searches for year after futile year to recover the child, and Edwards faces off repeatedly with a menacing Comanche warrior known as Scar (Henry Brandon). Of course, eventually he kills Scar and rescues the kidnapped child, who has grown into a young woman.[2] Wayne himself often spoke of Scar as a symbol of the "red man"—and thus, in his twisted right-wing ideology, of the Communist "new reds" who represented, for him, precisely the same threats to civilization as the Native Americans portrayed in his film.

Scar in *The Searchers* is notably portrayed in full masculine bravado with many wives and with scalps of white women hanging proudly in his teepee. His attire is that of the half-dressed Indian who is presented as a frightening phallic other man. For Eastwood, however, it was important to portray Comanche attire and dialogue with historical accuracy, to be respectful of the land and to be representative of a different mode of life, which was hostile to "White Man civilization" only as a response to the latter's cultural and territorial aggression. In *Josey Wales* we see two men confirming a bond that extends beyond the reach of race or tribe, a fraternity that honors a blood brotherhood that transcends cultures. It is Wales's directness, honesty, and courage that allow Ten Bears to recognize in him certain universal ideals of masculinity, of which the worst forms of narcissistic manhood, machismo, and overblown bravado are but pale, twisted images. In *The Searchers* the Comanche are nothing but ruthless barbarians who cannot be met man-to-man because there are no reasonable ideals that they will accept. Of course, *The Searchers* also includes an Indian buffoon, a comic character who wants nothing more than to sit passively in his rocking chair. To an extent at least, Lone Watie echoes this role in his interpretation of his own ironic position with respect to his native heritage, but unlike the caricature portrayed in *The Searchers*, Watie is completely committed to supporting Wales and his new family. While his commentary on the results of the "civilizing" process provides some enjoyable comic relief, he is much more than the butt of a joke. Indeed, as the film progresses Watie increasingly returns to himself, first by burning his clothes and ultimately by standing up for himself as a proficient gunman defending Wales against bounty hunters. After a particularly bloody gunfight, Wales remarks that he never worried about the opponents on his right, because he trusted Lone Watie to take care of them.

When Wales returns with the two kidnapped workers and shares his news of the treaty with the Comanche, the townspeople join them in the celebration, delighted at the prospect of peace with the Indians. Unfortunately, Wales knows that he can have no peace for himself, because the Union soldiers and many bounty hunters will still be after him—the price on his head makes him an attractive target for the many men who remain unemployed after the war. As he tells his friend Lone Watie, "Sometimes trouble just follows a man." Refusing to bring more violence on what has become a peaceful home, he sets out to settle the score on his own. Yet he hardly sets out before he is challenged on the road by the very Union soldiers responsible for the treachery leading to the price on his head. "You're alone now, Wales," they taunt him. But they are mistaken: Wales's friends have taken up positions with their guns and open fire on the soldiers, killing almost all of them. The captain who ordered the execution of the surrendering militia lives, however, though wounded. Helplessly the captain pulls the trigger of his gun, but it clicks away because its ammunition is already spent. Wales lets him keep trying, unwilling to kill a wounded, unarmed man. Finally, the captain desperately takes up his sword and lunges at Wales, but Wales manages to turn the sword back on him—killing him through his own unwavering aggression.

There is neither joy nor indifference in Wales's expression as he approaches the final confrontation with his foe, but rather profound sorrow. He is eaten up by traumatic flashbacks of his burning farm, of his wife's screams, of his son's scorched flesh. Yet even under this intense psychological pressure, he does not submit to rage this time; he simply approaches his rival calmly—guns in hand, but without firing. Trauma has not so destroyed him that he has lost contact with the ideals that make him a very different kind of man from the murderous officer before him. The scene brilliantly captures his refusal to become the perpetrator of dishonorable violence.

Meanwhile, the Texas Rangers question the townspeople about the fugitive outlaw Josey Wales—and Wales's new friends happily sign an affidavit asserting that they saw Wales killed in the gunfight earlier that day. Wales stands among the crowd, but there is no indication on anyone's part that gives away what they all know: Wales is standing right in front of Fletcher. As they leave, one Ranger hangs back: Fletcher, the weak or corrupt Confederate officer who brokered the deal to have his men slaughtered. He is certain that the people are lying to him, that Wales is still alive—but he pretends not to recognize Wales himself, whom the people address as "Mr. Wilson." "Mr. Wilson" asks Fletcher what he would do with Wales if he found him, and Fletcher responds, "I think I'd try to tell him, the war is over." As Fletcher turns to leave, Wales comments, "I guess we all died a little in that damn war."

In the closing scene, Josey Wales rides off alone. This is not the traditional, triumphant final ride of the cowboy, but rather the lonely ride of a man so psychically wounded that he cannot return to any place that would be called "home." Such a return, perhaps, would be impossible for him, as it would be too difficult to connect with the ideas associated with "normalcy" after enduring the intense trauma of losing everything and everyone he loved in life. But we do not actually know what happens to him; we only know that he rides off alone.

This film then is not only about the psychic illness caused by the trauma of war and how difficult it can be to heal from that trauma; it is also about the maintenance of ideals of humanity against traumatic pressures, so that there remains a "beyond" to the relationship between perpetrator and victim. As we saw in Sue Grand's analysis of evil, this relationship is a profound stalemate that often results from overwhelming trauma. Both Wales and Ten Bears have seen the things they loved the most totally ravished and brutalized; they have confronted in the most horrifying ways their own finitude and the limits of their power; but neither has given up on the ideals of masculinity that they both share. The recognition between them that they both hold true to these ideals allows an alternative to traumatic repetition, and it even opens the door for Wales to the possibility that he might once again honor life rather than death. Indeed, it is only after he meets with Ten Bears that he can reach out to the young woman Laura Lee (Sondra Locke), with whom he shares a single night of lovemaking before setting out from the ranch.

As in *Pale Rider* the female characters are not fully developed, nor is the connection with them any more than a brief retreat from having to face the world alone. It is perhaps a somewhat simplistic portrayal of a man able to reach out to another human being because he has experienced a kind of possibility of peace that was completely belied in the destruction of his earlier life. It is brief, and there is certainly no sign that Wales will totally come out of the disassociation imposed by trauma. Finding a way out of the horrifying trauma of war is obviously an overwhelming psychic undertaking, but if it's to be undertaken at all, it cannot be found in the deadly repetition of vengeance and violence. Even Fletcher recognizes this truth when he says that the war is over.

Firefox (1982)

After *The Outlaw Josey Wales*, Eastwood directed two additional, but less notable, war films before creating his more recent masterworks. The first is *Firefox*,[3] which begins with an aging Vietnam Vet, Mitchell Gant (Eastwood), peacefully running down a road in Alaska. His quiet is run interrupted by a descending helicopter, which triggers a full-blown traumatic flashback to the horrors of a war that will never cease to haunt him. Two military officers approach him as he cowers, his mind returned to the jungles of Vietnam. A pilot, Gant had been shot down and eventually rescued, but his most traumatic memory recalls the face of a young Vietnamese girl as she is consumed by napalm, an image that plagues him throughout the film. Because he is a brilliant pilot, despite his propensity for mental meltdowns, the military has tracked Gant down and ordered him back into active service to steal a secret Soviet prototype, which is reported to be the most technologically advanced fighter plane on the planet. Reluctantly, he agrees because he understands that he really has no choice in the matter.

In many ways, the film is very dated in its casual representation of the pervasive optimism associated with the early Reagan years, which were ostensibly a total recovery from the defeatism that followed the country's experience in Vietnam. What makes the film noteworthy is not the fact that Gant, despite all odds, successfully completes his dangerous mission deep into the heart of the Soviet Union, but rather that Gant expresses genuine horror at what he is called to do, horror that is truly uncharacteristic of military heroes of the period. As he makes his way through enemy territory, he is confronted again and again with the violence of a so-called "cold war": first, a man is beaten to death so that Gant can assume his identity; later, several dissident Russian scientists are executed for the crime of aiding his espionage in opposition to the oppressive government.

Of course, once he has taken the plane, the Russians are determined to shoot him down, both to recover what they can of the prototype and to prevent it from falling into enemy hands. The film ends with a long, daring action sequence highlighting the talents of Gant, a truly exceptional military pilot, as he outmaneuvers and outguns his Russian opponents. Indeed, the Reagan administration actually hailed *Firefox* as representative of the country's new optimism in the post-Vietnam era; the plane is captured, after all, through great feats of American heroism, seeming to herald the nation's ultimate triumph over Soviet Communism.

Yet throughout the film Gant suffers from the side effects of war, uncontrollable traumatic symptoms that nearly cost him his life on several occasions. These moments feature some of Eastwood's most brilliant acting. It is Eastwood's direction of himself in these meltdowns that makes the film one of his greatest and most effective portrayals of the personal devastation of war, despite the heroic optimism communicated by his ultimate success in stealing the plane. Indeed, Eastwood as director highlights throughout the film that Mitchell Gant is not the real hero of the story; rather the true heroes are the dissidents, many of whom are Jewish. They risk their lives every day in the fight against Soviet oppression, and it is their efforts that make it possible for him to capture the plane at all. One man assigned to protect Gant on his way to the plane explains that he is married to a Jewish woman who has been imprisoned; his efforts to bring down the Soviet Union are intended to make him worthy of her.

The film's purported optimism is belied throughout by the weaknesses and demeanor of Eastwood's hero. Far from the blank-faced "No Name" of the Spaghetti Westerns, Mitchell Gant is a tentative man, broken most unwillingly from his isolation and continually torn apart by post-traumatic symptoms. Though he is obviously a skilled pilot, his technical prowess and daring never fully overcome his personal struggle with his past or with what he needs to do to complete the mission. In this sense, the film sends a much more mixed message about war (even cold war) than the Reagan administration was prepared to see.

Heartbreak Ridge (1986)

Eastwood's second war film of the 1980s, *Heartbreak Ridge*,[4] was rather more conventional. It opens with Gunnery Sergeant Tom Highway (Eastwood) in jail, boasting with loud masculine bravado about his many successes with women in Vietnam. He gets into a brawl with another prisoner, leading to yet another disciplinary hearing over his lack of self-control. Although the opening credits roll over a backdrop of tragic war scenes that concludes with a tearful picture of an orphaned child, this early note does not harmonize easily with the plot narrated by the film. While Highway has clearly lost himself—he is constantly drunk, rowdy, and out of control—the story unfolds as a conventional narrative of a dysfunctional and troubled war hero who finally makes good on his duty.

Assigned to train a very unlikely unit of young marines—including an African American rock singer who actually robs Highway on the journey to the base before they even know each other—Highway successfully transforms them into fully trained marines, just in time for them to ship out for the invasion of Grenada. There they quickly become heroes, taking an enemy stronghold on their own initiative without proper orders from higher-ups in the chain of command. Indeed, their arrival on the island is fast and easy because the initial skirmish to take the beach decimates the opposing forces, leaving bodies scattered across the sand. Highway's attitude is cynical and cavalier as he takes a Cuban cigar from one of the enemy soldiers—implicating, by the way, that the soldiers were indeed connected to socialist Cuba.

Highway carries the cigar in his mouth, representing the classic image of daunting manhood. His unit's first and most important mission is to rescue United States citizens who are being held prisoner in the university. They find that the group includes several very attractive female students—who are, of course, all too interested in the young marines, their affections clearly portrayed as one of the side benefits of war. Later, Highway plays the cocky maverick before his superiors in the chain of command, defending his unit's taking an enemy position without orders, which he sees as a heroic action. His commanders point out, perhaps rightly, that one of his soldiers died before air reinforcements were available—a death that might have been avoided had Highway and his men played the role assigned to them within the broader plan for the battle. But Highway refuses to concede, and it is clear with whom the audience should identify.

The film also includes a secondary narrative track, which was notably absent in *Firefox*: Highway was a married man but a total disaster as a husband. During his return to base, we see a very different side of Tom Highway from the tough man who trains younger marines. He attempts to reconcile with his wife and makes at least some attempt at understanding women by perusing various women's magazines.

His clumsy attempts at conversation read, in fact, like a typical women's magazine quiz to evaluate a relationship: "Did we mutually nurture each other?" he asks about their marriage on one occasion, and later,

"Did we communicate in a meaningful way?" Aggie (Marsha Mason) rebuffs him at first, actually throwing him out of the house, because she has no desire to become involved with him again or with what he has come to represent. Finally, she explains how difficult it was for her while he was away in Vietnam. She never knew whether he was alive or dead, and she never wants to put herself through that kind of agony again. Still, when he returns from Granada, she is there to meet him with the other wives and girlfriends.

The film is not as profound in its engagement with the dilemmas of heterosexuality as are some of Eastwood's other early films, such as *Tightrope*, and certainly it cannot compare to his later work, such as *The Bridges of Madison County*. Still, it creates a similar ambivalence in its protagonist, which breaks up the narrative coherence of the film—a technique that Eastwood often uses to good effect to undermine the viewer's easy assumptions, but which seems to fall flat in *Heartbreak Ridge* because the two sides of Tom Highway never find a way to believably coexist. We know that Highway's past includes the battle of Heartbreak Ridge—a school of hard knocks that created the horrifying images with which the film opens—but we never return to this heartbreak in the main stream of the narrative. Instead, we follow Highway in his successful, relatively clean, and hardly traumatic leadership of the mission in Grenada. His only remaining heartbreak lies in the trials he endures to retrieve a broken marriage, and while these tribulations accurately highlight the destructive influence of war on family life, they hardly maintain the level of impact that the film seems to set up for itself. While Highway is certainly a man with two sides—one the swaggering braggart who cynically steals cigars from the dead in battle, the other a man who secretly reads women's magazines hoping to connect on some level with his estranged wife—these sides never really speak to each other, and as a result neither speaks effectively to the larger themes introduced by the film. The lack of coherence between these roles cannot easily be reconciled to complete a relatable character. Whereas *Firefox* was notable for Eastwood's brilliant direction and performance of a man in trauma, *Heartbreak Ridge* presents a more conventional portrayal of masculine bravado against which Highway's tenderness toward his wife is never very convincing. Highway is well within the confines of Oedipal complementarity that starkly define what a man is and what a woman is supposed to do.

Still, even if we regard the film, along with *Firefox*, as part of a mid-eighties celebration of the worse kind of masculine hubris associated with war and empire, it is important to note that even at his most conservative and conventional Eastwood cannot avoid the kind of ambivalence in his characters that belies the ostensibly positive tone of these films. Indeed *Heartbreak Ridge* was severely criticized by the Reagan administration because it was not rah-rah enough. Despite Eastwood's long association with the Republican Party, the ethical struggles he portrays in his films prevent him from making a purely positive, conservative Hollywood film; he is simply too subtle a director to draw with broad strokes characters whose masculinity is heralded and never questioned.

However, he has truly come into his own with his more recent critical work on the subject of war, producing two genuine masterpieces that openly embrace his ambivalence toward the life of a soldier. In *Flags of Our Fathers* and *Letters from Iwo Jima*, as we shall see, he simultaneously honors the courage and valor of men on both sides of the battlefield even as he questions on a truly profound level whether any political purpose was really worth their sacrifice. These films are timely indeed, for in the terms of today's political debates they exemplify the sense in which a person can respect and support the troops—the men and women who give their lives on the battlefield—while also questioning the legitimacy of the purposes that send them there or the governments that turn them into tools of war. Indeed, Eastwood's critique is all the more profound for the fact that he sets his films in the context of World War II—perhaps the last conflict that a majority of Americans unabashedly view as, from the American perspective, a "just war." His material raises his film above the many valid criticisms of a given war, instead aiming his critique at the very idea of war by presenting from both perspectives—American and Japanese—showing us that the complex interplay of courage and fraternity, along with the abusive instrumental rationality of warring governments, is what produces the "heroes" amid the horror of war. Ironically, his masterful war films call upon us to imagine—however impossible it may seem—a world without war. Indeed, an aspiration for peace can hope to make sense of the sacrifices that came before. Let us turn now to consider these films in more detail.

Flags of Our Fathers (2006)

Most of us are familiar with the famous photograph by Joseph Rosenthal that heroically frames six men as they struggle to hoist a large American flag atop Mount Suribachi on the island of Iwo Jima. Indeed, perhaps even more familiar than the photograph itself is the Marine Corps War

Memorial in Washington, D.C., which reproduces the image as an enormous bronze statue. It stands as one of our most significant war memorials.

I have been privileged to become friends with a marine who as a young man fought at Iwo Jima, and his response to questions about the battle has always been very similar to the response of the veteran John "Doc" Bradley as depicted in *Flags of Our Fathers*[5]: he remains silent, simply shaking his head. Another friend who served in the army infantry during the war has also been reluctant to share his experiences; he has only remarked that of the approximately 600 men who embarked with his unit only twelve returned alive. At the time, he was only eighteen years old. Both of my friends have asked me not to mention their names in this book, largely because one of the most profound and tragic experiences of the war for each of them was the total annihilation of individuality. Therefore they want it on record that as individuals they were nothing special. War transforms men, as one of my friends has said, into nothing more than "government issue"—the term behind the familiar but seemingly cryptic abbreviation, "G.I." *Flags of Our Fathers* is to my mind a truly American masterpiece. It is profoundly American in two senses: first, it deals with one of the most significant and memorable battles of World War II; and, second, it grapples with a distinctly American wartime response that has our government and media transforming men into myths of war, and glorifying them as heroes.

Flags opens to a nightmare sequence in the mind of Doc Bradley, who desperately shouts out the name "Iggy"—a friend of his who died on the island of Iwo Jima, as we later discover. The nightmare landscape is a ravaged moon, shot in black and white with startling flashes of color. Eastwood will use similar imagery throughout to communicate both the memory and the reality of war. Doc wakes still shouting the name and, as he collapses later on the stairs of his home, dying from a heart attack, he still gasps Iggy's name as if somehow he will be reunited with his friend at last.

The film is based on a book that was written by John Bradley's son, James, who admits that he did not begin to understand his father's silence about the war until after he was gone. His father never shared his feelings about that day on Mount Suribachi or about his fame in the aftermath of that battle, and he refused to comment on the famous photo depicting him and his comrades as heroes. After his father's death, however, James Bradley is determined to learn more about what had become such a significant event for his father, hoping even to learn why he was so silent about it. He began by interviewing the photographer who took the famous picture, who explained the profound impact that Doc had had on the men around him—though no one, including the photographer, had expected the photograph or the men in it to become the mythic figures that they became.

But the film flashes back to provide a visual account of the story behind Doc's nightmare. A medic, Doc (Ryan Phillippe), is called out of his foxhole to help a wounded soldier. Though Doc had actually trained to be a barber in civilian life, he was assigned a medical position and took to it well. His companion, Iggy, who shares the foxhole with him, is terrified at Doc's intending to leave, but Doc cannot shirk his duty to help the men on the field. Eastwood films the scene in black and white to bring to life the shadowy reality of war, which is remembered and often experienced as if it were a black-and-white photo, because in a sense war drains the color from the world only to violently thrust it back through the horrible reality of severed limbs and gushing blood, bursting flames and bombshells. Eastwood shoots all of these things in color with dramatic effect.

Tending his patient, Doc is interrupted by a confrontation with a Japanese soldier whom he must kill before he can continue to assist the wounded American soldier. By the time he returns to his foxhole, Iggy has vanished. Despite warnings from another soldier to keep quiet, Doc desperately calls his friend's name hoping to find where he has gone. The film will return again and again to Doc's haunted memory of Iggy's disappearance, gradually unfolding the story of what happened to Iggy and giving the audience a feeling for why the loss of his friend haunts him so. While some critics have bemoaned the lack of narrative coherence in *Flags*, the thematic point here is that war itself breaks up any possibility of narrative coherence, both on the battlefield and in the memories that disrupt the lives of soldiers long after the war has passed. Thus, the film proceeds through three subjective temporal points of view: James Bradley's contemporary encounters with the history of his father's traumatic past, shot in color; flashbacks to war scenes, which are almost always shot in black and white; and color depictions of the publicity tour of the men who raised the replacement flag at Mount Suribachi. Even though they did not raise the first flag, the men were hailed as heroes in order to generate funds desperately needed to continue the war. Cycling between these three points of view, we are engaged in all three stories simultaneously: a son struggles to understand his father through fragments of a story, which, now that his father is gone, can never be whole. The flag-raisers, whose viewpoints we see through the eyes of the son, show us what it meant to them to be used as war heroes when they knew they were not even the ones who had raised the first flag. Finally, we as viewers attempt to understand our own complex historical relationship to war heroes and symbols of war that represent men struggling to survive. The film can have no overarching coherence because the very real themes with which it engages have no coherence of their own.

The film moves back and forth in time so that we ourselves join James Bradley in trying to make sense of what happened. Thus, after reliving Doc Bradley's nightmarish remembrance of Iggy's disappearance, we return to the beginning when the young men head off on the boat to Iwo Jima. We meet the other two main characters from the publicity campaign based on the flag-raising photograph: Rene Gagnon (Jesse Bradford) and Ira Hayes (Adam Beach), a man as proud of his Pima Indian heritage as he is of his enlistment in the marines. Though the other soldiers playfully refer to Ira as "the chief," being a marine is the first time he has felt equal to those around him.

For a moment, the film seems to settle into a conventional narrative in war movies, showing the eager young soldiers bravely marching into the heat of war. The men are in good spirits as they hail the air force, which is flying ahead to bombard the shores of Iwo Jima in preparation for the landing that rapidly approaches. Shortly, however, the easy introduction to war is broken when one excited young man loses his footing and falls overboard. The others, including Doc and Ira, try to throw him a life preserver, but it is too late; the boat is going too fast. Another man comments, "Oh, they'll pick him up," but it is all too clear that no boat will stop for this young man, no pilot will break formation in the lead-up to the invasion to rescue one unfortunate sailor. He will be left to die, alone, far out in the ocean. Doc mutters to himself, "So much for 'no man left behind.'"

"No man left behind" is one of the military's favorite slogans, and it is among Hollywood's favorite war myths. Think for instance of the blockbuster *Saving Private Ryan* (1998), in which an elite military force is sent to retrieve one young private from the heart of the fighting in WWII Europe because he is the only surviving brother of the four who went to war. As the story goes, Private James Ryan (Matt Damon) must be returned alive to his widowed mother because of a general's deep concern for her grief. This particular Government Issue must survive for the sake of his mother.[6] When I took my infantry friend to the film, he lasted all of forty-five minutes before asking me in disgust to never expose him to that kind of "bullshit" again. Yes, bullshit. While the film is loosely based on the sole survivor policies developed by the military during World War II—and more particularly on the story of the Niland brothers, one of whom was shipped home when his three brothers were believed dead—the United States military has never expended such resources as the film depicts to live up to the "no man left behind" ideal.[7]

The reality of war is that the infantry is routinely marched onto the battlefield only to be mowed down by machine gun and artillery fire, left to die an agonizing death with hardly a thought from their superiors as to who they were or how they died. The "private," we should recall, derives from the same root as deprived and deprivation, and in the military context it means "without rank" or deprived of rank. A marine corps private wears no uniform insignia. Yet in the myth bolstered by *Private Ryan*, the young enlisted man is so important that the highest ranks of the military order an elite squad of eight men to risk their lives— indeed, ultimately to give their lives, all eight of them—for the sole purpose of finding and recovering him. The film opens with the aged Private Ryan visiting the grave of Captain John Miller (Tom Hanks), who led the mission to save him; Ryan wonders if he is worthy of all of the lives that were lost trying to save him. The film would like us to believe that he is, or at least that he represents the ideals of a military that would risk everything to save the life of one young man whose family has already suffered too much. But the story is, as my friend puts it, bullshit. And as a result, the film is a glorification of war even in its depiction of the horrors of hand-to-hand combat, the desperation in the faces of dying men, and the brutality of what it takes to kill a man. Though *Private Ryan* gives us a disturbingly graphic image of war— indeed, more graphic in many of its details than either *Flags* or *Letters from Iwo Jima*—its straightforward message that the military stands for undiluted honor and nobility without a hint of ambivalence results in a film that undermines any critique we might otherwise read into it.

Eastwood very frankly debunks the myth of *Saving Private Ryan* by showing what actually happens when a man falls overboard. He does not film this simple truth in order to criticize those in command—to suggest that they are at fault for not going back—but in order to show that in the business of organized killing, the human beings who fight are necessarily deprived, to a certain extent, of their humanity and individuality. They are, as if by definition, expendable. This fundamental truth is inseparable from the reality of war, and Eastwood's honest portrayal of it forms his general indictment against the glorification of war. His relentless exposure of the effects of the trauma of war forces us to understand the circumstances into which we send our young men and women when we as a society deploy our military against an enemy. In these movies, Eastwood the director presses us very profoundly toward a policy of restraint insofar as he shows us that war is never as glamorous as many films (and certainly governments) would have us believe.

As the Japanese open fire against the American invasion, all hell breaks loose, and Eastwood brings the viewer into the confusion with the use of a scrambling hand camera, which disrupts our ability to maintain a coherent perspective outside the action on the battlefield. We hear a confused mix of heavy breathing, trampling feet, and meaningless screams, and now and then we are reunited with Doc Bradley as he begins his desperate efforts to tend the wounded around him. Unlike *Saving Private Ryan, Flags of Our Fathers* is filmed in a way that does not separate the audience from the action; it is part of the action, with a sense of having to duck from gunfire and dodging exploding rounds of artillery. Indeed, when I first saw the film in the theatre, a woman next to me became so disoriented and frightened by the incoherent point of view that Eastwood thrusts onto the audience that she became nauseated and I had to help her to the restroom. One can only imagine how much worse it must be for the men and women who were actually fighting in the trenches, experiencing the raw reality of what we saw.

As a director, Eastwood is well aware that he can never fully portray the horror of war, not even by denying his audience the safety of a steady perspective. His film technique is not really intended to give us an accurate idea of what the soldiers experienced, but rather to disrupt our position to the extent that as we glimpse the horror of war, we must allow our imaginations to falter before it. We must recognize the real events of war as something that we cannot know, something that cannot be understood or accepted or glamorized because it falls outside the bounds of what the human mind can sort into a coherent experience. Losing all of our reference points, as well as the capacity to interpret the information delivered by our senses, we might barely grasp for a moment the ultimate horror of living through an event that cannot be represented by words and images. We might understand why Doc Bradley and others simply fall silent before what they cannot comprehend themselves, let alone communicate to others.

Eastwood also plays with the limits of the audience's imagination to deepen our understanding of Doc's traumatized reaction to his friend

Iggy's death. When Iggy disappears from the foxhole, Doc is obsessed with finding him; even decades after his friend has been killed, he wants to restore his life to the moment when Iggy disappeared so that he could prevent what happened. When Iggy's body is discovered, Doc is taken to where Iggy lies on the battlefield, down into one of the caves where the enemy had taken him. The audience never sees what was done to Iggy, and in this approach to depicting this scene Eastwood makes a strong break from cinematic realism. What we do see is Doc over-whelmed with horror, falling to his knees before what remains of his friend. His terror strikes us dramatically, because we are compelled to imagine what reality could so completely break a man who looks upon it; we are forced to imagine everything that Iggy meant to Doc; we must struggle to grasp what it means for their friendship to be brutally dis-solved before our eyes. From our safe haven in the theatre, any actual image of a dismembered corpse—no matter how gruesome—would risk the possibility that we would be underwhelmed, and our reaction or lack thereof would have broken our identification with Doc's heartbreak and agony. His expression would suddenly become dramatic, and we would recognize it as the performance it is, not empathize with his (very real) pain. By playing on our imagination, Eastwood reverses the logic of cinema, giving primacy to our identification with Doc and forcing us to imagine our own best friendship obliterated by violence, our own worst nightmare of mutilation realized. As a result, we confront not merely the dismembered body of a soldier slain in battle, but also an inscription onto Doc Bradley's unconscious that he cannot escape.

Let's turn now to the central (if somewhat divided) narrative line of the film, in which Eastwood recounts the events surrounding the famous flag-raising on Mount Suribachi. The book by James Bradley uncovers, through interviews with others, Doc's personal sadness and ambivalence about the publicity stunt that the flag-raising ultimately became. Doc's feelings were premised in large part on the public misconceptions of what actually happened that day, including the fate of the other three men who—with Doc, Ira Hayes, and Rene Gagnon—were sent to erect the replacement flag. Our understanding of Doc's motivation grows along with his son's, as he slowly puts together an account of why Doc never came to terms with the striking contrast between the battle as it was portrayed on their publicity tour and the true horror of combat on Iwo Jima.

Two flags were raised on the island that day. The first was erected by Hank Hansen, Ernest "Boots" Thomas, Harold Schrier, James Michaels, and Charles W. Lindbergh. The flag signified the Americans' successful capture of Mount Suribachi, and it was a proud moment for all the soldiers involved; across the island and on the boats surrounding it, every soldier who could see the flag erupted in cheers at the prospect that their nightmare was coming to an end. Yet shortly after the first flag was raised, an arriving general decides that he wants the flag for a souvenir. As a result a second group is sent to remove the first flag and raise another; Ira Hayes, Franklin Sousley, Doc Bradley, Harlon Block, Michael Strank, and Rene Gagnon climb the summit of Mount Suribachi to complete their mission. While the first flag-raising had been captured on film by Staff Sergeant Louis R. Lowery, it is Joseph Rosenthal's perfectly framed photograph of the second, more staged event that goes down in history to represent the victory at Iwo Jima.

Though the Americans have captured the mountain, turning the tide of battle in their favor and effectively winning the island, the conflict continues for many days—indeed, until almost all of the Japanese soldiers are killed, many of whom take their own lives rather than suffer the shame of surrender. Using flashbacks, the film then turns us back to what actually happened to those who raised the first flag. Hank Hansen, who helped raise the first flag, meets his end in Doc's arms. Despite Doc's heroic efforts to save him, the best he can ultimately do is to promise to return Hank's prized wristwatch to his worried mother, who is waiting for news of her son. Of the men in the more famous flag-raising, three— Harlon, Mike, and Franklin—will not survive the war, and on the very day that Mike and Harlon die, Congressman Joseph Hendricks of Florida introduces the bill that will turn that famous photograph into a bronze war memorial. Franklin is shot in the back, and Harlan is, as a comrade put it, "blown into the air"—his body is sliced from his groin well into his torso, and as he dies, he lets out one strangulated scream: "They killed me!" Doc stands fast through it all as his friends are killed; he is horrified by death after death as he tries to piece together bodies and hold in crushed intestines, struggling against impossible odds to keep them alive.

It does not take long for the government to recognize the symbolic significance of Rosenthal's brilliant shot. The three surviving flag-raisers are quickly brought home to go on a war-bonds publicity tour, even though Ira, Rene, and Doc make every effort to tell anyone who will listen that they were not the first flag-raisers and that the original flag-raisers faced much greater risks when they took Mount Suribachi: they are the ones who should be hailed as heroes. Unfortunately, no one seems interested in what actually happened, because the American imagination has become so wrapped up in the striking poses of the second flag-raising photograph. Worse, however, is the fact that the slain Harlon Block does not receive his share of fame and recognition at all, since he has been misidentified in the picture as Hank Hansen, who participated in the first flag-raising, not the second one that is depicted in Rosenthal's photo. Harlon's mother, however, insists that she recognizes her son, declaring that she diapered and powdered that rear end—she would know it anywhere. She even goes so far as to leave her husband because he accepts the official identifications of the soldiers in the photo, seeing this as a betrayal. While the survivors know the truth, they do not know how to handle the publicity events in which they have been entrapped. As a result they miss early opportunities to correct the record. Worse, Doc feels compelled to concede that it was Hansen rather than Harlon in the famous photograph when a tour promoter introduces him to Hansen's heartbroken mother, who would like Doc to confirm her son's identity. Agonizing over his participation in the deception, Doc cannot bring himself to tell Mrs. Hansen that her dead son is not famous after all and therefore his death does not have the same meaning. He points to Harlon and lies, saying that it was indeed Hansen in the photo.

As Eastwood moves back and forth between the publicity tour and the horrific images of what really happened on the battlefield, we come to understand the suffering that is imposed by the flag-raisers' terrible silence surrounding the many truths that no one wants to hear. Ira Hayes, in particular, becomes increasingly distressed at the hypocrisy of the war-bonds tour. He never wanted to leave his military brethren in the first place; he wanted to stay on and fight by their side. Gradually unraveling beneath the weight of his guilt, he turns to alcohol. After getting into a fight when a bar refuses to admit him because he is a Native American, he is eventually dismissed from the tour and ordered to return to the front lines, which is what he wants to do anyway, but they do not even allow him to visit his mother before he goes.

As the war comes to an end, the heroes settle back into civilian life. Doc quietly takes over a funeral home and spends the rest of his life working as a mortician. Rene, rather enamored of his fifteen minutes of fame, seeks to call in the many favors offered when he was considered a celebrity, but none of the promises are kept and none of the offers come through. Working one odd job after another, he too falls into a life of relative obscurity and financial struggle. Ira, meanwhile, maintains a certain level of notoriety, not only through his constant minor arrests but because he tries to recreate himself as an activist for Native American rights. In a last redemptive gesture, he walks and hitchhikes across the country—almost fifteen hundred miles—in order to visit Mr. Block to tell him the truth: his wife was right to recognize a backside that had appeared in one of the most famous photographs in history. After walking over one thousand miles, he simply walks up to Harlan's father, tells him the truth, and walks away. Ira dies not long after his trek, probably from exposure or alcoholism; perhaps also, we could say, from a broken heart.

At one point, James Bradley looks directly into the camera—at the audience—with a profound sadness on his face. He has been true to the memory of Doc, his now dead father, by seeking the real story behind his father's silence about Iwo Jima. Yet even as he pieces the story together, he never completely unravels the paradox of his father's silence. Clearly this event was not one that Doc sought to share with his son or with anyone else in his family. It was nothing for him to be proud of, and certainly not something to turn into a set of manly lessons for his son. Yet Doc, after all, did nothing of which he should be ashamed—he fought valiantly and put his life on the line many times to save the men around him. Ultimately, the author James Bradley, along with Eastwood the director, wants us to understand what Doc told his son right before he died—there were no heroes in Iwo Jima, just men trying to survive and watch out for each other. Doc played a role, however reluctantly, in one of the myths that make war appear glamorous and rewarding.

A hero is a fantasy. "Heroes"—at least as they are portrayed in Hollywood—do not scream. They do not, like the flesh-and-blood human beings who go to war, struggle to make the best of a nightmare so that they and their friends might hope to come home alive. No, "heroes" stand above the anguish and heartache of war. They come through it all as if they could not die or suffer—as if the thousands of bodies strewn about them were merely the minor supporting characters in a scripted drama all their own. Hollywood, of course, is all too familiar with heroes of this sort; and in one of the most tragic ironies imaginable, Ira, Rene, and Doc are asked to participate in the filming of a feature hailing the virtues of a fictional hero at Iwo Jima. A John Wayne film, *The Sands of Iwo Jima* is doubly ironic in that it both imagines a "hero" unlike anyone who actually fought in the battle and deprives the three soldiers of any dignity they have left by denying them any agency or bravery of their own: Sergeant Stryker (Wayne) orders the flag-raising with the three real-life marines huddled around him; indeed their main function in the film is to take their orders from the Hollywood-contrived "hero" of the film. In Bradley's book, he records his father's bitterness about the whole affair. In Doc's words, as recalled by a fellow marine:

> They didn't get us off to California to help make the picture. All that was a cheap publicity trick to get a little free advertising for the movie. . . . We were out there only two days, and most of that time was spent fooling around. I think they only took about two shots of the flag-raising, and that only took about ten minutes. If you think you will see real action like Iwo Jima by seeing the picture, I really think you will be sadly disappointed. Chief Hayes says they have the picture so fucked up he isn't even going to see the movie.[8]

Again, the men had been used, cheaply, to represent something they never meant to portray: "heroes," John Wayne–style. Eastwood ends the film with an extraordinary image of the young men of Easy Company playfully jumping up and down in the water like the children they were. That was how Doc wanted his son to remember him and his friends—in the water, imagining for a moment that the war was not tearing apart their lives. War does not produce heroes, because its participants are only men—and tragically many of those men are still boys. As James Bradley reflects on what he has learned of his father's life:

> I will take my dad's word for it. Mike, Harlon, Rene, and Doc— the men of Easy Company—they just did what anyone would have done, and they were not heroes. Not heroes. They were boys of common virtue. Called to duty. Brothers and sons. Friends and neighbors. And fathers. It's as simple as that.

To honor their memory, perhaps we can do nothing more significant than to refuse to think of them as heroes, as images and ideals that tend to justify and glamorize what it means to go to war. By relinquishing our need for this fantasy, we can recognize the genuine honor and sacrifice of the flesh-and-blood human beings who are sent to the front lines to fight our wars for us.

In this book, we have often explored the significance of parenting, particularly of fatherhood, in many of the movies that Eastwood has directed. In the same scene in which Doc tells his son of the young men playing in the water, he apologizes to him for not being a good father.

His son insists that he was the best father a man could have. Under the fiction of "Father knows best" of course, real men are supposed to be in total charge of the lessons that they teach their sons, particularly the lessons tied in with the masculine dramas of war and violence as they are supposed to be endured. But the trauma of war leaves Doc unable to provide lessons; instead he must remain silent. Obviously he cannot communicate these lessons because he does not want to create a fantasy of masculinity for his son. He does not want to play or even pretend to be the father who knows best. Here again we see the Oedipal myth of the potency of paternity, which is undermined by a man who seeks to retain his integrity by remaining silent before a false heroism that he refused to claim. We only know Doc through his son, and it is perhaps that Doc's humility before his inability to save his friends that serves as a powerful reminder that there are no such things as phallic men who can conquer all and live up to the Hollywood version of heroism. Doc could continue to play the hero—he is asked to do so time and time again on Memorial Day—instead he always asks his son to say that he is fishing. And it is in that refusal to continue to play the role of the hero that the son takes away from his father as the ultimate lesson on the devastation of war.

Flags of Our Fathers should be considered an American masterpiece, but it has not received the critical praise that it deserves. Some critics have complained that Eastwood's broken narration makes the film confusing. Indeed, it is rather difficult to watch, but not because the viewer has trouble following the narrative line. Rather, it is difficult on a moral level because it confronts us with the reality that heroes are produced in spite of themselves, sometimes even at great expense to their sense of themselves as real human beings with stories to tell. The film confronts us with the profoundly paradoxical truth that "heroes" are manufactured; in this case against the protests of the men who are being molded for this purpose. The brilliance of Eastwood's film is that he runs us up against what cannot be told but can only be grasped retrospectively as a son's love dismantles the contradictions and ambivalence of his father's life. It is Eastwood's ethical fidelity to Doc's simple lesson that there are no heroes that explains his framing of the film as a series of disjointed narrative tracks—the story of Iwo Jima and the story of the "heroes" who represent it cannot be assembled into any straightforward plot line because they are not, in fact, in any way compatible scenarios, even for the men who lived through them both. Certainly Eastwood's film is deeply respectful toward these young men who fought so bravely and who cared so deeply for one another. But it also takes us to a world without heroes because the fantasy that heroes exist at all is used to prop up the mythical glamorization of war. *Flags of Our Fathers*, in this sense, is an anti-war movie in the truest sense of the word: it does not oppose this or that war for being ill-planned or unjust. Rather it questions the very possibility that anything noble or honorable can come from the violence of war.

With this in mind, we turn now to the twin piece to Eastwood's *Flags of Our Fathers*. Another masterpiece, *Letters from Iwo Jima* crosses the battle lines to discover the stories that animate the lives of Japanese soldiers who are hopelessly defending the island against the American invasion.

Letters from Iwo Jima (2006)

Letters from Iwo Jima[9] has received more critical acclaim than *Flags of our Fathers*, perhaps because, on a surface level, it presents the more conventional story of a dedicated general in impossible straits. The film opens with the discovery of letters, which were left behind on the island of Iwo Jima by the Japanese soldiers who died there, among them the letters of General Tadamichi Kuribayashi (Ken Watanabe). Kuribayashi manages the defense operations of the island, ordering his men to dig into caves and holes when he realizes early on in the battle that there is no hope for air support; direct conflict on the beaches, therefore, will be entirely futile. Indeed, Kuribayashi knows that they are hopelessly outnumbered, so the best he can do is to hold the island as long as possible, stalling the American advance to the mainland. Understanding that he will not survive the battle, he prepares to die the honorable death of a Japanese soldier—and he is determined to make a respectable example for his troops.

Kuribayashi, we learn, had once traveled to the United States, and he fondly remembers his visit. Kuribayashi and his compatriate Baron Nishi (Tsuyoshi Ihara) are portrayed as cosmopolitan men who are not wrapped up in any shallow stereotypes of nationalism; yet they remain dedicated patriots who accept the Japanese code of honor that prefers a death—even suicide, if necessary—to surrender. Nishi was an equestrian Olympic medalist, who met such movie stars as Mary Pickford and Douglas Fairbanks when he was in the Olympics. Eastwood refuses to simply stereotype the conventions of Japanese discipline and loyalty by sentimentalizing the soldiers at Iwo Jima; neither does he neglect their deep desire to survive even against the knowledge that survival would mean almost certain disgrace.

One of the things that make *Letters* so extraordinary is that we are returned to scenes we should recognize from *Flags*, this time from the standpoint of the Japanese. In *Flags* we saw guns peeking out from the caves occupied by the island's defenders; in *Letters* we see the faces behind those guns. We get to know the men who hold them. The narrative unfolds around two young soldiers, Saigo (Kazunari Ninomiya) and Shimizu (Riyo Kase). Shimizu has been deployed to Iwo Jima as a kind of death sentence after he failed to maintain the strict discipline required of his position with the dreaded Kempeitai military police—he had defied orders by refusing to shoot a dog. Saigo is a young baker with a pregnant wife, who was drafted into the war against his deep desire to remain with his wife and unborn child. He is optimistic about the outcome, but his wife does not share his optimism—after all, she has not seen anyone return from the front lines, and she knows that Japanese soldiers are sworn to die before they surrender. Indeed, Saigo's promise to return home following the war, which he makes to his unborn baby as he lays his head on his wife's stomach, portrays a very different view of what really matters in a man's life over and above conventional Japanese military honor. Saigo plays a somewhat comic role in the film; he continually butts up against military regulations and social conventions, landing him in constant trouble with his superiors.

Eastwood uses this comic device to add depth to the character of General Kuribayashi, portraying him as an understanding commander who proves that discipline does not always demand harshness, nor even the strictest application of the rules. He saves Saigo from reprimand or death on three occasions, on the first of which Saigo objects to the meager rations offered to sustain him. An officer prepares to beat Saigo for his insubordination and laziness, but Kuribayashi intervenes, rebuking the officer and suggesting that he cannot so easily dispense with his soldiers.

The full force of what it means to fight and die against impossible odds is highlighted by the dramatic fall of Mount Suribachi, the capture of which signals the beginning of the end for that Japanese at Iwo Jima. Kuribayashi has ordered his men to hold the mountain as long as they can before retreating to a less strategic position, but less senior officers on the scene do not believe the order has been received correctly. According to the honor code, they should kill themselves on the spot for the shame of losing their position. With tears in their eyes, many men follow the orders of their immediate commander, throwing themselves on hand grenades to make their last moments swift, if gruesome. Saigo, however, refuses to follow these instructions, arguing that they should follow the orders received from General Kuribayashi—orders preferable to him, as we know, because he has made a promise to return home and will do everything in his power to honor it. Shimizu also hesitates, even though he believes Saigo is wrong to disobey a direct order. Another officer decides to take matters into his own hands, intending to behead Saigo and then kill himself, but at the critical moment Kuribayashi shows up to reinforce his orders in person: it was in fact his command to retreat and continue the battle. Thus, he saves Saigo yet again.

While we have seen in *Flags* that the Japanese were under orders to brutally dismember slain American soldiers in order to terrify their comrades, Eastwood reminds us in *Letters* that brutality and coldhearted killing occur on both sides of the battlefield—likewise humanity and kindness. When a young, wounded G.I. is captured, Japanese soldiers carry him into a cave for medical treatment, even when it is clear he must be dying. Baron Nishi sits by and entertains the prisoner, cheering him with stories about the Olympics and parties with movie stars. The young man eventually dies, and Baron Nishi discovers a letter on his body. Here Eastwood focuses on the faces of the young Japanese soldiers as they listen to Baron Nishi read the American's letter and recognize so much of themselves in what they hear. Soon the men endure a ferocious attack, which blinds the Baron so that he feels no alternative but to end his own life. Saigo and Shimizu were among the men who heard Baron Nishi read the American's letter and they discuss how this enemy of theirs is not so different from either of them—his mother, in fact, reminds them of their own mothers. In that moment, they lose the sense of what they have been fighting for. Who is this enemy who has been portrayed to them as so brutal and terrifying, if when they finally confront him he turns out to be a young man little different from themselves? They decide at last to surrender: Shimizu goes first, but as Saigo prepares to follow him, he is interrupted by Japanese officers and cannot make his escape. As it turns out, it will be better for him: although Shimizu has peacefully surrendered, his American guards balk at the prospect of remaining through the night to watch over Japanese prisoners. In a brutal and cold-hearted violation of justice and law, they murder their charges out of no motive greater than sheer, unapologetic boredom.

Thus, we have seen brutality on both sides of the war, and Eastwood permits us no easy illusions about justice on the battlefield. The Americans are no more demonized than the Japanese, because Eastwood portrays the impersonal violence of war as simply part of what it means to engage in the business of killing.

Kuribayashi saves Saigo a third and final time when he orders Saigo back from the fighting while his comrades lead the final charge against the Americans. The assignment is honorable enough: Saigo is charged to clean up the camp, to ensure that valuable strategic information is well hidden or destroyed before the Americans take the base. Before taking his last stance against the U.S. Army, Kuribayashi jokes with Saigo that good things come in threes.

Kuribayashi salutes his men as he prepares to lead them into a hopeless charge. He assures them that they will be honored for the sacrifices that they will make as well as for the ones that they have already made. At last, proudly, he does not order the charge—he leads it. When he falls wounded, his friend and assistant drags him from the heat of battle; but Kuribayashi orders his friend to behead him. Weeping, the man prepares to follow his superior's orders, but he is shot by an American soldier before he can do so. At that moment we discover that Saigo has survived the night. He runs desperately down the hill to be with the general, who chuckles softly and mutters, "You again." Kuribayashi asks Saigo if he is still on Japanese soil, and when Saigo confirms that he is, Kuribayashi asks to be buried in a place where the Americans will not find his body. The general takes out his gun and shoots himself, ironically ending his life with the Colt .45 that he was given as a present in the United States.

Following the general's instructions, Saigo buries the body where it will not be discovered. When he returns, he confronts a group of American soldiers, one of whom holds the Colt .45 that Kuribayashi used to kill himself. Enraged at the soldiers' disrespect, Saigo blindly swings a shovel about him as the confused Americans attempt to calm him down; they finally succeed in knocking Saigo unconscious. Overwhelmed by the course of recent events, Saigo futilely lashes out at the Americans.

The film ends with Saigo on the beach, wounded and going home, smiling because he knows that he will keep his promise. Michael Kimmel, in the afterword to *Manhood in America: A Cultural History*, says that when the war ends, it is time for men to go home, to end their fantasy of the lone hero in the heat of battle (or just capitalist competition) and to accept the many obligations associated with the very idea of going home.[10] Saigo is going home in all of these senses.

Flags of Our Fathers and *Letters from Iwo Jima* are best seen back-to-back, since they often echo one another in their portrayals of a single historical event from the two very different perspectives of what were at the time mortal enemies on the battlefield. But just as Eastwood has shown us that there are no heroes in *Flags*, in *Letters* he portrays the face of the so-called enemy. Thus, we are confronted with enemies that are not, in the end, the trumped up evil monsters that we have been trained to see them as, but rather young boys and brave officers doing the best they can to succeed (or survive) the most impossible circumstances that a human being can face. The true horror of war is that our "heroes" and our "enemies" are all the same flesh-and-blood human beings; it is just as terrible to kill as to be killed.

Hero
I am a hero
I am fighting for my country—
I strut around in a bloody uniform
Look at me—a soldier
Look at me—a bloody hero

I am tough
I've got a rifle
I am a soldier
I am a fucking hero

So what?
Who wants to wear a uniform?
Who wants to be a bloody soldier?
Who wants to be a fucking hero?

Heroes die.[11]

We are returned to the image of the boys as they run to jump and play in the water. They helped each other and stood by each other, and we see the risks that they took to do so. But here there are no vestiges of the imagined Hollywood fighter who does not cares at all about his survival and is indifferent to his own ruthlessness and the horrors of war surrounding him. Instead, on both sides of the battle, we see young men who are truly horrified by the violence around them, the torn bodies and the damaged souls. We also see young men who very much want to survive; Saigo seriously tries to surrender in order to keep his promise that he will home to his wife. The sentiment of war movies often relies on the stereotype of the men who do what they have to do for "us," and it is as the "us" that we are supposed to root for our side and get the warm feeling that we truly are safe because these great men are out there doing their duty.

But in *Letters* and *Flags*, we see the war from both perspectives—American and Japanese—so the viewer of both movies is left in the uncomfortable position of not knowing who to root for, of wondering who the good guys are and why the bad guys need to be killed. It is the dissolution of the simple identification of "We are on this side and therefore we identify with the soldiers on our team" that is broken up by the two films taken together as an interpretive unit. There are no sides anymore, only the nightmarish reality of war that leaves the viewer questioning the very idea of identifying with a side at all. Eastwood's daring as a director is to show us a historic battle and all the traumatic effects that it has on the men that fight in it, even when they bravely accept their destiny, as in the case of Kuribayashi. The breakup of an easy identificatory standpoint effectively undermines the conventional narrative structure of war movies, in which the necessity of war is taken for granted and is often a benefit to the development and growth of the men who fight it. In Eastwood's model, the war is no benefit to these men but only a nightmarish reality from which they can never escape and before which they fall silent: there is nothing good to say about being a produced hero in the battle of Iwo Jima. War is no longer portrayed as what makes a man "a man," but rather as what can shatter him, leaving him in the isolation of one who can never relate to others the horrible reality of living in the chaos of the battlefield.

7

Shades of Recognition:
Privilege, Dignity,
and the Hubris of White Masculinity

As I have mentioned throughout the book, many of Eastwood's most important meanings are captured in the dramatic details—in *how* he tells his story as much as *what* he tells. In *Million Dollar Baby*, for instance, the central narrative is told entirely from the perspective of a black man, whose voice we hear from almost the very beginning to the end when he closes the film with his own conclusions. It is almost unheard of for a Hollywood film to tell a white man's story from the perspective of a black man who interprets the action for the viewer.[1] We have also seen how Eastwood has profoundly redone the "colored" sidekick of the traditional Western, making him more of an equal of the white protagonist of *Unforgiven*. In this chapter we will discuss three films—*White Hunter Black Heart*, *True Crime*, and *Bird*—from very different genres and with very different narrative lines, but with one key feature in common: they all explore the issue of race. At least two of them also connect white racism to the hubris of masculine narcissism, which does not recognize limits and therefore tends to confuse fantasy with reality.

Before we turn to these films, however, I want to speak somewhat generally to the issue of race as it appears in the *Dirty Harry* films, though Eastwood directed only the last film in the series. As Dennis Bingham has correctly noted, the popularity of Dirty Harry among both white audiences and audiences of color has much to do with Callahan's ambivalent relationship to authority.[2] Even though Callahan has a badge, he clearly does not represent the establishment; he is rather a white working-class hero, who often aligns himself intentionally with society's outsiders. As Bingham points out, in *The Enforcer* he even cooperates with a group of black revolutionaries.[3] I agree with Bingham's point that throughout the series, Callahan's identification with minorities, outsiders, and even revolutionary groups is closer to white paternalism than to the kind of equality granted to Morgan Freeman's characters in *Unforgiven* and in *Million Dollar Baby*. However, I would like to emphasize that whether Callahan's associations with people of color reflect his own ambivalent antiestablishment attitudes or something deeper, they have clearly set him up in a position that is strikingly different from the stereotypical role of the white do-gooder. It would, of course, be somewhat ridiculous to claim that Harry Callahan or the Dirty Harry films are genuinely antiracist. Still, by the time he directs *Million Dollar Baby*, Eastwood has challenged in a variety of ways the cinematic conventions that dictate that white people tell the stories and black people are merely the minor characters the white people meet along the way.

White Hunter Black Heart (1990)

In *White Hunter Black Heart*[4] Eastwood plays director John Wilson, who is shooting a film on location in Africa, and the character Eastwood has created delivers a striking example of the hubris that is so integral to the white male narcissism, which we have discussed throughout this book. Wilson, it seems, has become so obsessed with the idea of shooting an elephant that he neglects the duties required to produce his own film; he puts them off time and time again while he indulges in his fantasy conquest. Pete Verrill (Jeff Fahey), a white screenwriter, becomes increasingly impatient with the constant delays in the making of the film; he is outraged as well about the director's perverse fantasies of conquest and inhumane treatment of the Africans whom he drags along as guides. Ultimately, Verrill proclaims that the elephants Wilson wants to kill are possessed of far more dignity than he is.

The outcome of Wilson's hunt is truly tragic. Finally within range of an elephant, Wilson tries to shoot it but fails, sending it on a violent rampage. His African guide bravely leaps in front of him to protect him from the attack, and the guide is brutally mauled as the elephant tosses him into the air. The elephant and Wilson survive; the black guide does not. The villagers are absolutely horrified and grief-stricken as they carry the body away for a burial ceremony, while Wilson finally returns to shoot his film. He slowly climbs into the director's chair and gives the order to roll cameras at last.

Eastwood uses the role of director as a metaphor; it is just like white male narcissists to think that they can direct the world and its animals as if they are directing a film. Eastwood is, of course, a known critic of big-game hunting, but what he emphasizes in this film is the carelessness arising from the fantasy that the world can be owned and controlled, that everything that exists appears only as an object to be manipulated and used. Wilson confuses a job with an identity, and as he climbs back into the director's chair, it is not at all clear whether he has learned anything at all. Business will go on as usual, though a man has suffered an unnecessary death in the service of Wilson's aggressive ambition. His unconscious assumption of privilege both as a white man and as an individual who is crucial to the making of the film—at least in the eyes of his colleagues, who could not see how to go on without him—reflects a profound hubris, because he refuses to recognize the suffering it imposes on others.

The film is particularly interesting because it draws these parallels without portraying Wilson as an overt bigot or racist. Indeed, Wilson considers himself a liberal individual who treats people fairly. However, he clearly cannot see the African villagers as anything other than tools for his use, much as he considers it the duty of his actors and actresses to perform on his whim and therefore tolerate his endless delays. Eastwood shows us that racism and masculinity, as rooted in phallic fantasy, are in a sense two sides of the same coin; whiteness becomes a taken-for-granted sign of privilege, which comes with a fantasized authority.

True Crime (1999)

True Crime[5] explores a very different kind of masculine hubris. Steve Everett (Eastwood) is a womanizing reporter and recovering alcoholic with little remaining credibility after he stubbornly insisted on the innocence of a rapist who turned out to be undeniably guilty of the crime. Like John Wilson of *White Hunter Black Heart*, Everett has been careless in his treatment of others—including women, his employers, and the people who are affected by his writing—who unwillingly get caught up in his narcissistic fantasies: others seem to exist for him either incidentally or purely to satisfy his own purposes. Now that he has been relegated to human interest stories, he is assigned to interview Frank Louis Beechum (Isaiah Washington), a young black man who is awaiting execution for murdering a pregnant teenager years before.

Eastwood draws a clear contrast between Everett and Beechum by portraying each man in the context of his relationships with others. Beechum is doing everything he can to hold his family together. On the day before his execution, he comforts his daughter and tries to give his wife, Bonnie (Lisa Gay Hamilton), as much strength and love as possible. He is a good family man and a faithful Christian. The contrast to Everett's womanizing and indifference to the feelings of those around him is striking indeed, but Everett is also committed at this point to righting some wrongs—including, if he can, the mistake he made in the rape case, which he attributes to his drinking. He quickly suspects that something has gone terribly wrong in Beechum's case. He does not believe the man is guilty of murder, and this time he thinks he can prove it. His initial interest in cracking the case has nothing to do with freeing Beechum; he is thinking mainly about salvaging his own sagging career.

Only one eyewitness identified Beechum as the killer. When he interviews the witness, Everett realizes that the accountant could not possibly have seen a gun in Beechum's hand, because there was a grocery stand that stood between the two men at the time of the incident. As we flash back to see the story unfold from the accountant's point of view, we understand that he made a connection—*black man and gun*—without actually seeing what happened; and we understand that Everett can clearly see through the racist assumption, if only because he is desperately interested in a story that might salvage his career.

Everett, who quickly abandons the human-interest angle of the story, commits himself to a full investigation of the crime but endeavors to do it quickly, because Beechum does not have long to live unless Everett can prove his innocence in one day. Though Everett's professional drive and instincts have been restored by the challenge, Eastwood continues to contrast his Everett's carelessness in his personal relationships with Beechum's unswerving devotion to his family. Everett tries to seduce a much younger reporter, against her objections, even as he continues an affair with his editor's wife that increasingly strains his professional relationships. For all the impact on his work life, the affair apparently means nothing to him. It is a diversion, not a romance. In many of his relationships he seems to barely go through the motions of actual commitment or concern: while he agrees to take his young daughter to the zoo, she is treated to a whirlwind tour as he literally sprints past the exhibits, pushing her in a rented stroller into which she does not fit. She later falls out of the stroller and hurts herself. He rushed her through their day together, because he is so eager to question the accountant that he cannot brook any delays. Of course, we know that time is of the essence as Beechum's execution approaches, and if Everett's motive were really the pursuit of justice we could hardly be unsympathetic. But for now at least his only motive is to save his reputation as a journalist, so his impatience only bespeaks selfishness and narcissism.

When Everett learns that a third party was interviewed at the murder scene but supposedly saw nothing of the crime, he becomes convinced that it must have been the real killer. Desperately needing information but lacking the time to track it down himself, Everett hopes to learn more by raiding the files of the reporter who had worked on the case before him—the young woman he attempted to seduce, who has since been killed in a tragic accident. Breaking into her home, he is surprised to find her grieving father but in a classic display of indifference to others, he barely pauses to comfort the man, who goes on and on about the daughter he loved while Everett rifles unapologetically through her things. It is the father, however, who finds what Everett needs—the address of the other person who was present at the time of the murder.

Driving immediately to confront the mysterious witness, he is confronted by a group of rowdy black teenagers whose disruptive behavior is abruptly stopped by the middle-aged black woman living at the address. Everett remarks that he is relieved to find her still living there, to which she sarcastically responds, "Thought I might have moved to the suburbs?" He explains that he is looking for a boy, Warren, who turns out to be her grandson—and stresses that Warren may be able to save a man's life. But the woman becomes angrier still—she says when a "nice white girl" is murdered, the police and the reporters all come around looking for the black man who did it, but when her neighbors die, no one comes at all. She retorts, "Well I seen a lot of innocent folk get killed in this part of town. But it's funny, I ain't never seen you 'round here before." At last she tells Everett that her grandson Warren was also killed. Defensively, Everett tries to explain that he is just trying to get the facts—hoping that she might reveal some useful detail. But again she berates him: "I don't remember you coming looking for the facts when he was killed. No one came around looking for the facts then."

Everett heads home, defeated—without Warren he can think of no way to prove his case. His wife greets him and announces that she is leaving him. His casual mistress, the editor's wife, finally turned on him. He tries to convince his wife that he has changed—that he will change—but she has heard all this before and she wants nothing more to do with him. Setting her wedding ring on the table, she tells him frankly, "If that were a bullet, you would be dead." Taking the ring, he leaves in despair. At a dead end in his investigation and thrown out of his house, he falls back on alcohol and simply sits at a bar drinking and sulking. As he drinks, however, he is suddenly struck by part of Beechum's story in which he recalled the murder victim fingering a necklace—a necklace identical to one Everett saw Warren's grandmother wearing. At last he reconstructs the story as it must have actually taken place.

Warren, as his grandmother admits, was a junkie. In Everett's reconstructed flashback, Warren confronted the victim at the store register, demanding the little money she has and her necklace as well. But she was reluctant to part with the jewelry, a cherished gift, so in agitation Warren fired his weapon, grabbed the necklace, and fled. But this was all after Beechum had arrived: he had spoken to the girl, to whom he had lent a small sum of money, but he had graciously agreed to wait to be repaid. The murder took place while he was in the bathroom, and he only ran out after he heard the shot. He actually did everything he could to save the girl's life, but it was already too late—and at the worst possible moment the accountant walked in to find the black man, bloody and excited, stooped over the body of a dead white girl. He assumed the worst, though as Everett has already determined he could not have seen a weapon in Beechum's hand. Of course, Beechum fled—but why wouldn't he? A black man stooped over a dead white woman—in his mind, what chance did he have?

Having uncovered the truth, Everett must risk driving even though he has had a few drinks to fetch Warren's grandmother and take her to the governor's office in the desperate hope that Beechum can be saved. Fortunately, at this point Warren's grandmother is more than happy to cooperate with Everett because she realizes that an innocent black man's life is at stake, and she admits that she knew Warren had done something terrible without ever knowing what it had been. Frantically they drive to the governor's mansion—and meanwhile, we watch in horrific suspense as Beechum is strapped into the lethal injection apparatus, as the first call comes in confirming that all appeals have been denied, and as the first vial of poison empties into his system. Indeed, the second tube begins to drain as the red phone finally rings—Everett made it, certainly with no time to spare.

The guard answers the phone, and his first words are "It's too late." The warden, Luther Plunkitt (Bernard Hill), however, who has clearly had doubts about Beechum's guilt from the beginning, rushes to the table and rips the IV from Beechum's arm. Bonnie Beechum pounds desperately on the glass outside the chamber, screaming for her husband to stay awake. Eastwood's camera focuses on her wedding ring, reminding us, in these last moments, of the stark contrast between the Beechum and Everett families.

But we see no more. As the screen fades to black, we do not know whether Beechum lives or dies. Eastwood holds us in suspense, perhaps forcing us to consider the many moral implications of the similarities and differences between Beechum and Everett.

We fade back in to find Everett Christmas shopping, trying to find his daughter some toys but also trying to pick up the young female sales clerk. A few minutes later, he stands outside the store conversing with the African American Santa Claus who is about to end his shift— throughout the film Eastwood has worked with the belief in Santa Claus as a metaphor for rational faith and what it means to believe in miracles. At that moment we see Beechum at last, with his family—and we know that Everett succeeded in saving him. Of course, he never seemed to have much interest in whether justice was done. He was happy enough to restore his credibility and his career, to discover that he hadn't lost his "nose" for the truth. In the end, did he care about saving Beechum? Or was he only trying to save himself? Has he learned anything about himself and his own masculine hubris, or is he still as caught up in his own narcissism as when the film began?

Eastwood gives us mixed signals pointing in both directions: Everett flirts with the clerk and loses his wife, but his faith in the truth has turned out to mean something and he has redeemed one of his earlier mistakes. The film ends with a shot of Everett walking away to the tune of a song titled "Why Should We Care?" If Eastwood provides the glimmer of an answer, perhaps it is that by caring about others, or even just caring about the truth, men like Everett may stand the chance of breaking through an almost stereotypical masculine indifference to others to discover something—anything—bigger or better than themselves.

Is *True Crime* explicitly anti-racist? Certainly, as we have stressed throughout, the careless white man is contrasted intentionally with a devoted black family man—a blatant reversal of the all-too-common portrayal of black families as hopelessly dysfunctional. We should note a physical contrast between Everett and Beechum as well: while the critic Paul Smith complains that Eastwood's *Bird* contrasts almost perfect white bodies with Charlie Parker's declining physique[6]—a discussion to which we shall return shortly—in *True Crime* Beechum's healthy body stands out against the white protagonist's flabby waist and deeply lined features. More importantly, issues of race are subtly but consistently outlined throughout the film in a variety of themes and subtexts. The white accountant, of course, assumes that Beechum held the murder weapon because he is a black man who was found at the scene; and Warren's grandmother underlines the white authorities' indifference to murder when it happens in the black community—a regular, tragic affair. In the United States, at least, the death penalty is itself a highly racial issue, since the vast majority of the people we execute are black men.

Indeed, there is a certain hubris to the death penalty: we presume that we can so totally judge a man as to end his life. To disavow any possibility of identifying with him, along with any possibility of discovering that he is not guilty after all, is to deny our own flaws—even our own humanity. As we watch the vials of poison slowly drain into the body of Frank Beechum—killing him, as far as we know—he bravely locks eyes with his loving wife, and the full force of his death seems to condemn us all, as spectators, for tolerating a racist society in which we condemn so many young black men to die.

Bird (1988)

Eastwood's love for jazz has never been a secret, so it was no surprise when he decided to honor one of the greatest saxophonists of all time, Charlie "Bird" Parker, with *Bird*,[7] a film about Parker's life and work. Eastwood covers his early life rather briefly, showing him first as a child and then as a young man playing every musical instrument he could find. Fading out, we flash forward to find Charlie "Bird" Parker (Forest Whitaker) nearing the end of his tragically short life; he comes home from a gig, drunk and despairing over the death of one of his children. His despair is so intense that he tries unsuccessfully to kill himself with iodine. It is perhaps the greatest tragedy of all that Parker himself may never have appreciated the talents that his admirers recognize so clearly.

A terrible fragility seems to accompany Parker's kind of talent. Perhaps it is even a kind of symptom or side effect of intellectual or artistic distance from the world of convention, or the conventions of jazz as understood by others. Even the players who perform with Parker often find it too difficult to follow his original flights. In one of his early auditions, Parker takes off on his improvisational arc, only to be brought down by a drummer who is so frustrated by his inability to follow Parker that he tosses a cymbal at him to bring the young saxophonist back to earth.

Throughout the film, Eastwood will come back to this moment to symbolize Parker's interrupted originality and, indeed, his aloneness; he often substitutes another thrown object for the tossed cymbal, but he consistently reminds us that Parker pays a price for his originality.

Some critics (notably Paul Smith and Spike Lee)[8] have accused Eastwood of overemphasizing Parker's addiction to drugs and alcohol, undermining the depiction of his extraordinary musical genius. I think that this criticism is unfair, missing the significance of the thrown cymbal and the film's engagement with what it means to struggle to survive as a musician; on the one hand Parker is recognized by clubs that are named in his honor but on the other hand he constantly struggles to find work. As Parker's wife, Chan (Diane Venora), relates to his doctors after his suicide attempt, Parker is frustrated that he cannot find a wider audience to appreciate his music: bebop, as it was called, was still extremely controversial in the mainstream, and scary to many white people who rightly associated the music with black assertions of self, of independence. Throughout the film, Chan insists that her husband cannot be medicated or hospitalized, because he relies on his creativity and his passion for music—anything that interferes with his ability to fly, however well-intentioned, will become the ruin of him. Her appreciation and concern for him emphasizes the constant push and pull of drugs and creativity in Parker's life: it would be difficult indeed to tell an authentic version of his story without speaking to his addictions and their complex relationship to his musical talents.

Hooking up with the young Red Rodney (Michael Zelniker), Parker tours the south with Rodney's quintet. Here Eastwood has been accused of failing to emphasize the horrifying racism of the era. But of course Rodney must pass himself off as an albino—a white black—because the clubs would not allow an integrated band on stage, and Eastwood accurately presents the segregation of the clubs themselves: whites upstairs, black below. Elsewhere, the black men conceal themselves while Rodney buys groceries because the store has posted WHITES ONLY signs at the entrance. Still, the quintet's musical tour is a huge success in the south, where African Americans eagerly respond to the innovative new forms that have their roots in the African musical traditions that were passed down through hundreds of years of slavery—and indeed these musical traditions expressed the heart and soul of the black struggle for freedom in the South.

Returning to New York, the black men struggle for an audience despite their talents, and Parker must play weddings and bar mitzvahs—

the only gigs that Rodney can arrange for him, and the only way he can make a steady living. Meanwhile Parker and Rodney are hounded by crooked police who blackmail them for money and constantly harass them for names of junkies and drug dealers—more to collect on additional sources of dirty money than to get them off the streets. These and other problems associated with drugs are very much a part of Parker's story. He endlessly grapples with his addiction as a demon he would like to tame, unsuccessfully attempting several times to overcome his chemical dependencies. Parker also does everything he can to scare Red Rodney away from drugs, just as Dizzy Gillespie (Samuel E. Wright) fights hard to help Parker in his own struggles. As Gillespie tells his friend in the film, speaking of white racists and racist society in general: "Deep down they like it if a nigger turns out unreliable. I won't give them the satisfaction of being right. I'm a leader, a reformer, you are a martyr. They always remember the martyrs longer—but my secret is that if they kill me, it won't be because I helped them." But Parker's "unreliability" is as much due to his isolated artistic originality as to his struggles with addiction: a perfectionist constantly obsessed with his own ideas, he seeks restlessly to find ever more original musical concepts and surprising new ways in which to express them. Flying as a bird above the world, he loses sight of the worldly obligations that would tie him down or clip his wings.

In her brilliant novel *Jazz*, Toni Morrison shows us that jazz is more than just a musical form: It is also an allegory for the very blackness and wildness that whites simultaneously seek out and reject in themselves. They project all that jazz onto the black Other.[9] The music is both seductive and terrifying, and historically that meant that the most challenging aspects of jazz needed to be tamed before it could become acceptable in the white mainstream. But Parker desperately seeks out such acceptance, finding it for a time in Paris's more experimental artistic climate—and to some degree even later on his more successful tours in the United States. As his biographer explains, a jazz musician is only as good as his last performance, but each performance fades too quickly from memory:

> Bird may be the greatest, only he has to prove it. Over and over again. In clubs and in unheated dance halls, reeking of cheap perfume and sour sweating bodies, where the admission is $1.25 for studs and chicks are 50 cents. In cabarets and jazz clubs and places to jam, night after night, every night of the year, as he has been doing ever since he was fifteen years of age and stopped going to

high school and became a full-time professional musician in Kansas City. Bird is like a heavyweight champion who cannot afford to lose a single bout. He cannot afford not to work, not to play, not to show. He can goof, fail to make the scene, but the only thing he cannot afford to do ever is lose.[10]

Indeed, Eastwood shows us the extraordinary effort it takes to be a jazz musician as talented and original as Charlie Parker—one solo at a time. Though some critics have charged that Eastwood does not foreground Parker's music successfully enough, the fact is that Eastwood worked closely with Parker's friends and survivors to ensure that almost all of the music we hear in the film is either Parker's own rendition of the piece or an interpretation played by artists such as Red Rodney who knew him well enough to carry out his legacy as well as any musician can. Spike Lee's criticism was particularly harsh, asserting that too much time was spent on the drugs and not enough on the music—but we rarely see Parker's drug use at all. His continuing addiction is suggested by shots of paraphernalia at his bedside; there are no gratuitous depictions of the artist shooting up. Indeed, we might also note that Eastwood in no way associates substance abuse exclusively or even primarily with black men. As we have just seen in *True Crime,* many of his white characters have struggled with alcoholism, and theirs has not been the struggle of the frustrated artistic genius but rather the despair of white men who cannot handle the trauma of their own inevitable failure to live up to the absurd fantasies of white masculinity. Parker, however, deals with the paradoxical humiliation of a man whose talents outstrip the understanding of his audience and his colleagues alike—and he is regularly humiliated, as when he becomes so lost in his own world of music that a cymbal lands at his feet to awaken him to the fact that he is being laughed off the stage. Kenny Clark, a drummer, describes Parker's brilliant innovations:

Bird was playing stuff we never heard before. He was into figures I thought I'd invented for the drums. He was twice as fast as Lester Young, and into harmony Lester hadn't even touched. Bird was running the same way we were, but he was way out ahead of us. I don't think he was aware of the changes he had created. It was his way of playing jazz, part of his own experience.

Parker himself discusses how he pushed himself, working for years to develop his own theories of jazz improvisation on the saxophone:

I'd been bored with the stereotyped changes that were being used all the time. I kept thinking, *there's bound to be something else*. I could hear it sometimes, but I couldn't play it. Well, that night I was working over Cherokee, and as I did I found that by using the higher intervals of a chord as a melody line and backing them with appropriately related changes, I could play the thing I'd been hearing. I came alive.[11]

Parker cared very deeply about the development and progression of jazz as an exciting, living art form. One of the saddest moments of the film is when Parker returns to one of his New York City haunts and listens in dismay as a younger jazz musician forsakes the edgy improvisational greatness of bebop for a catchy and repetitive style well-suited to the dancing of his primarily white audience.

Much has been written about how the early precursors of rock-and-roll were really "tamed jazz"—and Eastwood draws out the depth of Parker's disappointment with these developments. Along with the death of his daughter, this shift in the music he loved—the music he helped to create—seems to press him into his final tragic decline. Feeling that he has lost touch with the world or that the world has lost touch with him, Parker succumbs to his addictions and his health deteriorates. As I have already written, Parker's struggles as a musician and his struggle against drugs are, in a way, one and the same, though this should in no way be taken to mean that drug abuse is required in order to be a great jazz musician. Indeed, Dizzy Gillespie is among the few musicians rightly considered Parker's peer, and he considered himself a lifelong reformer who refused drugs himself and educated others about what drugs do to the black community. While I have strongly disagreed with Spike Lee's reading of Eastwood's film, I profoundly respect Lee's own work on jazz in which he effectively demonstrates the power of jazz independent from the personal trials of many of its greatest musicians. But to simply try to take drugs out of the life of Parker and some of the other great jazz musicians may be to create a kind of fantasy land in which the profound struggles of black jazz musicians are in a certain sense disregarded.

Perhaps on some level Spike Lee fails to understand Eastwood's film as a true homage not just to an art form but to a personal hero, one whom Eastwood dutifully portrays in all of his brilliance and complexity. Of course, to some extent Lee's unease seems to arise from concerns about the very concept of a white man making a movie about black music or, for that matter, about a black man whose life was marked in every way by his race as much as by his talent. We should take this concern seriously, as it strikes more to the heart of the issue than whether or not drugs should be omitted from the story of Parker's life: had the same film been produced by a black director, we might be more at ease with the idea that he or she would be true to the historical realities of drugs in the black community without painting the picture with the paternalistic brush of white superiority. Still, our unease raises a question without answering it: does Eastwood, in fact, portray Parker's addiction with the right combination of sensitivity and candor to make his engagement with drugs in the life of a black man historically and socially authentic?

I would argue that he does. Eastwood's film depiction of Parker's drug use is appropriate and authentic, I think, in a double sense: First, drug use was an integral part of Parker's story as it was for so many jazz musicians (though Eastwood is careful to make it very clear that many others militantly refused drugs and alcohol). Second, it speaks truthfully about the present dilemmas of drugs in America's urban black communities. Presenting the ethical and physical consequences of drug use candidly and honestly, Eastwood nevertheless refrains from adopting the stereotypes of white ideologues: Parker and his friends are not simply thuggish criminals who either do not know any better or do not care. On the contrary, they are intelligent men who understand their own addictions but cannot find any way to end them. Moreover, their drug use is connected not only to their complex relationship with their music but also very explicitly to the traumas of living under the heel of white racism. Indeed, the most despicable characters of the film are the white authorities who take advantage of these black men in their powerlessness rather than extending a hand to assist them. Thus, while we are correct to subject a white man's film about a black man's life to particularly careful scrutiny, I think that Eastwood's homage to Charlie Parker ultimately passes muster.

Indeed, would it not have been the height of hubris to simply "whiten" the problem of drugs in Parker's life, rather than attempting to understand his struggle within the subtle human context that connects his personal fragility to the very creativity that often puts him beyond comprehension? In this period, many jazz musicians like Parker felt that they were talking past the conventions of mainstream society—and if their music resembled a kind of madness to many offended ears, then the isolation imposed by this reception tended toward the kind of breakdowns that Charlie Parker and others endured. That thrown cymbal returns again and again to shatter his inspired rapture, ripping him vio-lently back to earth, only to experience the taunts of those who did not appreciate him.

Conclusion

None of these films is explicitly anti-racist in the sense that it takes the fight against racism as its principal aim and motivation. Yet each illumi-nates Eastwood's own engagement with race and the various issues facing white men (and women) as they confront it as an issue in their lives. In *True Crime* Eastwood contrasts the carelessness of a womanizing white alcoholic reporter's relationships to the deep devotedness of a black fam-ily man's relationship, challenging many of our stereotypes in his very profound portrayal of the decency and humanity of a black man who has been condemned by society to die for a crime he never committed. Some critics have accused Eastwood of using lighting and shadows in *Bird* to turn the features of Forest Whitaker as Charlie Parker into a kind of monster. Rather, I think the lighting effects in *Bird* are better explained as Eastwood attempting to visually capture the extraordinary burdens of a man who felt, as his biographer explained, compelled to perform at the peak of his ability night after night, proving himself still a better and more original artist than he was the day before.

In *White Hunter Black Heart* Eastwood makes the integral connection between fantasized phallic masculinity in Wilson's disregard for the lives and concerns of the people around him. The most tragic example of this is the African guide who dies to help Wilson fulfill his fantasy of shooting an elephant, but we also see Wilson's lack of concern for others in the many technicians and actors who wait on his whim to do their jobs. He shows us that a white man's racism is bound up in his narcissistic fantasies of himself as the omnipotent phallic hero; Wilson is so wrapped up in himself that he hardly bothers to notice the African people around him.

Eastwood never explicitly questions the realities of race, racialized thinking and categorization. He does not deconstruct the concept of race as a mere fiction, as some contemporary critics have done. He never calls on us to become "color blind" in the sense that this phrase has come to represent a mythic objective perspective outside the issues of race. And color blindness is undoubtedly a myth, because in the world as we know it considering oneself blind to color entails a special kind of hubris indeed. Moreover, as we know too well, only a white person can afford the luxury of pretending not to know what color means. But given the realities of race, in these three films Eastwood explores the complexity of how fantasies associated with white masculinity and the easy privilege that comes with it are integrally connected to the operations of racism.

Conclusion: The Last Take

As we have seen throughout this book, Eastwood the director addresses the most urgent and searing questions of ethics and politics today in his films—from the question of evil to the possibility of moral repair and reconciliation. He does so through familiar American genres in film, from the gunslinger West to the police beat, from the boxing ring to the mythic battle fields of our history's greatest war.

Particularly when they are produced by Hollywood, movie genres are profoundly tied in with the imaginary of what America supposedly is and what it stands for. I'm using the word "imaginary" here in a broader sense than the Lacanian psychoanalytic interpretation of the term, in which the imaginary is that stage in all of our lives when we are dependent on the eyes of the Other to interpret who we are and who we might be. Here I'm speaking of the imaginary of the images and symbols of collective life, which are such an intrinsic part of the myths of our nation that certain images almost immediately bring with them a dramatic story line with stereotypic characters who live up to these imagined mythic proportions. As we discussed in the Chapter 6, *The Sands of Iwo Jima* is a classic example not of the horrifying actuality of the Battle of Iwo Jima but rather of how this imaginary actually operates by presenting both stereotypic masculine characters and a simple narrative line of the American hero who always stands up and wins the day no matter how great the odds against him.

We also, of course, see another imagined American hero in the boxing genre, the working class boy who literally fights himself out of a horrible childhood by taking a brutal beating time and time again and ultimately ends up victorious. Here again we see the imaginary at work with particular masculine figures following a story that we easily recognize, knowing its beginning and ending before the film has even started. We only need to think of the Rocky films to remind ourselves how the boxing genre relies on an imaginary figure who points to and underscores one of the great founding myths of the United States—a working class boy can make it if he is only willing to suffer through the hard knocks of life. When, as an audience, we settle down before these films, we are comforted not only because we know what to expect but also because the familiar images and symbols reinforce some of the greatest myths of the imagined "reality of America"—myths that so often now belie the brutal truth of an unjust class structure, racial oppression and, of course, the extraordinarily brutal wars of empire.

The power of Eastwood's movies is that he works within these conventional genres but twists them in such a way that the imaginary of the audience is challenged rather than comforted because the easy story line falls away into a complex ethical engagement that undoes the familiar story. A central aspect of this challenge is the undoing of our identifying the hero with fantasized phallic masculinity. In Chapter 3 we discussed at length Jacques Lacan's insight on how masculinity is underscored by a fantasy of omnipotence that is a defense against the profound vulnerability, on the part of both men and women, to those who bring us into the world and leave their traces on our lives. Lacan himself almost always uses the phrase "symbolic castration" to indicate the ethical goal of his own interpretation of psychoanalysis, which is that both sexes must come to terms with the reality that there is no way to escape the vulnerability of our finitude and the limitation it brings with it.[1] Both men and women, of course, have to face the this fundamental truth but white masculinity follows a particular kind of trajectory, particularly because, as both white and masculine, it is embedded in fantasies that make omnipotence seem almost a real alternative.

In the movies we have discussed in this book, Eastwood over and over again returns to the terrible toll that this fantasized masculinity brings with it. Eastwood's characters struggle with their own dilemmas of masculinity in familiar contexts, but with the twist that the qualities of a good man are not taken for granted. Indeed, the stereotypes of masculinity that we have associated with traditional Oedipal complementarity throughout this book come to be associated with a hardened acceptance of violence, and even of aloneness, as the price of manliness.

Yet the specter that haunts all these movies and gives them their dramatic force is precisely this struggle to be a good man when what it means to be a good man can no longer be identified with the fantasy of phallic control and uprightness. Indeed, as we saw in *A Perfect World*, the idea of uprightness even when it involves Garnett trying to save Butch—first from an abusive father and then from himself—gives way to the seeming bitterness of humility when Butch realizes that what he thought he knew was the right thing to do has turned out so badly. But it is in this humility and vulnerability that Eastwood movies also open up at least a glimmer of another meaning of coming to terms with limitation. In the context of South Africa, Njabulo S. Ndebele writes eloquently about how the embrace of uncertainty and humility is the only way toward a common humanity in which what it means to be a man is not associated with omnipotence, revenge, and violence toward others who must be controlled under that very vision of absolute certainty.

> I have reflected much on this. What seems to happen in this situation is that at the point at which you recognize mutual vulnerability between yourself and an adversary that will not go away, you signal a preparedness to recognize that there might be new grounds for a common humanity, whose promise lies in the real possibility that you may have to give up something that has defined your reality handed down from a past that cannot entirely meet your best interests now and in the future. It is the humility that arises when you give up certitudes around what was previously the uncontested terrain of your value system and unsustainable positions derived from it. It is the willingness to embrace vulnerability of the kind that faces you when you learn to unlearn because there is so much more that is new to learn. Your new sense of comfort comes from the confidence that others who are on the opposite side are doing so too and are also experiencing vulnerability. It is about the capacity of abandoning certitudes acquired through a history of habit.[2]

Of course, to confront this vulnerability can indeed be frightening; yet without it there seems to be no way out of the endless cycle of revenge. In *Mystic River* Jimmy Markum can only restore his sense of self against its shattering, which was caused by the death of his daughter, by killing the man he mistakenly believes murdered his daughter. As result, he finds himself caught up in a trajectory of revenge from which there can be no escape. Alternatively, Sean Devine finally gives in to his vulnerability and his desperate need for his wife to return to him, and there is just a small glimmer of hope about what this difference might mean in the life trajectories of these men. Markum comes out strutting, clapping loudly at the parade but his daughter is dead and there will be no bringing her back. His wife, Annabeth, as we saw, is desperately invested in propping up the phallic fantasy he has to have of himself in order to go on living with the knowledge that he has murdered an innocent man.

Devine is uncomfortable: what does a man do when he does not hide behind the conventions of bravado that keep women in their place and unimportant in a man's life? Even though he is awkward, he still manages to reconcile with his wife and his small daughter. This is the vulnerability of which Ndebele writes, which, if one can painfully remain with it, might bring a transformation into conventional heterosexuality rooted in Oedipal complementarity. It is not only in *Mystic River* but in Eastwood's other films as well that the question of what it means to be a good man is considered in the context of a heterosexual romance and a man's efforts to explore sexuality beyond violence and fetishism. Indeed, what has made several of Eastwood's movies controversial—movies like *Tightrope* for example—is that they explicitly draw out the integral connection of masculine heterosexuality when it is bolstered by phallic fantasy and the violence that is integral to that fantasy. There is a subtle feminist message, even though I do not intend to claim that Eastwood is deliberately making this argument. The connection between male violence, including rape, and what we think of stereotypically as a "normal man" is put in clear display in *Tightrope*, where both the Eastwood character and his double are completely pulled in by the need to enact violation against women as a defense against their own vulnerability. We often find in Eastwood a secondary track to the main narrative line in which the effort to find a meaningful relationship with a woman challenges the Oedipal fantasies upon which a character may have previously relied or that he hides behind in order to bolster his own bravado.

In one of his most powerful movies—*Million Dollar Baby*—Eastwood portrays a love that doesn't fit into the customarily neat lines of Oedipal complementarity. Instead, conventional feminine and masculine roles are reversed. Dunn is the fix-it person; Fitzgerald is the boxer. Thus, the exact nature of the love between Dunn and Fitzgerald remains ambiguous throughout *Million Dollar Baby*. Though we understand that Dunn loves Fitzgerald, Eastwood blurs the lines between father and friend,

friend and lover. Here again Eastwood portrays a man in the worst possible ethical dilemma. He is asked by the woman whom he no doubt loves to kill her out of love. Here the anguish associated with accepting both our need for others and our responsibility to them, precisely because of our love for them, is illustrated when Dunn must put himself so at risk that he may never recover. Yet he has no choice but to follow through on what his love demands.

There is in *Million Dollar Baby* a second narrative track that we see again and again in Eastwood films—the issue of fatherhood itself—and this track is often associated with a subtle exposure of the fiction that Oedipal fantasy actually "works." Both Butch and Phillip in *A Perfect World* have fathers who have deserted their Oedipal responsibilities. In both *Absolute Power* and *Million Dollar Baby* the struggle both to repent for failure as a father and to repair the father-daughter relationship gives dramatic force to the relationships between the central characters. In *Absolute Power* the phallic power of masculinity is exposed in all its violence by an "outlaw," a thief, who is willing to leave his life of hiding from the law in order to accept responsibility to be a loving father to his daughter. In *Million Dollar Baby* there is a subtle suggestion that Dunn is actually called to help Fitzgerald because she offers him a chance to repair what he cannot repair with his own daughter. None of these movies offers a simple alternative to conventional Oedipal complementarity by giving us a hornbook on what it means to be a good father, but they all indicate where it must begin in the acceptance of vulnerability and humility before one's own failures and limitations.

Eastwood gives us no easy answers to the ethical questions that he raises in these films. Indeed, it would be the height of hubris to claim to solve questions as large as these, encompassing themes such as revenge, retribution, justice and moral repair. The power of Eastwood's work is that he presents his characters struggling honestly with ethical questions in all the complexity and urgency of real-life situations. His characters must act, and they inevitably make mistakes. He leaves us not with abstract discussions or easy resolutions. The relationships that arise in Eastwood's films call men to profound ethical decisions that cannot be decided through any formula or simple table of pros and cons. Often, there is simply no "good" solution to the problems, and his characters must learn to live with the inevitable guilt and shame of participating in complex relationships with other human beings.

Eastwood's films cut us to the core of our being, not because they show us what it means to be a good man but because they illustrate so powerfully what a struggle it is to even make an attempt. His films have, and I believe they will continue to have, a profound staying power in what they communicate about human relationships. They cut deeply beneath the surface of what we think we know about moral conflict and ethical commitment. The compelling depth of Eastwood's tragically scarred protagonists sears the flesh of the viewer, cuts more deeply than the salves of our psychic defenses can repair, and leaves an imprint on our very bones. On that note, I am reminded of Yeats:

Go guard me from those thoughts men think
In the mind alone.

Notes

Preface

1. Dennis Bingham, *Acting Male: Masculinities in the Films of James Stewart, Jack Nicholson, and Clint Eastwood* (Piscataway, N.J.: Rutgers University Press, 1994), pp. 163–245.

2. For an excellent definition that is particularly relevant to Eastwood's films and his working through stereotypic masculine ideals and genres, see Judith Butler, *Gender Trouble: Feminism and the Subversion of Identity* (New York: Routledge, Chapman and Hall, 1990), p. 147.

3. For a longer discussion of Walter Benjamin's notion of the phantasmagoria, see Drucilla Cornell, *Moral Images of Freedom: A Future for Critical Theory* (Lanham, Md.: Rowman & Littlefield Publishers, 2008), pp. 11–37.

4. Drucilla Cornell, "What Is Ethical Feminism?" in *Feminist Contentions: A Philosophical Exchange*, ed. Seyla Benhabib, et al. (New York: Routledge, 1995), pp. 76–106. I put ethical feminist in quotation marks because I have called myself an ethical feminist.

Introduction: Shooting Eastwood

1. *Dirty Harry.* DVD, dir. Don Siegel, perf. Clint Eastwood (Warner Bros. Studios, 1971).

2. Krin Gabbard, "'Someone Is Going to Pay'—Resurgent White Masculinity in *Ransom*," in *Masculinity: Bodies, Movies, Culture*, ed. Peter Lehman (New York: Routledge, 2001), p. 9.

3. *Play Misty for Me*, DVD, dir. Clint Eastwood, perf. Clint Eastwood, Jessica Walter (Universal Studios, 1971).

4. *Tightrope*, DVD, dir. Richard Tuttle, perf. Clint Eastwood, Geneviève Bujold, prod. Clint Eastwood and Fritz Manes (Warner Bros. Studios, 1984).

5. *A Perfect World*, DVD, dir. Clint Eastwood, perf. Clint Eastwood, Kevin Costner, Laura Dern (Warner Bros. Studios, 1993).

6. Lee Clark Mitchell, *Westerns: Making the Man in Fiction and Film* (Chicago: University of Chicago Press, 1996), pp. 4–5.

7. *Bronco Billy*, DVD, dir. Clint Eastwood, perf. Clint Eastwood, Sondra Locke (Warner Bros. Studios, 1980).

8. *Space Cowboys*, DVD, dir. Clint Eastwood, perf. Clint Eastwood, Tommy Lee Jones, Donald Sutherland, James Garner, Marcia Gay Harden (Warner Bros. Studios, 2000).

1. Writing the Showdown: What's Left Behind When the Sun Goes Down

1. *High Plains Drifter*, DVD, dir. Clint Eastwood, perf. Clint Eastwood (Universal Studios, 1973).

2. Lee Clark Mitchell, *Westerns: Making the Man in Fiction and Film* (Chicago: University of Chicago Press, 1996).

3. See Sue Grand, *The Reproduction of Evil: A Clinical & Cultural Perspective* (Hillsdale, N.J.: Analytic Press, 2000).

4. Mitchell, *Westerns*.

5. See especially the "Dollars Trilogy" featuring Clint Eastwood: *A Fistful of Dollars* (1964), *For a Few Dollars More* (1965), and *The Good, the Bad and the Ugly* (1966).

6. Grand, *The Reproduction of Evil*, p. 8.

7. Ibid, p. 6. Italics in original.

8. Ibid., p. 5.

9. Ibid., p. 4–5.

10. Ibid., p. 6.

11. See Walter Benjamin, *The Origin of German Tragic Drama* (New York: Verso Press, 1998).

12. Grand, *The Reproduction of Evil*, p. 11.

13. *Pale Rider*, DVD, dir. Clint Eastwood, perf. Clint Eastwood (Warner Bros. Studios, 1985).

14. See preface in Michael Kimmel, *Manhood in America: A Cultural History*, 2nd ed. (New York: Oxford University Press, 2006).

15. In *Culture of Masculinity* Kimmel refers to three ideal types of American men, particularly in the sense that they engage the ideals of manhood for white men; they are the genteel patriarch, the heroic artisan, and the self-made man.

16. *Shane*, DVD, dir. George Stevens, perf. Alan Ladd, Jean Arthur, Van Heflin, Jack Palance (Paramount Pictures, 1953).

17. *Unforgiven*, dir. Clint Eastwood, perf. Clint Eastwood, Morgan Freeman, Gene Hackman (Warner Bros. Studios, 1992).

18. Kimmel, *Manhood in America*, p. 213.

19. Elizabeth Bronfen, *Over Her Dead Body: Death, Femininity, and the Aesthetic* (Manchester: Manchester University Press, 1992), p. 219.

20. Sue Grand, *The Reproduction of Evil*, p. 159; Krin Gabbard, " 'Someone Is Going to Pay'—Resurgent White Masculinity in *Ransom*," in *Masculinity: Bodies, Movies, Culture*, ed. Peter Lehman (New York: Routledge, 2001), pp. 7–23, p. 9.

21. Sigmund Freud, "Mourning and Melancholia" in *Collected Papers*, vol. 4, *Papers on Metapsychology* (New York: Basic Books, 1954), p. 153.

22. Eastwood has used and transformed the all-too-familiar black sidekick that often mars the Western. As Michael Kimmel rightly notes, "By the mid-nineteenth century this new American male hero began to encounter another man, usually a man of color, as a sort of spirit guide to this world without women. . . . Literary critic Leslie Fiedler attributes this tradition on cross-race male bonding to a search for redemption for white guilt, but I believe it is also a way to present screens against which white manhood is projected, played out, and defined. The nonwhite stands in for women—as dependent child . . . male mother . . . spiritual guide and moral instructor . . . sometimes all at once. Their homoerotic passion is never the passion of equals; the nonwhite is either the guide and exemplar or the Rousseauian 'noble savage' who, in his childlike innocence, is more susceptible to the wiles of civilization" (Kimmel, pp. 44–45). But in *Unforgiven*, Logan is a full equal and friend to Munny, the hero, and this is just one of the many ways in which we see Eastwood working with a traditional figure using a traditional template of the genre, but only to make the character into something much more profound.

23. Michael Kimmel, *Manhood in America*, p. 213.

24. Dennis Bingham, *Acting Male: Masculinities in the Films of James Stewart, Jack Nicholson, and Clint Eastwood* (Piscataway, N.J.: Rutgers University Press, 1994), p. 164.

25. Ibid., p. 167.

26. Walter Benjamin, *The Arcades Project*, trans. Howard Eiland (Cambridge, Mass.: Belknap Press, 2002), p. 348.

27. Bingham, *Acting Male*, p. 236.

28. Chris Packard, *Queer Cowboys and Other Erotic Male Friendships in Nineteenth-Century American Literature* (New York: Palgrave Macmillan, 2005), p. 2.

2. Dancing with the Double: Reaching Out from the Darkness Within

1. *Tightrope*, DVD, dir. Richard Tuggle, perf. Clint Eastwood, Geneviève Bujold, prod. Clint Eastwood, Fritz Manes (Warner Bros. Studios, 1984).

2. Notably, this psychologist is played by an African American woman. In Eastwood's later work especially, he tends to quietly resist stereotypical Hollywood racism, which rarely portrays African Americans in positions of power or

authority, let alone positions in which white leading men seek them out for an educated opinion.

3. Dennis Bingham, *Acting Male: Masculinities in the Films of James Stewart, Jack Nicholson, and Clint Eastwood* (Piscataway, N.J.: Rutgers University Press, 1994), p. 216.

4. Jessica Benjamin, *Like Subjects, Love Objects: Essays on Recognition and Sexual Difference* (New Haven: Yale University Press, 1995), p. 178.

5. Ibid., p. 209.

6. Ibid., p. 196–97.

7. Jessica Benjamin, *The Bonds of Love: Psychoanalysis, Feminism, and the Problem of Domination* (New York: Pantheon, 1988).

8. Otto Rank, *The Double: A Psychoanalytic Study* (London: Karnac Books, 1989).

9. Dennis Bingham, *Acting Male*, p. 216.

10. Jessica Benjamin, "Beyond Doer and Done to: An Intersubjective View of Thirdness" in *Psychoanalytic Quarterly*, 73:5–46 (2004), p. 5.

11. *In the Line of Fire*, DVD, dir. Wolfgang Petersen, perf. Clint Eastwood, John Malkovich, Rene Russo (Sony Pictures, 1993).

12. Hannah Arendt, *Eichmann in Jerusalem: A Report on the Banality of Evil* (New York: Penguin, 1994).

13. *Blood Work*, DVD, dir. Clint Eastwood, perf. Clint Eastwood, Jeff Daniels, Wanda De Jesus (Warner Bros. Studios, 2002).

14. Anthony Easthope, *What a Man's Gotta Do: The Masculine Myth in Popular Culture* (New York: Routledge, 1990), p. 53. The quote continues: "This brings out the question of how it is not to be observed. It is not to be looked at with the eye of desire. This is precisely the look the masculine body positively denies, as if it were saying, 'whatever else—not that.' The hardness and tension of the body strives to present it as wholly masculine, to exclude all curves and hollows and to be only straight lines and flat planes. It would really like to be a Cubist painting, or whatever, but above all not desirable to other men, because it is so definitely not soft and feminine. Not smooth bones and muscle, not flesh and blood. The masculine body seeks to be Rambo, not Rimbaud" (Easthope, p. 54).

15. Judith Butler, *Gender Trouble: Feminism and the Subversion of Identity* (New York: Routledge, 1990).

16. Jacques Derrida, *Politics of Friendship* (New York: Verso Books, 1997).

17. *Sudden Impact*, DVD, dir. Clint Eastwood, perf. Clint Eastwood, Sondra Locke, Pat Hingle, (Warner Bros. Studios, 1983).

18. See Immanuel Kant, *The Metaphysics of Morals*, trans. Mary J. Gregor (Cambridge: Cambridge University Press, 1993), §460–461, pp. 252–253.

19. Immanuel Kant, *Religion within the Boundaries of Mere Reason and Other Writings*, trans. Allen Wood (Cambridge: Cambridge University Press, 1999), pp. 635–44.

20. Martha C. Nussbaum, "Equity and Mercy," *Philosophy and Public Affairs*, vol. 22, no. 2 (Spring 1993): pp. 83–125: 96.

21. See, for example, Thaddeus Metz, "Judging Because Understanding: A Defense for Retributive Censor" (Chapter 10, pp. 222–240).

22. Although it is, again, beyond the scope of this chapter, we will return to the debate between compatiblists and incompatiblists with respect to free will—that is, to the question of whether the notion of freedom can be naturalized in a way that is compatible with an assumption of causal (psychological) determinism, or whether we must retain a notion of freedom as a metaphysical capacity to defy natural causation in the pursuit of a moral purpose. See Drucilla Cornell, *The Philosophy of the Limit* (New York: Routledge, 1992) for an extended discussion of my own defense of incompatiblism as integral to understanding the limits of psychological determinism.

For a further discussion of the incompatiblist/compatiblist debate including a sustained critique of where compatiblism goes wrong in its assumptions about scientific knowledge as well as in its construction of moral obligation, see a forthcoming dissertation by Elric M. Kline, "Freedom's Paradox: Hoping against Hope in a Freedom of the Will."

23. Paul Smith, *Eastwood: A Cultural Production* (Minneapolis: University of Minnesota Press, 1993), p. 133.

24. *The Gauntlet*, DVD, dir. Clint Eastwood, perf. Clint Eastwood, Sondra Locke, (Warner Bros. Studios, 1977).

25. See Drucilla Cornell, *Beyond Accommodation: Ethical Feminism, Deconstruction, and the Law* (Lanham, Md.: Rowman & Littlefield, 1999).

3. Ties That Bind: The Legacy of a Mother's Love

1. *The Bridges of Madison County*, DVD, dir. Clint Eastwood, perf. Clint Eastwood, Meryl Streep (Warner Bros. Studios, 1995).

2. *Breezy*, DVD, dir. Clint Eastwood, perf. William Holden, Kay Lenz, Roger C. Carmel (Universal Studios, 1973).

3. Robert James Waller, *The Bridges of Madison County* (New York: Grand Central Publishing, 1992).

4. *Something's Gotta Give*, DVD, dir. Nancy Meyers, perf. Jack Nicholson, Diane Keaton, Keanu Reeves, Frances McDormand (Sony Pictures, 2003).

5. Susan Bordo, *The Male Body: A New Look at Men in Public and in Private* (New York: Farrar, Strauss, and Giroux, 1999).

6. Although Benjamin has clearly borrowed a great deal from G.W.F. Hegel's concept of recognition, her psychoanalytic work revises Hegel's insight considerably in that she addresses how recognition (more specifically the third) denotes the possibility of a break from Oedipal complimentarity. See Hegel's famous dialectic of recognition in *The Phenomenology of Mind*, Chapter 4. Simply put, the third for Hegel (*aufgehoben*) is found in legal marriage and/or the child

produced by the couple. (See Hegel, *The Philosophy of Right*, the section on the family.) For a profound and amusing examination of Hegel's stiff understanding of sexual difference as complementarity and his affirmation of the thirdness of marriage, see, generally, Jacques Derrida's *Glas*. In *Bridges*, Robert Kincaid explicitly resists this stiff notion of family, rejecting the notion of ownership in marriage.

7. Bordo, *The Male Body*, p. 143.

8. Ibid., p. 143–44.

9. Kaja Silverman, "Masochism and Male Subjectivity," *Camera Obscura* 17 (May 1988): 31–36.

10. See generally Jacques Lacan, *The Four Fundamental Concepts: Book XI of the Seminars of Jacques Lacan* (New York: Norton, 1998). For an excellent discussion of Lacan's concept of the symbolic order, see Charles Shepherson, *Vital Signs: Nature, Culture, Psychoanalysis* (New York: Routledge, 2000), pp. 37–39, 62–69.

11. For a longer discussion, see Drucilla Cornell, *Between Women and Generations: Legacies of Dignity* (New York: Palgrave Macmillan, 2002), p. 209n52.

12. As I have argued elsewhere, Gurewich's reinterpretation of the Oedipal myth provides a mental space in which to understand ourselves as ethical subjects of the law, so that we can and should call this law dignity. See Cornell, *Between Women and Generations*, p. 56–57.

4. Psychic Scars: Transformative Relationships and Moral Repair

1. See Jessica Benjamin, "Beyond Doer and Done To: An Intersubjective View of Thirdness," *Psychoanalytic Quarterly* 73 (2004): 5–46. For another excellent discussion of the complex issues involved in trauma, see *Trauma: Explorations in Memory*, ed. Cathy Caruth (Baltimore: Johns Hopkins University Press, 1995).

2. *A Perfect World*, DVD, dir. Clint Eastwood, perf. Clint Eastwood, Kevin Costner, Laura Dern (Warner Bros. Studios, 1993).

3. *Absolute Power*, DVD, dir. Clint Eastwood, perf. Clint Eastwood, Gene Hackman, Ed Harris (Warner Bros. Studios, 1997).

4. For a much longer discussion of femininity as masquerade, see Drucilla Cornell, *Beyond Accommodation: Ethical Feminism, Deconstruction, and the Law* (Lanham, Md.: Rowman & Littlefield, 1999), pp.105–106.

5. *Million Dollar Baby*, DVD, dir. Clint Eastwood, perf. Clint Eastwood, Hilary Swank, Morgan Freeman, (Warner Bros. Studios, 2004).

6. F. X. Toole, *Rope Burns: Stories from the Corner* (New York: Ecco, 2001), p. 9.

7. Ibid., p. 12.

8. Samuel Menasche, "In the Ring," in *New and Selected Poems*, ed. Christopher Ricks (New York: Library of America, 2005), p. 180.

9. Emmanuel Levinas, "Ethics and the Face" in *Totality and Infinity: An Essay on Exteriority*, trans. Alphonse Lingis (The Hague: Maritnus Nijhoff Publishers, 1981), pp. 194–220.

10. Menasche, "Grief," in *New and Selected Poems*, p. 25, italics in original.

5. Parables of Revenge and Masculinity in *Mystic River*

1. *Mystic River*, DVD, dir. Clint Eastwood, perf. Sean Penn, Tim Robbins (Warner Bros. Studios, 2004).

2. Karen Horney, "The Value of Vindictiveness," *American Journal of Psychoanalysis* 8 (1948): 8.

3. Ibid.

4. Ibid., p.10.

5. William Ian Miller has rightly noted that the point of view of the avenger is usually the controlling one. See "Clint Eastwood and Equity: Popular Culture's Theory of Revenge" in *Law in the Domains of Culture*, ed. Austin Sarat and Thomas R. Kearns (Ann Arbor: University of Michigan Press, 2000), p. 172.

6. Anthony Easthope, *What a Man's Gotta Do: The Masculine Myth in Popular Culture* (New York: Routledge, 1990), p. 20.

7. Ibid., p. 84.

8. Miller, "Clint Eastwood and Equity," 169.

9. Ibid., pp. 174–175. See Robert C. Post, "The Popular Image of the Lawyer," *California Law Review* 75 (1987), pp. 379, 382. The law, represented by the bureaucratic and legalistic restrictions on prosecutors as well as by the odor of corruption, is seen as an impediment to justice. For an account of how Hollywood films portray the legalistic ethic of prosecutors as impediments to justice, see Roger Berkowitz, "The Accusers: Law, Justice and the Image of Prosecutors in Hollywood," *Griffith Law Review* 13 (2005).

10. So pervasive is the need for vengeance to be justified that *The Star Chamber* (1983), one of the few classic films that break with tradition to show an act of vengeance gone bad, must abandon its avenging heroes once their errors are brought to light.

11. For an excellent discussion of revenge in Hollywood westerns, see Peter French, *The Virtues of Vengeance* (Lawrence: University of Kansas, 2001).

12. Something like this yearning for paternal security through limitless strength likely girds much of the support for President George W. Bush's foreign policy as well as for the liberal welfare state. See also Carl Schmitt, *Theodor Däublers "Nordlicht": Drei Studien über die Elemente, den Geist und die Aktualität des Werkes* (Berlin: Duncker & Humblot, 1991).

13. For the distinction between excuse and justification, see Chapter 10 in George P. Fletcher, *Rethinking Criminal Law* (New York: Oxford University Press, 2000). First published 1978 by Little, Brown.

14. French, *The Virtues of Vengeance*, p. 32.

15. Romans 12:19.

16. See Shai Lavi, " 'The Jews are Coming': Vengeance and Revenge in Post-Nazi Europe," *Law, Culture, and the Humanities* 1 (2005): 282–301.

17. Not every animal, Nietzsche writes, has the right or the capability to make good on its promises. See Friedrich Nietzsche, "*Zur Genealogie der Moral*" in *Kritische Studienausgabe*, eds. Giorgio Colli and Mazzino Montinari (München: Deutscher Taschenbuch Verlag GmbH, 1988), p. 291.

18. See Karl Shoemaker's description of the vengeful nature of the French king Louis the Fat, in "Revenge as a 'Medium Good' in the Twelfth Century," *Law, Culture, and the Humanities* 1 (2005): 333–58.

19. Percy Ernst Schramm, " '*Mythos' des Königtums*," in *Kaiser, Königtum, und Päpste*, vol.1 (Stuttgart: Anton Hiersemann, 1968), 68ff.

20. Victor Ehrenberg, *The Greek State* (Oxford: Oxford University Press, 1960), pp. 66–67, 76.

21. Ernst Kantorowicz, *The King's Two Bodies* (Princeton, N.J.: Princeton University Press, 1966). Similarly, Jean Bodin argues that all kings depend upon the claim that their power comes "not from the Pope, nor from the Archbishop of Rheims, nor from the people, but rather from God alone." Jean Bodin, *Les Six Livres de la Republique* (cited in Giorgi Agamben, *Homo Sacer*, trans. by Daniel Heller-Roazen (Stanford, Calif.: Stanford University Press, 1998), pp. 101–2.

22. This is how Giorgio Agamben interprets Carl Schmitt's thinking on sovereignty, by reducing sovereignty to a logical relation of indistinction. See Agamben, *Homo Sacer*, p. 28: "The exception is the structure of sovereignty."

23. See generally Michel Foucault, "Politics and Reason," in Lawrence D. Kritzman, *Michel Foucault: Politics, Philosophy, Culture, Interviews and other Writings 1977–1984*, trans. Alan Sheridan (New York: Routledge, 1998), 62ff.

24. Ibid., pp. 66–67.

25. See A. R. Johnson, "Hebrew Conceptions of Kingship," in S. H. Hooke, *Myth, Ritual, and Kingship: Essays on the Theory and Practice of Kingship in the Ancient Near East and in Israel* (Oxford: Clarendon Press, 1958), pp. 207–8.

26. See Chapter 3 in Danielle Allen, *The World of Prometheus: The Politics of Punishing in Democratic Athens* (Princeton, N.J.: Princeton University Press, 2000).

27. Compare Philippe Nonet, "Antigone's Law," *Law, Culture, and the Humanities* 2 (2006): 314–35.

28. Compare our understanding of Devine's fortitude grounded in a sense of finitude with Jennifer Culbert's account of humble resolve in "Reprising Revenge," *Law, Culture, and the Humanities* 1 (2005): 302–15.

29. Sigmund Freud, *Three Essays on the Theory of Sexuality*, trans. James Strachey (Basic Books, 2000).

30. Drucilla Cornell, *At the Heart of Freedom* (Princeton, N.J.: Princeton University Press, 1998), 8ff.

31. See Drucilla Cornell, *The Imaginary Domain* (New York, Routledge, 1995).

32. Sean's effort to let Lauren be together with him in her difference from him can rightly be understood along the lines of Aristotle's definition of friendship. For a fascinating effort to build a politics upon the Aristotelian ideal of friendship—i.e., of letting the friend be as different and yet the same—see Jill Frank, *A Democracy of Distinction* (Chicago: University of Chicago Press, 2004), 143ff. Against the humility of friendship stands the logic of sovereignty. The struggle for sovereignty, as Patchen Markell writes, is one that lurks in the modern ideology of identity and, specifically, masculine identity. Patchen Markell, *Bound by Recognition* (Princeton, N.J.: Princeton University Press, 2003), 113ff.

33. Jacques Lacan, "On Feminine Sexuality, The Limits of Love and Knowledge" in Jacques Alain-Miller, *Seminar XX, Encore: On Feminine Sexuality, The Limits of Love and Knowledge*, trans. B. Fink (New York: Norton, 1998). Although there is a great recent outpouring of literature on masculinity in film, much of it relies on Lacan both implicitly and explicitly. See, for example, Easthope, *What a Man's Gotta Do*. See also Mary Ingram, *Men: The Male Myth Exposed* (New York: Arrow, 1984).

34. Markell, *Bound by Recognition*, p. 113.

6. Militarized Manhood: Shattered Images and the Trauma of War

1. *The Outlaw Josey Wales*, DVD, dir. Clint Eastwood, perf. Clint Eastwood, Chief Dan George, Sondra Locke (Warner Bros. Studios, 1976).

2. *The Searchers*, DVD, dir. John Ford, perf. John Wayne, Vera Miles (Warner Bros. Studios, 1956).

3. *Firefox*, DVD, dir. Clint Eastwood, perf. Clint Eastwood (Warner Bros. Studios, 1982).

4. *Heartbreak Ridge*, DVD, dir. Clint Eastwood, perf. Clint Eastwood, Marsha Mason, Everett McGill. (Warner Bros. Studios, 1986).

5. *Flags of Our Fathers*, DVD, dir. Clint Eastwood, perf. Ryan Phillippe, Jesse Bradford, Adam Beach. (Dreamworks Pictures, 2006).

6. *Saving Private Ryan*, DVD, dir. Steven Spielberg, perf. Tom Hanks, Tom Sizemore, Edward Burns (Dreamworks Pictures, 1998).

7. In reality, sole survivor policies serve primarily to prevent family members from serving in close proximity, such as on the same ship, so as to minimize the likelihood of family tragedies in which several family members perish in the same attack. Such regulations were drafted after the Sullivan brothers were all killed in the sinking of the USS *Juneau* during World War II. As for Sergeant Frederick Niland, no elite unit was sent to retrieve him from the front lines. Rather, he made his own way back to camp after parachuting off target, at which point he was informed of the death of his brothers and shipped back to the United States to complete his term of service without engaging in combat. It was later discovered that his brother Edward, presumed dead, was actually captive in a Japanese POW camp in Burma.

8. James Bradley, with Ron Powers, *Flags of our Fathers* (New York: Bantam Books, 2001), p. 322.

9. *Letters from Iwo Jima*, DVD, dir. Clint Eastwood, perf. Ken Watanabe, Kazunari Ninomiya, Tsuyoshi Ihara, Ryo Kase (Warner Bros. Studios, 2006).

10. Michael Kimmel, *Manhood in America: A Cultural History*, 2nd ed. (New York: Oxford University Press, 2006).

11. *A Secret Burden: Memories of the Border War by South African Soldiers Who Fought In It*, ed. Karen Batley (Johannesburg: Jonathan Ball Publishers, 2007), p. 97.

7. Shades of Recognition: Privilege, Dignity, and the Hubris of White Masculinity

1. I can think of one other notable exception to this general Hollywood rule, and it makes for an interesting comparison with *Million Dollar Baby*. In *The Shawshank Redemption* (1994), Ellis Boyd "Red" Redding (Morgan Freeman) narrates the story of Andy Dufresne (Tim Robbins), a white accountant who was wrongly convicted of homicide but eventually escapes from Shawshank Prison. Interestingly, like *Million Dollar Baby* the film deals with issues of deep moral repair. Whereas the black man in *Million Dollar Baby* actually pushes the white male character down the path of his own redemption, in *Shawshank* the white man is innocent from the beginning while the black man is a confessed murderer who is inspired by the white man to give himself a second chance at life. While *Shawshank* should be rightly credited for portraying a positive African American narrator, *Million Dollar Baby* goes further by making Freeman's character an important part of the moral heartbeat of the film. *Shawshank* concludes after Redding reads an inspiring letter from his friend Dufresne; in *Million Dollar Baby* it is Eddie Dupris who writes a heartfelt letter to Frankie Dunn's daughter.

2. See in general Dennis Bingham, *Acting Male: Masculinities in the Films of James Stewart, Jack Nicholson, and Clint Eastwood* (Piscataway, N.J.: Rutgers University Press, 1994).

3. *The Enforcer*, DVD, dir. James Fargo, perf. Clint Eastwood, Tyne Daly (Warner Bros. Studios, 1976).

4. *White Hunter Black Heart*, DVD, dir. Clint Eastwood, perf. Clint Eastwood (Warner Bros. Studios, 1990).

5. *True Crime*, DVD, dir. Clint Eastwood, perf. Clint Eastwood, Isaiah Washington, James Woods (Warner Bros. Studios, 1999).

6. Paul Smith, *Eastwood: A Cultural Production* (Minneapolis: University of Minnesota Press, 1993), pp. 238–240.

7. *Bird*, DVD, dir. Clint Eastwood, perf. Forest Whitaker, Diane Venora, Michael Zelniker (Warner Bros. Studios, 1988).

8. Smith, *Eastwood: A Cultural Production*, pp. 235–36; Eugene Novikov, "Clint Eastwood Thinks Spike Lee Should Shut His Face," Cinematical weblog,

June 6, 2008, http://www.cinematical.com/2008/06/06/clint-eastwood-thinks-spike-lee-should-shut-his-face.

9. Toni Morrison, *Jazz* (New York: Penguin, 1993).

10. Studs Terkel, *Giants of Jazz* (New York: New Press, 2002), p. 172.

11. Ibid., p. 171.

Conclusion: The Last Take

1. See Chapter 3. Also see generally Jacques Lacan, *The Four Fundamental Concepts: Book XI of the Seminars of Jacques Lacan* (New York: Norton, 1998).

2. Njabulo S. Ndebele, "Learning to Give Up Certitudes: Vulnerability in Our Mutual Need" in *Fine Lines from the Box: Further Thoughts About Our Country* (Houghton: Umuzi, 2007), p. 221.

Filmography: Clint Eastwood as Director

Play Misty for Me (1971, Universal/Malpaso, U.S.)

High Plains Drifter (1973, Universal/Malpaso, U.S.)

Breezy (1973, Universal/Malpaso, U.S.)

The Eiger Sanction (1975, Universal/Malpaso, U.S.)

The Outlaw Josey Wales (1976, Malpaso for Warner Bros., U.S.)

The Gauntlet (1977, Malpaso for Warner Bros., U.S.)

Bronco Billy (1980, Warner Bros., U.S.)

Honkytonk Man (1982, Malpaso for Warner Bros., U.S.)

Firefox (1982, Malpaso for Warner Bros., U.S.)

Sudden Impact (1983, Malpaso for Warner Bros., U.S.)

Pale Rider (1985, Warner Bros., Malpaso, U.S.)

"Vannessa in the Garden" (1985, an episode in Steven Spielberg's
   Amazing Stories, Amblin Entertainment, U.S.)

Heartbreak Ridge (1986, Malpaso for Warner Bros., U.S.)

Bird (1988, Warner Bros., Malpaso, U.S.)

White Hunter Black Heart (1990, Malpaso/Rastar for Warner Bros.,
   U.S.)

The Rookie (1990, Malpaso for Warner Bros., U.S.)

Unforgiven (1992, Malpaso for Warner Bros., U.S.)

A Perfect World (1993, Malpaso for Warner Bros., U.S.)

The Bridges of Madison County (1995, Malpaso, U.S.)

Absolute Power (1997, Malpaso, Castle Rock Entertainment, Columbia Pictures, U.S.)

Midnight in the Garden of Good and Evil (1997, Malpaso, Silverstone Pictures, Warner Bros., U.S.)

True Crime (1999, Malpaso, The Zanuck Company, U.S.)

Space Cowboys (2000, Malpaso, Clipsal Films, Mad Chance, Village Roadshow Pictures, U.S.)

Blood Work (2002, Malpaso for Warner Bros., U.S.)

"Piano Blues" (2003, an episode for the documentary miniseries *The Blues*, Road Movies Filmproduktion, Vulcan Productions, U.S.)

Mystic River (2003, Malpaso, NPV Entertainment, Village Roadshow Pictures, Warner Bros., U.S.)

Million Dollar Baby (2004, Malpaso, Lakeshore Entertainment, Albert S Ruddy Productions, Warner Bros., U.S.)

Flags of Our Fathers (2006, DreamWorks SKG, Warner Bros., Amblin Entertainment, Malpaso, U.S.)

Letters from Iwo Jima (2006, Amblin Entertainment, Dreamworks SKG, Malpaso, Relativity Media, U.S.)

Changeling (2008, DezArt Cinematic, Imagine Entertainment, Malpaso, Relativity Media, U.S.)

Gran Torino (2008, Double Nickel Entertainment, Gerber Pictures, Malpaso Productions, Matten Productions, Media Magik Entertainment, Village Roadshow Pictures, Warner Bros., U.S.)

Index